PSYCHOANALYSIS LISTENING TO LOVE

PSYCHOANALYSIS LISTENING TO LOVE
Passion and Bonds

Simonetta Diena

Translated by Harriet Graham

R Routledge
Taylor & Francis Group

LONDON AND NEW YORK

First published 2018
by Routledge
2 Park Square, Milton Park, Abingdon, Oxon OX14 4RN

and by Routledge
711 Third Avenue, New York, NY 10017

Routledge is an imprint of the Taylor & Francis Group, an informa business

British Library Cataloguing-in-Publication Data
A catalogue record for this book is available from the British Library

Library of Congress Cataloging-in-Publication Data
A catalog record has been requested for this book

ISBN: 978-1-78220-455-8 (pbk)

Typeset in Palatino LT Std
by Medlar Publishing Solutions Pvt Ltd, India

To
Giancarlo,
for ever

CONTENTS

ACKNOWLEDGEMENTS

The author wishes to thank the following for their kind permission to reproduce their works within this book.

"Remembrances of Marie A." from *Die Hauspostille* by Bertolt Brecht © Bertolt Brecht Erben/Suhrkamp Verlag.

© 2018 Museum of Fine Arts, Boston, for the photographs of the painting and watercolour by John Singer Sargent:

Mrs Fiske Warren (Gretchen Osgood) and her Daughter Rachel (1903)
Oil on canvas
152.4 × 102.55 cm (60 × 40⅜ in.)
Museum of Fine Arts, Boston
Gift of Mrs. Rachel Warren Barton and Emily L. Ainsley Fund
64.693

Corfu: Lights and Shadows (1909)
Translucent and opaque watercolour, with wax resist, over graphite on
paper
Sheet: 40.3 × 53.1 cm (15⅞ × 20⅞ in.)
Museum of Fine Arts, Boston
The Hayden Collection-Charles Henry Hayden Fund
12.207

The poem "Cascando" by Samuel Beckett, reproduced with kind permission from Faber & Faber.

Extracts from *Stranezze 1957–1976* by Sandro Penna © 2017 Mondadori
Libri S.p.A.

ABOUT THE AUTHOR

Simonetta Diena, psychiatrist and psychoanalyst, is a full member with training functions of the SPI (Italian Psychoanalytical Association) and the IPA (International Psychoanalytical Association). For many years she has worked in the field of eating disorders and her publications have appeared in national and international journals and in collected volumes dealing with the problems connected with these disorders. She teaches at the Istituto Italiano di Psicoanalisi di Gruppo (IIPG) in Milan and, since 1999, is a Fellow in the IPA Research Training Programme. For years her research has focused on art and psychoanalysis and she has authored a number of essays on this topic as well as articles published in national and international journals. She lives and works in Milan.

PREFACE

Francesco Barale

Simonetta Diena asked me to write a "psychoanalytic" Preface to her book *Psychoanalysis Listening to Love*, but this impassioned yet light book of hers is already so rich in psychoanalytic spirit that I really do not want to spoil its consistent grace with too many further considerations about psychoanalysis.

An already wide-ranging psychoanalytic phenomenology of love life is waiting to be enjoyed by the reader in the book's twelve chapters: from primary love up to love in old age. Every time, Diena takes her cue from the many ways in which the passions of love are reactivated in the analytic situation, energising the dynamics; a dense weft of reflections is woven around this guiding thread in which clinical practice is starred with a rich repertory of literary, poetic, artistic, and musical references.

It must be said that the love experience is undoubtedly a somewhat complex phenomenology: the object of a thousand-year-old chain of reflection—both Western and Eastern—which alone would be enough to immediately knock out of play any ambitions for academic completeness. Well aware of what she is dealing with, Simonetta Diena wisely steers clear of losing herself in this wealth of material. Also because, from this immense corpus of cogitations (suffice to think of the quantity of references that provide the backdrop to the eighty entries in Roland

Barthes' *A Lover's Discourse: Fragments*), the experience of love would in any case appear to be, despite everything, somewhat resistant to letting itself be captured by systematic treatments. It is a remarkable affair. On the one hand, it comprises several elementary ingredients inherent to humankind, of which every person feels they have immediate evidence in some way, and, on the other, a hotchpotch that continues to surprise us and catch us unaware with unexpected proposals. It is even difficult to write or talk about it, because there always seems to be an over-abundance or an under-abundance of language, compared to the task at hand.

Notwithstanding, the psychoanalytic situation is a privileged place that allows us to observe how the experience of love continues to unfold its "natural" ingredients in multiple and unexpected forms, marked by an intrinsic conflictuality, between intermittences, contradictory urges, and complex blends of diverse components: to remain in a classical vein, suffice to think of the combination between libidinal and aggressive components, co-present since the dawn of time in every action of love; or the blending of narcissistic aspects and object aspects.

The love experience implies inevitable, unavoidable, and interminable change, dictated at the same time by need and impossibility. It is a powerful and indispensable matrix of bonds, aggregations, and constructions. It is the begetter of life, if we want to see it in an optimistic light—"*E' il sol dell'anima, la vita è amore*" ("Love is the sunshine of the soul, 'tis life itself!"), sings the Duke of Mantua in Rigoletto...—or at least the instigator of well-curbed illusions (if things go well...), capable of "pushing the night further away" (Milite, 2005) or at least for a while longer. But its path is anything but straight. It is a labyrinth that calls for "psychical expenditure" (Freud, 1905d, p. 148), as it has been described. Its entire course is veined by a trace of the impossibility of ever being able to achieve that complete fulfilment, for which it was originally triggered, which fuels it, and within whose illusion it is formed.

It will come as no surprise that this contradiction between need and intrinsic impossibility was the focus of one of the very last, enigmatic reflections of Freud. Besides, any love investment is after all a "false connection", at least if it is considered from the point of view of the original need from which it stems.

The vitality of amorous life depends precisely on the ability to get by in that tangle of components, contradictory ingredients (libidinal and aggressive, pre-oedipal, oedipal, and post-oedipal...), and impossible demands that characterise the paths of love, and that this book so know-ledgeably delineates. It depends on the capacity of men and women, restlessly and pleasurably immersed in that tangle, to find the right bal-ance (or a skilful oscillation) among all those different ingredients: enjoy-ing it, maintaining the love investment while recognising its limits and inevitable disappointments, balancing narcissistic and object aspects, and avoiding idealisation pathologies while maintaining all the time the ability to fuel that pinch of illusion and well-curbed idealisation. All this is essential not only for the love investment but also, in general terms, for the prospect of maintaining open and vital the signifying horizon of our existences, and of keeping alive the idea that the games are never definitively played out, that things can always be different, and that the contingent spaces within which they have been built up are susceptible, perhaps in small measure, to being opened up again.

And then, for quite a long time, the miracle of intimacy, triggered by being in love and by sexual attraction, calls for attention to be paid to the emotional and affective situation; for patience and tenacity... "skill".

On those same ridges, the possibility of avoiding the different drifts in the psychopathology of amorous life is also played out. After all, Simonetta Diena's work stems precisely from a sympathetic encounter with varied forms of love's suffering and its multiple failures. And on this point too, how immense would the wealth of traditional reflection be, through which this book sails its particular course! Among the many classics and the many important contributions (starting with Freud...), Diena's work reminded me of a slim volume written by a number of authors, edited some years ago by Carlo Maggini (2001), which was entitled *Malinconia d'amore* ("Lovesickness"), a reference to the flip side of love, its inescapable companion—melancholy—which traditional psychopathological thinking assigns to the vicissitudes of love, and subtitled *Frammenti di una psicopatologia della vita amorosa* ("Fragments of a Psychopathology of Love"). In the various declinations of that frag-mented psychopathology, much attention was paid to a theme that is very present in Simonetta's book: the matter of idealisation, so intrinsic to the passions of love, so essential to falling in love, and often so dif-ficult to hold in check.

When touching on this, the terrible phrase laying bare the quin-tessence (and fragility) of the idealising pathology of love in *Madame Bovary* inevitably comes to mind: "Never touch your idols: the gilding will stick to your fingers" (Flaubert, 1857, III, ch. 6, p. 263). So, is nothing true? Is it all just a matter of ephemeral illusions, dazzling the senses, just an alluring void? Precisely the great nihilistic narratives, such as the sublime novels by Flaubert, for example, let us glimpse the intensely powerful nostalgia for what might have been and was not, for what has been lost, or simply for what has remained inaccessible "on the other side of life" (Céline, 1932, p. 7), in between the lines, unsaid. Even the "cynical" finale of *Sentimental Education* treads this path. And Céline too… and even the conclusion of *Dangerous Liaisons*. Precisely for this reason, though, precisely for what they evoke in between the lines, these narratives still talk so powerfully to our spirits, in which they continue to trigger intense contradictory emotions with their apparent assumptions. Paradoxes of those inevitable blends of impossibility and necessity… of those fatal illusions…

Undoubtedly this already complicated matter is still more so in current times. Times of turbulence, uncertainty, confusion; of the disintegration of social, symbolic, and normative structures that traditionally acted as a collective picture and frame to the personal vicissitudes of amorous life, providing the schemas, the culturally shared channels of identification. Suffice to think of what has been called the "subversion of the sex-gender system" (Butler, 1990) and the chaotic liberation at the same time—on those ruins and in that widespread identity uncertainty—of both a modern archaism and a turbulent anarchism of love. Thanks to this, these times are also characterised by a fundamental paradox that ends by weighing heavily on the love relationship. In fact, it now evolves in a symbolic void of forms and collective organisers that manages in some way to sustain and guarantee it, in a sort of concluded disenchantment. It is certainly more fragile and evanescent, but also more or less fatally charged with a surrogate and exorbitant narcissistic importance, precisely thanks to its flimsiness.

In a beautiful book of some years ago, with the significant title *Normal Chaos of Love*, Ulrich Beck and Elisabeth Beck-Gernsheim summed up the question like this:

> The direction in which modern developments are taking us is reflected in the way we idealize Love. Glorifying it in the way we do acts as a counterbalance to the losses we feel in the way we live. God, or priests, or class, or neighbours, then at least there is still You. And the size of the "You" is inversely proportional to the emotional void which otherwise seems to prevail.
>
> (Beck & Beck-Gernsheim, 1990, p. 33)

What an unbefitting narcissistic pressure weighs on the already fragile relationships of love, deprived of their containers and their collective supports! On parental relationships, on couple relationships…

Almost forty years ago, in his prophetic way, Roland Barthes introduced his *A Lover's Discourse: Fragments* with the following words:

> The lover's discourse is today of *an extreme solitude*. … Once a discourse is thus driven by its own momentum into the backwater of the "unreal", exiled from all gregarity, it has no recourse but to become the site, however exiguous, of an *affirmation*.
>
> (Barthes, 1977, p. 1)

For these underlying reasons too, the reflections on the passions of love proposed in this book may be very useful since they originate from the special analytic state of profound sharing. Diena's thinking, pursued with such grace and empathy, succeeds in restoring to us in an enlightened way the trace of the experience under discussion—rather than losing sight of it (as so often happens in "scientific" texts): that experience "that was living and true" (Caproni, 1995, p. 204, author's translation).

A last point: on preparing to read her book, it dawned on me that Simonetta Diena was being decidedly courageous to psychoanalytically tackle the "passions of love". This subject is not only enormous in general terms, but, also in psychoanalysis, if one were to treat it with ambitions of systematicity, would test the entire corpus of psychoanalytic thinking. Some years ago, Otto Kernberg wrote a memorable book about this, with a title only slightly different from Diena's, *Love Relations: Normality and Pathology*. An extremely knowledgeable "treatise". What else might one still have to say? I read Diena's book and, immediately afterwards, re-read the one by Kernberg (1995). And I thought that Simonetta's courage had been put to good use. Let me explain: Kernberg's book is a mine of clinical doctrine. In fact, I continue to propose it to my students. In it, everything holds together: a systematic theoretical apparatus, a wealth of clinical materials, and a brilliant way of inventively integrating different approaches and models. Diverse dimensions that this book only touches upon are thoroughly dealt with there (for example, the aggressive components, but also certain aspects and components of sexuality and eroticism). But in Diena's book, the reader is not looking for something similar to Kernberg's. In comparison, her book, to turn to Caproni's lyrical words once again, "becomes a feather, becomes a sail" (Caproni, 1995, p. 204, author's translation). It is something quite different and, above all, proposes another way—incomparable but complementary to the other—of psychoanalytic listening. There is no claim for systematicity or for exhaustiveness. Diena offers us thoughts that, in the moment in which they enlighten us about important aspects of mankind's experience of love, make us feel its marginal edges, its zones of shadow, its intrinsically contradictory and unresolved aspects; they render it for what it is, wholly irreducible and mysterious.

And we must ask ourselves, though, if this too might not be considered a strength. As Marcel Proust wrote: "The hard and fast lines with which we circumscribe love arise solely from our complete ignorance of life" (Proust, 1919, part 2, p. 85).

Francesco Barale is a psychiatrist and psychoanalyst; full member and training analyst of the SPI and the IPA; Director of the Department of Applied Health and Psycho-Behavioural Sciences at the University of Pavia; Director of the Psychiatry Service in the San Matteo Polyclinic of Pavia.

What place does the subject have in love?

Salvatore Natoli

What can we say about love? In the first place, can we express it in words? Well, if we list all the discourses about love that history has handed down to us over the centuries, then it certainly can be. Indeed, it has been discussed and mulled over since the dawn of time. Perhaps because Eros—to use the words of Phaedrus in Plato's *Symposium*—"is held in honour because he is one of the most ancient ... So Love's great antiquity is widely accepted" (*The Symposium*, 178b–c; pp. 9–10). And it is not just debated, it gets debated until the cows come home because there are so many and so many different ways of loving it is impossible to fully grasp its nature. So that rather than defining it, one can describe it; or—we might say—in describing it, it is better defined.

And this is exactly what Simonetta Diena does in this book, from a psychoanalytic stance and recounting many clinical cases. In these chapters, love is presented from a variety of perspectives, allowing us to go deeper into the experience of it and to grasp it more fully, as far as one can. Love is so varied and capricious that it can even fade into something else, though keeping the same name; it can become ambiguous without the subjects involved even realising. That is why love is where the issue of truth is frequently raised. *True love* is an everyday expression, although it suggests that it is really nothing of the kind or, at least, one has a premonition about its precarious nature; one has doubts about it and fears its flimsiness.

So what, then, is love? *First love*—and the real first love—is a force that begets; it is Lucretius' *alma Venus*, the:

> Pleasure of men and gods (*hominem divunque voluptas*) … for every species comes to birth/conceived through you, and rises forth and gazes on the light (*genus omne animatum concipitur*).
>
> (Lucretius, *The Nature of Things*, I, ll. 1–10; p. 3)

For many reasons, she is the Freudian libido rightly understood as a basic energy, a generative force, and therefore an all-permeating drive. Indeed, all love stories, but—I will go further—all individual vicissitudes and interpersonal relationships are nothing but manifestations of this fatal force that has the power of law. When skilfully fashioned, Eros is a force that begets forms and, in his turn, aspires to immortality. To say it with Plato's words, it is: "Reproduction and birth in beauty (*tokos en kalo*) … Because reproduction is the closest mortals can come to being permanently alive and immortal" (Plato, *The Symposium*, 206e; p. 44).

On the other hand, if it is badly managed or inhibited, it re-emerges as a perversion, which, according to Nietzsche, is something that happened in Christianity—or, better, in a certain type of Christianity: "Christianity gave Eros poison to drink—he did not die of it, to be sure, but degenerated into vice" (Nietzsche, 1886, p. 105, no. 168).

Eros is therefore as all-pervading as he is metaphorical; each time he takes on different, varying forms that are difficult to quantify. To give an idea of this, I will offer a brief list: maternal love, filial love, love-pleasure, passionate love, lost love, love missed out on, impossible love, infantile love, mature love, and so on. Along with their respective pathologies, of course, such as satyriasis, sadism, masochism, narcissism, possessive jealousy, incapacity to bear its loss, over-reactive violence, love turning to hate (but was that love?). As we can see, there are many diverse types of love, but the *ways* of loving are even more numerous and varied. For this reason, *discussing* love—even constructing theories about it—is something quite different from its immediate expression, the love of the person who loves and who, in loving, talks of himself. And yet, even though it might seem strange, even in this case an amorous vocabulary precedes the subjects and not only that: it allows them to air their feelings and therefore to communicate them and make them understandable to others. Forms—I would also say rituals—express desire, sensual pleasure, expectation, the absence of love; how one suffers when dependent; and what can we say about the kiss more than the kiss, or bodies, the caress, the embrace?

As far as experience goes, all this is absolutely individual but is nevertheless inscribed in the codes of love, otherwise it is never recognisable, not even to the lovers themselves (for more on this, see Barthes, *A Lover's Discourse: Fragments*, 1977). Barthes is right; there is a mould for love, but according to the Greek meaning of the word: it must not be taken as something static, "but rather in its gymnastic or choreographic acceptation" (Barthes, 1977, p. 3). It is not a code to conform to but rather a collection of figures to be brought into play at one's pleasure, as fancy takes you and depending on the circumstances. Love is expressed in gestures and figures, and "the figure is the lover at work. Figures take shape insofar as we can recognise, in passing discourse, something that has been read, heard, felt" (Barthes, 1977, p. 4). Understood in this way, "amorous *dis-cursus* … turns like a perpetual calendar, an encyclopedia of affective culture" (Barthes, 1977, p. 7).

Stories of love are, after all, stories—indeed *love stories*—and perhaps only poets have the words for them because, in fact, they do not talk of love but instead "make it talk"; they grasp love in all its fluctuations and almost mime it. Here in this book and in its most intense moments, the author turns to poets and also to the cinema to talk of love. It seems clear to me that talking about love is something different from love that *talks of itself*: the two issues move along different planes even if, given the object (love), these planes converge. This book seeks the point of convergence: in shifting one plane onto another, it attempts to give as much importance to theory—the psychoanalytic contributions about love—as it does to clinical practice (Freud's clinical cases), where the word is left to the so-called patient or, more pertinently, to the subject involved in the experience. But where is this subject? What is his place in love? The book explores this, and it would be quite out of place for me to add more; I will thus limit myself to a few comments stemming from the most common forms in which love suddenly manifests itself, and so I say: *love/pleasure; love/passion; love/fidelity*. But is the same love expressed in these three forms? Or does one exclude the other following a true/false dichotomy? Or again, even if different, do they have anything in common so that we can say that they are three faces of the same experience? And they call it love, one says; but how and when is it really love? These interrogatives explain why an experience at first sight so elementary and obvious becomes so problematic; why love stories are so often unresolved and why it is precisely love that causes pain.

Already in ancient Greece—but not only there—the question of whether happiness corresponded or not to pleasure, and in this case to pleasure *par excellence*—meaning love—was the object of long and unresolved controversy. Let us recall Plato's celebrated opening to *Philebus*:

> Then let us begin with the goddess herself, of whom Philebus says that she is called Aphrodite, but that her real name is Pleasure … and with her, as I was just now saying, we must begin, and consider what her nature is.
>
> (Plato, *Philebus*, 12, b–c)

Pleasures are manifold and various but *the* pleasure is Aphrodite, love in its physical, carnal dimension that seizes hold of men in their entirety and subjugates them. Which leads to a perfect match between love and pleasure: in this case, to love means to look for pleasure and this closely corresponds to Freud's sexual instinct–pleasure principle dynamics. This love can be an attachment to a single source of pleasure—one person—or to various sources of pleasure. What is common to both cases is "the attachment to pleasure", better if not bound to a single source and therefore not tied to any person in particular. This is Lucretius' *vulgivaga Venus*, the "vagabond Venus", who takes her pleasure wherever she finds it and is bound to nothing if not to pleasure itself: "Nor does the man who gives the slip to Love lack for its fruit;/Rather, he enjoys it without penalty or pain: (*sine poena commode sumit*)/Pleasure's unalloyed not for the lovesick, but the *sane*" (Lucretius, *The Nature of Things*, IV, ll. 1073–1075; p. 139).

These are key lines because Lucretius, perhaps without even wanting to, introduces the difference between love and pleasure. Love, in fact, is to be avoided because it makes a subject's personal satisfaction depend on the other and this leads to pain. It should be noted that for those who love in this way, Lucretius uses the word *miseris* ("lovesick"): one suffers loss of the other, one is obliged to beg for love. On the contrary, sensual pleasure—pure pleasure—is clearer "for the sane". ("Sane", for Lucretius, meaning "wise men".) Love is a sickness. At this point, love is no longer identified absolutely with pleasure—understood as "disastrous lust" ("*dira libido*"; IV, l. 1046; p. 138)—and alludes to something else, or better, to another way of loving.

And so an impalpable shift occurs from *love for pleasure* to the *pleasure of love* but not so much and not only of love as such, but of love for someone who is not perhaps absolute but certainly specific: the *you alone* of love. There cannot be love without pleasure, but here pleasure transcends and becomes something else, it becomes *passion*, which "Took me with such great joy of him", as Dante's Francesca says in *The Divine Comedy* (vol. 1, *Hell*, Canto V, l. 104). Here pleasure in the other transmutes into a *bond*, into need of the other and only of him/her. The pleasure of love is heart-breaking; it makes one suffer, and even draw pleasure from this suffering: the well-known *pangs of love*. This way of feeling is alien to those who seek only for pleasure—and it is unimportant whether they look for it in many bodies or in just one—; in any case, the other is always instrumental in pleasure, being nothing more and nothing less than just being a body. But once satisfied, desire is not placated but returns with equal vehemence and urgency, to use once again the words of Lucretius: "But then the fever starts again, madness must soon return" ("*redit rabies eadem et furor*"; IV, l. 1117; p. 140). Pleasure looks for variety but finds repetition until strength wains and: "This also—one lives ever at the other's beck and call" ("*sub nutu degitur aetas*"; IV, l. 1121; p. 140).

And yet even the person who goes in search of pleasure, in order to really enjoy it, is obliged to enter into purely *fictitious relationships*; in fact, little can be obtained from the other if he/she is not involved, if in some way he/she is not recognised. In many cases, seduction is nothing but this: a *passepartout for pleasure*; which is, indeed, made up of stories, casual adventures, *stolen kisses*. Don Giovanni is our master. Unless one does not limit oneself uniquely to consuming pleasure. In that case, it corresponds to the release of a natural need—like every animal appetite—which could turn into an obsession; or, more prosaically, it is a compensation, a tax to pay against solitude and the lack of love. Along with Nietzsche, I would never dream of denying the right to pleasure, nor, here, do I intend to express opinions about it; I only want to emphasise that in the search for pleasure *alone*, the other as *the other* can only represent an encumbrance, which clamours to be removed. And so I ask: can pleasure alone be called love? I will skirt around the answer to say: well then, passion is the perfect opposite.

I have dwelt at length on love/pleasure because I think that today the search for fleeting opportunities or for furtive love is more widespread and frequent than the increasingly rare, literary, grand passions. At least in the Western hemisphere. But, despite this, the idea that passion is the seat of love and that without passion there cannot be love is still deeply entrenched. And, in fact, I applaud the fitting choice of Goethe's poem "Selige Sehnsucht"/"Blessed Longing" as the epigraph for Chapter Five, "Fatal love". So difficult to translate, the second word—*Sehnsucht*—has here been rendered as "longing". In love/passion you do not know—at least on first impressions—why you fall in love. Passion, in fact, entails suffering, a falling prey to the other. As we know, passions are overwhelming, though it is not known where they spring from nor even to where they lead. But lovers do not worry about such things in the slightest because you simply live passion. And passion yearns for complete union: "New desire unbounded/Rends you, that you may beget"/"Auf zu *höherer Begattung*" (Goethe, 1819, "Blessed Longing"). Just you, only you, and forever. Passion demands oneness because, while pleasure can be shared and distributed, this does not hold good for passion. Passion yearns for eternity: it is the highest pleasure and a peak at which one would always want to remain. One burns with passion; one suffers an almost alchemical transformation; one experiences the Dantesque *trasumanar* (to transhumanise, to go beyond the human; *The Divine Comedy*, vol. 3. *Paradise*, Canto I, l. 70). But this state is too high for us, for our bodies, for our finite forces; in fact, at the highest point, we are suffused with the feeling that we will not be able to make it, we will surely yield. Which leads to torment. As Rilke writes:

> Weren't you astonished by the caution of human gestures
> on Attic gravestones? Wasn't love and departure
> placed so gently on shoulders that it seemed to be made
> of a different substance than in our world? Remember the hands,
> how weightlessly they rest, though there is power in the torsos.
> These self-mastered figures know: "We can go this far,
> This is ours, to touch one another this lightly; the gods
> Can press down harder upon us. But that is the gods' affair."
>   (Rilke, 1923, "The Second Elegy", ll. 69–74, p. 15)

Exactly, it is up to the gods: in fact, if all measure of time is lost at the very peak—it practically comes to a stop—when it inexorably takes up its rhythmic beating once again, lovers do everything they can to detain it in *long goodbyes*, but they do not have the power to stop it. It does not surprise us that in its bid to make love eternal, romantic literature could do nothing but let lovers die. And this book shows exactly how passion—fatal love—ends by becoming in actual fact impossible love. We are made of time and we can draw on flashes of eternity only in passing—*per transitum*—and, as we know, passions die down and loves wane. The only type of eternity that man can bestow on love is that of making it last. If passion in its fusional nature suspends differences and illudes/deludes, in order to last love has to come to terms with truth, and recognise the other's irreducible diversity, which not even the greatest love can negate.

From where, how, why passion bursts forth is something that still remains a mystery. But in igniting the senses, in merging with the other, do we really recognise him/her for what he/she is? Do we love someone and model them on us, in equal measure to our desire? To turn to Rilke's words once again:

> It is one thing to sing the beloved. Another, alas,
> to invoke that hidden, guilty river-god of the blood.
> …
> Not for you, girl so aware of him, not for your mouth
> did his lips curve themselves into a more fruitful expression.
> …
> … relieved, he nestles
> Into your sheltering heart, takes hold, and begins himself.
> But did he ever begin himself, really?
> (Rilke, 1923, "The Third Elegy", ll. 1–2, 16–17, 23–25, p. 17)

Indeed, "*Aber began er sich je?*/But did he ever begin himself, really?" (l. 25). Nothing has probably really begun. And the perceptive poet writes:

> Yes, you did frighten his heart; but more ancient terrors
> Plunged into him at the shock of that feeling.
> (Rilke, 1923, "The Third Elegy", ll. 20–21, p. 17)

It is the "hidden river-god of the blood": the subject never gets the better of passion; passion always overcomes him. But when the other emerges and imposes himself in his difference, when one realises that this person differs from the image we have created of him—and which perhaps disappoints us—passion evaporates and, in evaporating, any reasons that might have motivated us to proceed along a common path disappear.

To use a stock phrase, we can only say: "It was wonderful". In the pages of this book, we are beautifully shown how passion—fatal love—in actual fact ends by being impossible. Or is transformed. As Simonetta Diena writes (Chapter Five):

> Fatal love cannot stand up to everyday frustrations. Fatal love yearns for the absolute, for infinity without time. On returning, through the analytic process, to a shared temporal state, to the before and to the after of a coherent and logical narration, Elisabetta [a clinical case] gave up this type of passion ... in exchange for a daily life full of interests, relationships, and also passions—small, normal, human passions.

Indeed, passion is by no means destined to disappoint; in fact, it can be an *opportunity*, the decisive encounter, the best way for leading us to the other; it can wake us to the fact that one is made for the other, and make us feel that that person is necessary for completing our life since otherwise it would remain incomplete. Lastly, it is a means for discovering together the joys of a shared life. At this point, *love-passion* mutates into *love-alliance*. But does passion die in this alliance? Not at all; indeed, it is the best way for endowing it with continuity. Just as passion does not rule out pleasure—but removes it from being dispersed by transforming it into a totalising experience—so the alliance bestows history on this passion, without any lessening in pleasure. Fidelity confers on passion the only eternity possible: to keep it alive in time. As T. S. Eliot says: "Only through time time is conquered" (1935, "Burnt Norton", II). Time is conquered because, if it is not conquered, it simply consumes us. But fidelity is quite different from routine; indeed, it demands constant renewal, especially in front of whatever might spark separation. Time by itself steals the *aura* from passion and breaks the spell; so, too, the exertions of the everyday, becoming used to the other whose presence is taken too much for granted so that it can unintentionally turn into mutual indifference; where the other returns to appearing necessary, perhaps, when he is not there. In addition, there are external temptations; today's mobility offers such easy opportunities for going out; and, finally, there is proof itself of our pain, which can renew the alliance, but also break it, when reproaching the other with blame. Life is this, but when being faithful, love recognises the other, preferring and *choosing him/her*.

Thus the seal of love is friendship: passion's yearning for eternity turns into a *bond* for life and for death. And here we must cite Catullus' "Poem 109", which is quite above suspicion regarding the vehemence of passion, but in which the vocabulary of passion begins to be transposed into that of friendship:

> You dangle before me, my love and life, the prospect
> That this love of ours will be cherished and last forever.
> Great Gods, make it that she can promise truthfully,
> And say it sincerely and from her heart
> So that we may live our whole lives
> By this everlasting pact of sanctified love.

As we can see, here passion starts to become a promise: it is no longer only *pathos*, the spontaneously experienced, but a commitment of love. But what is the secret to making this love last? "So that we may live our whole lives/By this everlasting pact of sanctified love." Note the words everlasting (*aeternum*), pact (*foedus*) of sanctified love (*sanctae ... amicitae*). The Roman elegy knew this well; Propertius knew it when he wrote: "Should I be ashamed to live content with [just] one girl-friend?" (Propertius, *Elegies*, 2.30B, l. 23; p. 64).

If Propertius speaks of shame, it is clear that even then love-friendship was something to be laughed at and certainly not common. Indeed: "In love devotion counts for much, and faithfulness (*fides*)" (2.26B, l. 27; p. 58), which has little to do with the institution of marriage, which in itself is concerned with patrimony. And Propertius continues: "One faith, one day, shall carry us both off" (2.20, l. 18; p. 50); and it is only that type of love that can make lovers say: "But paired in misery and shared love we'll be forced/To weep on *one another's shoulder*" (1.5, ll. 19–30; p. 8; author's italics). Here, there is a shift from the *delectatio* to the *dilectio*: in Latin, both terms mean *pleasure*, but the first signifies sexual enjoyment and also recreation, or pastime, whereas the second also denotes love but in the form of caring for and looking after someone, from *diligo* meaning to love but also to appreciate, esteem, and honour. Certainly a pact is honoured, but above all it is the person and the dignity of the other that we would never allow ourselves to offend. These are the verbs that make love long-lasting.

But we also know that alliances dissolve and love-friendship in itself is absolutely no guarantee of the *forever*. We change and life changes us, and it comes to pass that—as we know—relationships that before seemed to resound in unison or that, in any case, found some sort of harmony, are no longer on the same wavelength. Over time, latent aspects unknown to us, desires that we never had before, ideas that we would never have dreamt could come to mind emerge. You thought you knew yourselves and then, almost without realising it, you start to become alien to each other. Leaving aside caprices, new passions can always burst into flame—and do burst into flame—opening up unexplored horizons, bringing sensations of a budding youthfulness in the world, a new beginning. Now, if it is true that passion can never last or have any history unless it is transformed into love-friendship, it is also true that no alliance can be renewed if passion dies. To love means feeling unconditionally transported by the other, I would say need of the other. It means *suffering*; but it also means *doing* something; it is a reciprocal taking custody of the other, leaving the other his/her freedom intact. Why? Because he/she can *always choose me again*, want me forever.

In discussing love-friendship, I have used the term *dilectio*, caring for and looking after, which signifies love taking custody. First love, then, is a mother's love: first, at least chronologically, it psychologically provides the model for all future loves. And from this, Simonetta Diena (Chapter Two) takes her cue in this book on love:

> On the beach a small child wanders away from his mother towards the water's edge. After a few uncertain steps, he swivels round towards her, looks at her intently, and says: "You watch me, ok?" Reassured, he moves off with greater determination towards the sea. Meanwhile his mother never takes her eyes off her son for an instant.

I will not attempt a deeper psychoanalytic reading of this story, nor go into the mother's preverbal function, the pact between mother and child that is a relationship of reciprocal subjectivisation. I am not competent to do so and, besides, it is all in the book. For my part, I will concern myself only with the semantic nature of the looks exchanged. To look into each other's eyes: what does that tell us? There is always the splendid spark of that first glance, but also the trust in being able to look at each other again, in being able to read the words in the eyes of the other: "You can always trust in my love". And if not in mine, who then will you ever be able to trust? Passions are frequent, perhaps intense, but fleeting—as Rilke illustrates:

> But we, when moved by deep feeling, evaporate; we breathe our-
> selves out and away; from moment to moment our emotion grows
> fainter, like a perfume.
>   (Rilke, 1923, "The Second Elegy", ll. 18–20, p. 11)

Love-friendship is not like this but, on the other hand, is not so frequent. "All things excellent (*omnia praeclara*) are as difficult as they are rare (*tam difficilia, quam rara*)", as Spinoza says (*Ethics*, Book V, P42; p. 181). At this point, I leave the question open as to what true love really is.

Salvatore Natoli is Ordinary Professor of Theoretical Philosophy, Faculty of the Sciences of Formation, University of Milan Bicocca.

INTRODUCTION

O tell me the truth about love

Some say love's a little boy,
And some say it's a bird,
Some say it makes the world go around,
Some say that's absurd,
And when I asked the man next-door,
Who looked as if he knew,
His wife got very cross indeed,
And said it wouldn't do.

When it comes, will it come without warning
Just as I'm picking my nose?
Will it knock on my door in the morning,
Or tread in the bus on my toes?
Will it come like a change in the weather?
Will its greeting be courteous or rough?
Will it alter my life altogether?
O tell me the truth about love.

—W. H. Auden (1938)

In *Yoshe Kalb/The Sinner*, written in Yiddish in 1932, Israel Joshua Singer, brother of the better-known Isaac Bashevis Singer, describes the first meeting between the novel's two main characters with these words:

> Malkah ... made the visit brief and rose to go. Just as she reached the door, and stretched out her hand, it was opened from the other side and she stood face to face with Nahum. They started and made an attempt to ignore each other ... For an instant they looked at each other, a wild, unconscious joy lighting their faces. Then, catching themselves up, they looked away, and remained standing.
>
> (Singer, 1932, p. 69)

The novel continues, depicting how Malkah and Nahum—both married and, what's more, in-laws by way of their recent, respective marriages— would never ever be able to get together, despite being consumed by an irresistible, violent passion, which would never be slaked. And in fact the novel offers their passion no solution, except in the final destruction not only of both of them but also their entire worlds. Malkah dies, and with her the child in her womb, Nahum's son. And Nahum, at the end of this gripping novel, which is based on a true story, is censured and condemned because:

> You know not what you do; there is no taste in your life or in your deeds, because you are a dead wanderer in the chaos of the world!
>
> (Singer, 1932, p. 244)

Yoshe Kalb narrates an *amour fou*, an overwhelming passion, both sensual and mystic. As well as offering a fascinating panorama of the life of a world that is no more, and the violent conflicts between the Hasidic Jews of Galicia and the enlightened Jews of Germany, the contrasts and conflicts between sense and sensibility and between passion and reason, the novel also metaphorically portrays man's impotence to decide his own fate, to live within himself, with his own choices, without being trapped in forced exile from a non-existent homeland. According to Ethel Person (1991), the key psychological elements of love are idealisation and the desire to be united with the beloved. We could therefore argue that when you cannot love your love object you are forcefully exiled from your own self, alienated from your deepest feelings, forced to deny the truest parts of yourself. You become a double of yourself, a nothing in the chaos that the world around you has become. Forced to deny your deepest drives and hide what you experience and feel, you stop existing. The conflict between "Sense and Sensibility", to quote Jane Austen (1811), does not exist. It is impossible to combine the reality principle with the pleasure principle in a way that is adequate and satisfactory, and to make room for one's own passions within the boundaries that can ensure the survival of one's own ego. From this viewpoint, we could argue that passion stems from and develops in an intermediate space between the libidinal and narcissistic structures of the ego, that is, between drives and projective identifications.

In Ovid's *Metamorphoses*, one of the best-known mythological tales is that of Apollo and Daphne. Apollo had boasted he was the best at using a bow and arrow, and Cupid, wanting to take revenge on his pride, shot the god with a golden dart that could make gods and mortals alike fall madly in love with the first person they would set their eyes upon; he also shot the nymph Daphne, whom Apollo fancied, with a leaden dart that would make her shun love. As soon as the nymph, shot by the leaden arrow, caught sight of Apollo, she began to flee. So Apollo started to pursue her, until Daphne got near a river, begging her father Peneus (probably the river itself) to help her. Daphne turned into a laurel tree, escaping Apollo's love forever. Defeated, the god decided to make this tree evergreen, considering it as sacred to him and representing a sign of glory meant to adorn the head of the best among men (the victorious generals on Capitol Hill), those capable of exciting undertakings.

In this myth, it is interesting to note that Apollo, a victim of an impossible love that is beyond his reach, and suffering for this loss, regains possession of an aspect of himself by transforming the lost love in a sign of glory for victorious war campaigns. In the tormenting mixture of recovery and loss involved in every love story, this repossession is indispensable in order not to be destroyed and to escape lovesickness, the suffering for love.

One of the most common metaphors of love is the comparison with an illness that only the possession of the love object can cure. Also Freud (1917a, p. 143) talked about it as one of the three conditions in which "the Ego is not master in its own house". Passions of love belong to

Figure 1. Apollo and Daphne, life-sized Baroque marble sculpture, by Gian Lorenzo Bernini, executed between 1622 and 1625.

human nature; they constitute its most intimate essence; they are what man needs to survive. As Havelock Ellis (1937) argued:

> It is more passion, more passion and fuller, that we need. It is more passion and ever more that we need if we are to undo the work of Hate, if we are to add to the gaiety and splendour of life to the sum of human achievement, to the aspiration of human ecstasy.
>
> (Ellis, 1937, p. 61)

Or as Freud (1914c, p. 85) maintained: "We are bound to fall ill if, in consequence of frustration, we are unable to love."

But although literature and psychoanalysis talk about love as being something comprehensible and universal, in that it can be understood and identified, it is nevertheless obvious from both that there are many different ways of loving as well as different types of love.

And in these pages we will discuss this universal but at the same time singular nature of the experience of love, or, in other words, the profound and intimate trait, the unique ingredient, that makes love possible.

So this book talks about love, about how we fall in love, why we fall in love, and how much we suffer the pangs of love when we cannot love or be loved. It does not aim to define passion, which by its very nature escapes definition or, rather, gracefully conforms to it for a moment but then breaks loose, leaving its victims high and dry.

Instead, here we intend to talk primarily about how all this is experienced, tackled, shared, and worked through during the analytic experience.

Several times Freud advanced the notion that a woman in love was no subject for analysis, as though love absorbed every other conceivable libidinal investment. Today this clinical impression has been amended, due especially to clinical matters being very different now.

In his clinical practice, an analyst is constantly participating in the infinite vicissitudes and sufferings of his patients' love lives. In fact, love is one of the most perplexing yet at the same time the most natural emotional states to go through in the life of a human being. It so strongly attacks our illusion of being autonomous and independent, of not needing anybody, and yet we never ask ourselves why we persist in tormenting ourselves with it in such a way, always seeking for someone to love and to be loved by. Would it not be simpler to be satisfied with just loving ourselves?

Why can Malkah and Nahum (and many other leading characters of literary masterpieces) not resign themselves to their fate?

Already one hundred years ago, in "On narcissism: an introduction", Freud postulated that:

> Here we may even venture to touch on the question of what makes it necessary at all for our mental life to pass beyond the limits of narcissism and to attach the libido to objects. The answer which would follow from our line of thought would once more be that this necessity arises when the cathexis of the ego with libido exceeds a

certain amount. A strong egoism is a protection against falling ill, but in the last resort we must begin to love in order not to fall ill, and we are bound to fall ill if, in consequence of frustration, we are unable to love.

(Freud, 1914c, p. 85)

In other words, it is what the poet professes: "Beloved by none, it is sad to live" (Thomas Haynes Bayly, 1844). And one dies of this sadness, we might add.

We know that the need to love and be loved can be read as a *prototype* of every human need and every relationship between human beings. To be loved is wishing to be seen, known, recognised for what we are in our deepest and most hidden inner selves, in our wildest desires to live and be free. It is a need for *knowledge, gratitude, and recognition*. If you cannot love the object of your love, you are condemned to perpetual exile from a non-existent homeland.

Love goes through our lives and permeates our stories. Many philosophers, writers, poets, and psychoanalysts have undertaken the challenging quest of understanding the intimate nature of passions; however, although love has been the object of a great number of studies and research, of tales, poems, paintings, and even buildings, although it has been investigated throughout the centuries and by the most diverse cultures, despite all this, its elusive nature cannot be fully explained. We keep trying to understand what remains a mystery: "The language of love is impossible, inadequate, immediately allusive when one would like it to be most straightforward; it is a flight of metaphors", as Julia Kristeva put it (1983, p. 1).

What is that thing we call "love"? First of all, love indicates and represents the existence of someone on whom one becomes imprinted, and to whom one remains attached. Love is "a violation of our illusion of our independency ... the mysterious alchemy of mutual interpenetration with the subjectivity of the other" (Grotstein, 2000, p. 153). Love is when there is a normal and adaptive idealisation in which each lover donates his or her own self to the other, "the yearning to be forever united with another person" (Bergmann, 1987, p. 259). "Love is a point of intersection between desire and reality. Love reveals reality to desire and creates the transition from the erotic object to the beloved person" (Kernberg, 1995, p. 45, quoting the poet Octavio Paz (1974, p. 190), and his "overwhelming conciseness").

We cannot say that psychoanalysis has developed a definition of love of its own, although passions and their agonies are often at the centre of many patients' analyses. Freud suggested that Eros was so strong a force that in effect it tricked its victim into loving, so that mating could take place, a sort of chemical mechanism, a Darwinian evolutionary plan to preserve the species. Although psychoanalysis has not yet produced a definition of love of its own, and although in psychoanalytic literature references to love are surprisingly scarce, we can try to explain, though not really "*If this be love*", at least what occurs intrapsychically when one falls in love and what can turn a passion or an unspeakable grief into a softer and more shareable love.

Although, as Green writes: "I think that art, mainly literature and especially poetry, undoubtedly gives a better introduction to the knowledge of love, which we grasp by intuition ... To date, science has not contributed anything to our understanding of the core of the love experience" (2005, p. 5). Which, I might add, is what the famous aria by Cherubino reveals in Mozart's *Le Nozze di Figaro*: "*Voi che sapete che cosa è amor, donne vedete se io l'ho nel cor*" ("Ladies, you who know what love is, look to see if it is in my heart"). This line by Lorenzo Da Ponte (1785) remains surprisingly true: many people wonder if the emotion they feel is love and seek the answers outside and not inside themselves.

Often, in my work as a psychoanalyst, I have been involved with patients needing help because they did not understand why they were suffering, for they did not recognise that lovesickness was trapping them, or because they were not able to overcome a prolonged and per- sistent unhappiness caused by an unsatisfactory and frustrating love. Frequently, these patients appear to be stuck, prisoners of a love invest- ment that could not be satisfied, for which they could not find a future, and which, in spite of all this, they pursued with much determination and obstinacy. The reason why they would ask for help was the pro- longed and persistent unhappiness caused by this unsatisfactory and frustrating investment. In these patients, however, the need to over- come the frustration caused by an impossible love would not emerge; they would rather wish to find some illusory solution through which the loved one would at last come back to them, or would become aware of their love and of the mistake of not reciprocating it. If I could have offered them a powerful love potion, they would have used it, but anal- ysis travels other paths.

The roots of love are already there in early infancy. However, primitive childhood experiences alone are not sufficient to explain the complex and infinite vicissitudes that passion encounters and develops during our lives. When we fall in love, we stage the experiences and the unconscious phantasies of our past life through the mechanism of projective identification. Therefore, love plays a key role in the formation of idealisation, and in the development of illusion and disappointment, but in time the idealisation changes with the changing of the individual and society.

While not seeking to proffer a definition of love, many analysts have nevertheless discussed the reasons, vicissitudes, ways, and consequences that drive humans to love. For the sake of brevity and clarity, I will summarise here a few fundamental concepts in psychoanalytic thought over the years, taking key contributions by authors who have explored these aspects as my reference point and discussing their work.

In this book, I aim to broach the question of the two levels—oedipal and pre-oedipal—of love relations, which coexist and overlap in every matter of love, although with shifting importance according to the individuals involved and the objects of the love investment.

Unlike other authors, I do not think we can effectively distinguish between a mature, adult love and an infantile/adolescent, romantic, passionate, and idealised love. I believe that both exist and expand in the love relationships, on different levels, and at varying degrees of intensity according to the moment. Consequently, I find myself in perfect agreement with Kernberg (1974a) when he points out that the ability to fall in love and to continue being in love depends on having attained two fundamental developmental milestones: first, to arrive at mastering one's pre-oedipal dynamics, and, second, to successfully overcome the oedipal conflicts. Since we are dealing with developmental paths that are by no means necessarily linear, pre-oedipal elements and unresolved oedipal conflicts will always be left within us that, in the unfolding and evolving of our lives, will go on to determine the personality and character of each one of us, including inevitable pathological elements.

* * *

I have divided the book into a number of chapters. In the first, I deal with the psychoanalytic contributions that are, in my opinion, the most important and meaningful on this topic, attempting to summarise some fundamental concepts of psychoanalytic thought, taking as my reference point those authors, starting with Freud, who have best explored these elements, in order to discuss their work.

The second chapter discusses the earliest mother–child relationship, and attempts to construct a correspondence between this relationship, the patient–analyst relationship in analysis, and subsequent first love relationships. Therefore, in "Ways of seeing: the role of vision" we take a look at the first imprinting of love, stemming from the meeting with the mother, through a theoretical reading of Winnicott and Bion.

Instead, the third chapter attempts to tackle what we might call the romantic preliminary question in favour of the sensual experience, in art and above all in clinical work, with regard to what we might call mature, or adult, love. I have called this chapter, for reasons that will become clear on reading it, "Nostalgia, or 'something to love'".

The third and following chapters find their starting points in clinical situations that have offered me cues for tackling various aspects of love, vicissitudes that syncretically sum up assorted kinds of passion.

In chronological order, we come to the fourth chapter, "The unbearableness of being abandoned", which describes how in certain situations one cannot accept the end of a love story and one persists for too long in its grip thanks to mechanisms of pathological denial, with dramatic and destructive implications for the subsequent development of one's own existence.

The fifth chapter explores the question of "Fatal love", that yearning for romantic unhappiness, typical of the Western novel's way of living and imagining love with the recurrent, inexorable involvement of death as its unavoidable and only solution.

In the sixth chapter, "Transference love: 'There really was absolutely nothing to be done...'", I discuss transference love—a well-known situation—and its fundamental importance if tackled well and used during the entire evolution of the therapy.

The seventh chapter, "Maternal love: 'Flowing-over-at-oneness' (F. Tustin)", describes maternal love understood as the love for a lost mother. It is a complex chapter, which differs from the earlier "Ways of seeing" because it describes the consequences of the early loss of the first love object. It is an anomalous discourse because in general we prefer to talk of maternal love in the sense of a mother's love for her son or daughter. But, as I try to describe, it is the inexorable nature of the love that a son or daughter has for his or her mother that then bestows meaning on the whole of his or her affective life.

In the eighth chapter, "Love in old age", love is represented in many ways. At times, it is a fierce and persistent desire for what has been lost, for what could not be developed, due to defences, anxieties, and resistances to drives that at that moment seemed unbearable. At times, instead, it is the revenge for a right long repressed and denied, the right to be recognised in one's own possibilities for loving and being loved, a right that was suffocated by repressive education, or by political/social/economic beliefs. At times, it is an excruciating nostalgia for something that has been once but that was lost long ago, widowhood that is still impossible to bear, perhaps decades later, not yet replaced by other forms of affection.

And then in the ninth chapter, a subject that is very common in clinical practice will be explored, "Making choices; not making choices", or, in other words, why it is seemingly impossible to choose between two people who at first sight both appear to be the object of the love investment.

The tenth chapter concerns the "Incapacity to love". With all its many declinations, this subject could become a book by itself, but I have chosen to include it all the same in this collection because it is a common experience in our clinical practice and something that can often be resolved, or therapeutically adjusted.

The widespread social acknowledgement of diversity has produced a huge change in approach in recent years towards homosexuality. The eleventh chapter, "The homosexual universe and physical perfection", does not, therefore, discuss the sexual orientation of homosexuals but, instead, a number of constant elements that have appeared with greater frequency in the clinical material of gay loves.

During a final re-reading of this book, I added a short twelfth chapter, "Love on the silver screen", because I realised that I have made so many references to films, novels, poems, and the opera that they could in fact stand as a group alone among my Passions of Love.

I would like to point out, though, that, in choosing this abundance of quotations from poems and works of art in general, my choice was not based on their purely aesthetic elements, in other words the most successful bits, or, to put it differently, their "most beautiful" lines, from a standpoint of aesthetic enjoyment. Instead, I chose works that made me think like an analyst, that is, they placed me in a position of analytic listening as well as of pure poetic and aesthetic enjoyment. I frequently find these situations again in my clinical practice, and indeed refer back to them, as they have assumed universal value, like all true poetry. One thing in particular convinced me to choose these particular excerpts: the impulse I felt on reading them to change them, to intervene in the story line, altering the protagonists' destiny, intervening after all as an analyst, confronted with the Greek Fates, relentless tragedy.

Poetry is not just a collection of events seen and remembered, but, aided by imagination, is a much deeper reading of them. John Keats spoke of "negative capability" to describe that mysterious moment "when man is capable of being in uncertainties, Mysteries, doubts, without any irritable reaching after fact & reason" (Keats, 1817, p. 156). This is the capacity to tolerate doubt and the sensation of infinity, the "negative capability" that Bion, repeating Keats' words exactly, has so rightly called our attention to, the: "Capacity of the unconscious—negative capability, when a man is capable of being in uncertainties, Mysteries, doubts, without any irritable reaching after fact and reason" (Bion, 1970, p. 125).

A work of art needs to have internal coherence; this coherence may not correspond to the logic of the Unique and Absolute Truth, but is required in order to accept suspended attention, the negative capability that is so essential in every analysis, for every patient. For these reasons, I chose films and novels, or operas, that shone the spotlight on diverse characteristics of love's passions and that allowed me to remain suspended, while reflecting that the protagonists could have had different destinies, that the plots could have pursued different paths. In other words, I chose works in which the same suspended concern unfolds that we experience during analysis, and that cannot exist without this "negative capability" that Keats talks of.

Generally speaking, I like to think that a film director chooses one particular ending instead of another, and I also like to think, like many of my patients, that the finale or the plot could, though, have played out differently. There is in the spectator and reader a negative capability to remain suspended for the whole duration of the work. How will it end, we often ask ourselves when we are not completely gripped by something. Instead, when we are totally hooked, we accept the path chosen by the author and gratefully follow it; grateful because someone else is taking the trouble, in our place, to disentangle tangled skeins, conflicts, desires, dreams, and needs. In analysis, this work is the task of the analytic couple. The passions of love that account for a large part of literature, poetry, or opera can be found with exactly the same story lines in our clinical cases. Art imitates life; life imitates art. I sometimes think that on the silver screen a certain plot would not be credible, and yet, here I am, listening to it live. Vice versa, I sometimes rediscover clips of clinical vignettes on screen. As an analyst, I find this comforting, since it introduces the possibility of perhaps being able to modify the plot of the story narrated by the patient—"A sail passes by, pushing the night further away" (Milite, 2005)—to transform the apparently inevitable destiny of that particular issue.

A certain capacity can be appreciated in mature loves and their narratives that an attentive analyst picks up on at the start of an analysis, like a passionate reader of a novel. This is the ability to generate an illusion in the reader, the spectator, the protagonist, which is felt as both real and not real at the same time.

In the confused mixture of emotions that are felt in love, idealisation of the other is essential for keeping the relationship alive over the years. If this idealisation, this loving illusion, can at the same time have one foot in reality, and accept its limitations, and the other in phantasy, the powerful libidinal force that keeps a relationship going, then we have good probabilities for successfully maintaining reassuring and familiar love relationships that appear to continually renew themselves. Otherwise we repeatedly find ourselves up against unhappy nostalgia and love for passion, rather than passion for love. In other words, endlessly seeking the idealised yearning that the impact with reality regularly shatters, since reality can stand nothing that has anything ideal about it.

Finally, I cannot avoid making a last mention of an important aspect of love life in Western culture. Denis de Rougemont discussed this in his famous book *Love in the Western World* (1939), when he suggested that the romance of Tristan and Isolde was a "myth", or rather a story that summed up in a simple way a number of more or less analogous situations. Robert Graves (1954) defines myth as a cultural continuum present in all Indo-European populations, whose traces can be found from the Vedas to the Bible, to Gaelic myths, and postulates that all rituality stems from man's need to master the Earth's cycle. In the strict sense, myths express the rules of conduct of a social or religious group; they are symbolic narratives of life and death, the origin of the gods, sacrifices, and taboos. To close with de Rougemont: *"But the most profound characteristic of a myth is the power which it wins over us, usually without our knowing"* (1939, p. 19; italics in the original).

There is a profound bond between life and literature. In a more recent book, *Deceit, Desire and the Novel: Self and Other in Literary Structure* of 1961, René Girard states that the triangle established between the individual, the desired object, and the mediator is a constant, pivotal scheme in a novel's structure. The man would be incapable of desire without the help of a model, whether aware or unconscious of this, and the object or aim of his desire is proposed to him or imposed by a third, who acts as mediator. Girard calls this model "mimetic desire". It would seem that in order to proliferate, our desire for love has need of an influential intermediary, so that men are persuaded to desire what others desire. Many world-famous literary characters have offered myths to love and passion. Anna Karenina, Natasha, Madame Bovary, and, why not, many characters brought to life by Barbara Cartland, have been sources of inspiration in real life and not only vice versa.

With this in mind, I would like to quote a passage by Amos Oz (2003) describing life in Jerusalem in the 1940s:

> We were surrounded by Russians of every sort. There were many Tolstoyans. ... Our neighbourhood Tolstoyans (whom my parents referred to as "Tolstoyshchiks") were without exception devout vegetarians, world-reformers with strong feelings for nature, seekers after the moral life, lovers of humankind, lovers of every single living creature, with a perpetual yearning for the rural life, for simple agricultural labour among fields and orchards. ... Some of them were Tolstoyans who might have stepped straight out of the pages of a novel by Dostoevski: tormented, talkative, suppressing their desires, consumed by ideas. But all of them, Tolstoyans and Dostoevskians alike, in our neighbourhood of Kerem Avraham, worked for Chekhov. ... The area where we lived, belonged to Chekhov.
>
> (Oz, 2003, pp. 3–4)

From a psychoanalytic point of view, I sometimes find myself tempted to shuffle the cards, especially in clinical practice. What would Anna Karenina's life have been like in a novel by Jane Austen? She would certainly not have committed suicide, in my opinion. And Emma Bovary, how would she have ended up in a play by Pirandello? Can we introduce different narrative elements into analysis? (I will quote Nino

Ferro (2002) on this in the pages that follow.) Can we postulate literary solutions that differ from the obligatory course of repetition compulsion? Can we replace yearning for the Absolute with something that is more relevant and accessible to the everyday life we are, after all, called to live? This book also describes these alternative narrative attempts, veined by the desire to rediscover within our very depths the freedom to choose, even in front of commonly accepted and prevailing models, in order to fully respect our passions and our loves.

CHAPTER ONE

Theoretical psychoanalytical contributions

Freud, and the relationship between love and genitality

It is a general conviction among scholars that few aspects of Freud's work have been as little understood and as much distorted as his contributions to the understanding of love. Some of these factors derive from the fact that Freud never attempted to provide a specific definition of love. And yet we can say that Freud, struck by the intensity and violence of transference love, as well as by its irrefutable rapport with falling in love, believed that the unconscious search for the oedipal object made up part of every normal love relationship, and fuelled the underlying current of desire towards the love object and its idealisation. For Freud, therefore, the pivotal position of the Oedipus complex in the unconscious content of loving desire is what is called into question in the somewhat extensive explanation of the nature of love.

In *Three Essays on the Theory of Sexuality*, Freud observes that: "There are thus good reasons why a child sucking at his mother's breast has become the prototype of every relation of love. The finding of an object is in fact a *refinding* of it" (1905d, p. 222). Together with *The Interpretation of Dreams* (1900a), *Three Essays on the Theory of Sexuality* (1905d) is the text that Freud most enriched and clarified during its successive editions, although maintaining the same structure. In studying these essays from the point of view of the current state of psychoanalytic practice, Anna Ferruta (whose 2012 article in *The Psychoanalytic Quarterly* I am indebted to for this introduction to *Three Essays on the Theory of Sexuality*) raised two points that pose questions for our clinical practice: the all-pervading presence of sexuality in the subject's psychic manifestations and the link between infantile sexual experience and the structuring of the psychic apparatus.

I will pause at length on this paper by Ferruta because I believe—along with many other authors (for example, Bergmann, 1987)—that every subsequent consideration of Freud's concerns about the relationships between sexuality and love, affection and sexuality, object choice and narcissistic choice cannot disregard this original work.

Infantile sexuality

In his first essay, "The sexual aberrations", Freud starts out by analysing the psychopathology, to arrive, in the other two essays, at the physiological description of the psychic apparatus's functioning in relation to psychosexual development ("Infantile sexuality" and "The transformations of puberty"). The richness of detailed, pertinent descriptions about the sexuality of children bears witness to the author's extraordinary curiosity and capacity for observation.

We may conclude that the clinical practice of psychoanalysis was Freud's main source in his discovery of infantile sexuality. His own self-analysis and accounts given by patients enabled him to describe the many forms of sexual pleasure connected not only to erotogenic zones but to the whole body, as shown by the displacement of pleasure in the symptomatology of hysteria:

> There are predestined erotogenic zones, as is shown by the example of sucking. The same example, however, also shows us that any other part of the skin or mucous membrane can take over the functions of an erotogenic zone, and must therefore have some aptitude in that direction. Thus the quality of the stimulus has more to do with producing the pleasurable feeling than the nature of the part of the body concerned.
>
> (Freud, 1905d, p. 183)

Research carried out by Didier Anzieu (1985), on the function of skin as a containing envelope and communicative film with the non-self object is a development of these Freudian intuitions: the infantile sexual impulse as the element of both narcissistic and object functioning.

Sexual pressure may be released through the relationship with an object (thus autoerotic), but not only:

> It must, however, be admitted that infantile sexual life, in spite of the preponderating dominance of erotogenic zones, exhibits components which from the very first involve other people as sexual objects. Such are the instincts of scopophilia, exhibitionism and cruelty, which appear in a sense independently of erotogenic zones; these instincts do not enter into intimate relations with genital life until later, but are already to be observed in childhood as independent impulses, distinct in the first instance from erotogenic sexual activity.
>
> (Freud, 1905d, pp. 191–192)

Lastly, Freud addresses affection as a characteristic present in children during the latency period, when they are removed from the very roots of the sexual drive:

> Their sexual aims have become mitigated and they now represent what may be described as the "affectionate current" of sexual life. Only psycho-analytic investigation can show that behind this affection, admiration and respect there lie concealed the old sexual longings of the infantile component instincts which have now become unserviceable.
>
> (Freud, 1905d, p. 200)

The third essay, "The transformations of puberty", has the most arduous task in linking the experience of infantile sexuality to the structure of the psyche as a whole. The theory of genital primacy appears inadequate: "The starting-point and the final aim of the process which I have described are clearly visible. The intermediate steps are still in many ways obscure to us. We shall have to leave more than one of them as an unsolved riddle" (Freud, 1905d, p. 208).

The theory of genital primacy is presented and then continually questioned in favour of an implicit awareness of a necessary and continuous restructuring of psychic functioning, with regard to the experience of encountering the object.

The enigma posed by lust—the tension that, unlike hunger, is not quenched upon satisfaction—remains unresolved, thus indicating a direction for valuable advancements in the area of the relational: "We remain in complete ignorance both of the origin and of the nature of the sexual tension which arises simultaneously with the pleasure when erotogenic zones are satisfied" (Freud, 1905d, p. 212).

So we may say that the fusional nature and dependence of the mother–child pair form a primitive matrix of the loving experience that is then lost as a conscious memory in early childhood and re-experienced in adolescence and adulthood.

Bergmann (1987), who writes extensively on love in *The Anatomy of Loving*, often refers to this passage when he describes love as evoking memories and desires from a primitive, symbiotic phase in the child's life. He believes that Freud's idea of "re-finding" was influenced by Plato's thoughts on love, expressed above all in the *Symposium*. As a good classicist, I can only agree with this statement.

In fact, Plato is undoubtedly the most influential and important scholar of love in classical culture and, in my opinion, Freud was greatly influenced by his theories on love. Besides, Plato's *Symposium* continues to influence our own theories on love, even unbeknown to us. The *power of love* in the *Symposium* is represented as something that is present in all nature and all human beings. Aristophanes declares:

> Imagine that Hephaestus with his tools stood over them while they were lying together and asked: "What is it, humans, that you want from each other?" If they didn't know, imagine that he asked next: "Is this what you desire, to be together so completely that you're never apart from each other night and day? If this is what you desire, I'm prepared to fuse and weld you together, so that the two of you become one. Then the two of you would live a shared life, as long as you live, since you are one person; and when you died, you would have a shared death in Hades, as one person instead of two." ... The reason is that this is our original natural state and we used to be whole creatures: "love" is the name for the desire and pursuit of wholeness.
>
> (Plato, *The Symposium*, 192d, 3–193a: p. 26)

How well we know that the desire to fuse together, to be just one with the loved person, can be understood as the intense yearning and regret for the primitive symbiosis with the mother, even if no conscious memory of this remains, as I stated above.

The content of the earliest phantasies at the very start of romantic passion certainly re-echo the emotional quality of the earliest experiences with the mother. For many human beings, the theme of *re*-finding the object evokes a sort of mystic fusion with the loved one, associated with the idea of romantic love. Suffice to think of expressions often used in these circumstances: "He/she has found his/her other half" or "He/she has met his/her twin spirit".

Freud further develops his ideas about love in "On narcissism: an introduction" (1914c). He uses the term *anaclitic* for rediscovering/re-finding the object prototype of the first loving investment, the mother, calling this type and source of object choice the "attachment" type, or "object choice *of leaning-on*" type, then going on to introduce a second type of love object choice, the narcissistic love object. And he proceeds to clarify:

> We have, however, not concluded that human beings are divided into two sharply differentiated groups, according as their object-choice conforms to the anaclitic or to the narcissistic type; we assume rather that both kinds of object-choice are open to each individual, though he may show a preference for one or the other. We say that a human being has originally two sexual objects—himself and the woman who nurses him—and in doing so we are postulating a primary narcissism in everyone, which may in some cases manifest itself in a dominating fashion in his object-choice.
>
> (Freud, 1914c, p. 88)

Freud introduces a second method of finding an object—through a narcissistic attachment that is based on a person's identification with his or her own self as it is found and re-experienced in other people. In describing a narcissistic object choice, Freud (1914c, p. 90) outlines four ways in which a person may love, according to that type. These include: what he himself is, what he himself was, what he himself would like to be, and someone who was once part of himself. The example Freud chooses in describing loving what "he himself is" is in the love a person has for himself.

For Freud, being loved and loving represent both the goal and the satisfaction of the narcissistic object choice: not being loved lessens the sense of self, while being loved heightens it.

Narcissistic love, therefore, becomes love for another person that is modelled on love for oneself. It is no longer just re-finding an object of the past (the mother), but also an object that represents what we were in the past. The only moment in which a person can completely sacrifice the love for him/herself is when he/she is in love, and this is because part of the investment towards the other (external object) also represents an investment towards an internal self. One loves the other also for how much this other represents what we are or would like to be. In normal conditions, there is a certain tension between the ego and the ideal ego because the ideal ego always clamours for a bit more than what the ego is capable of offering. The fortunate lover sees his self-esteem repaired or heightened when the object of his love also loves him, confirming and seeing in him his ideal of his ego. In the more extreme cases, says Freud, with another beautiful expression: "The object has, so to speak, consumed the ego", and "The whole situation can be completely sum-marised in the formula: *The object has been put in the place of the ego ideal*" (1921c, p. 113; italics in the original).

In 1921, with *Group Psychology and the Analysis of the Ego*, Freud sum-marised what we can call his third theory of love (Bergman, 1987). It is evident that what mattered most to Freud was that the link between love and sex should not be lost.

> Libido is an expression taken from the theory of the emotions. We call by that name the energy, regarded as a quantitative magni-tude (though not at present actually measurable), of those instincts which have to do with all that may be comprised under the word "love". The nucleus of what we mean by love naturally consists (and this is what is commonly called love, and what the poets sing of) in sexual love with sexual union as its aim. But we do not separate from this—what in any case has a share in the name "love"—on the one hand, self-love, and on the other, love for parents and children, friendship and love for humanity in general, and also devotion to concrete objects and to abstract ideas.
>
> (Freud, 1921c, p. 90)

* * *

On the other hand it is also very usual for directly sexual impulsions, short-lived in themselves, to be transformed into a lasting and purely affectionate tie; and the consolidation of a passionate love marriage rests to a large extent upon this process.

(Freud, 1921c, p. 139)

In the above passages, Freud is affirming that love is something more than the manifestation of sexual libido because the whole ego is involved. This type of love, mature love, can be attained when a state of satisfying genital development has been reached. In this case, the possibility for loving can be protracted over time, well beyond the immediate satisfaction of sexual impulses. We will see in the following pages how this relationship between love and genitality (intended as a level of development) will undergo profound changes in the authors who come after Freud.

Balint, and the theory of primary love

Primary Love and Psychoanalytic Technique is a collection of essays that appeared in 1952 (although written by Balint between 1930 and 1952) about three closely connected topics: human sexuality, object relations, and psychoanalytic technique. Not all the articles are equally interesting. Read today, they may seem boring at times and at others decidedly outdated but, in my opinion, they contain a number of highly interesting points.

What is *primary passive love* or the *primary object relationship* for Balint?

It is an original impulse, the source of every subsequent normal or pathological development. For Balint, the earliest mother–child relationships would be placed in a happy and ecstatic expectation of love and satisfaction, which goes from child to mother, without any perceptions of reciprocal obligations: a boundless, omnipotent possibility to receive on the child's part; an infinite, limitless capacity to give on the mother's. In Balint, affection is no longer, as in Freud, an *aim-inhibited libido* (as we will see below), but an autonomous impulse, which no longer has to be distinguished from genitality. On the subject of affection, see also Ambrosiano and Gaburri (2008) when they discuss the drive to exist, alluding to affection as a specific quality of primary care. So too, in Balint, genitality emerges as an autonomous impulse, linked to the reproduction of the individual and the species. Man's destiny, for Balint, is in fact bound to the primary object relationship: only the affectionate, punctual gratification of the need for passive love will allow the child to achieve any progressive growth within his examination of reality, up to tackling the adventure of genitality as an adult. Instead, the absence of this primary love will force him to travel the paths of the neuroses, perversion, or psychosis.

In his essay "Critical notes on the theory of the pregenital organisations of the libido" (1935, in 1952a, p. 51), Balint proposes studying "the development of object-relations, i.e., the development of love".

It is difficult to translate this essay into modern words since it is also rich in concepts about biology and drives. In part, I refer to the preceding paragraphs devoted to Freud's opus for an understanding of Balint's work, whereas in others I confess to being struck by a number of apparently outdated concepts, which, however, contain fundamental intuitions for psychoanalytic theory and practice. For example, when he describes those patients who "do not love, but want to be loved". The claim for gratification of such a need is wholly problematic, and is often manifested in a violent way and with a great psychical expenditure, as though it were a question of life or death. The fear of being abandoned derives from this tendency. Balint highlights the misinterpretation that this request encounters, because it is read as a form of aggression and innate sadism. Instead, for Melanie Klein this misinterpretation is linked to the theory of the predominance of destruction in the earliest years of life. However, Balint continues, and I find this quite brilliant: "Ill-nature, malice, wickedness, even sadism can be analysed, cured, or what comes ultimately to the same thing: they have their antecedent. It is suffering that makes one wicked" (Balint, 1935, in 1952a, p. 62).

The other misinterpretation concerns passion. The way the drive is manifested is confused with its goal: it is believed that desires, whose gratification is claimed so passionately, belong to a healthy instinctual life, while impassioned instinctual goals lead to disturbed development, to the *confusion of tongues* of which Ferenczi speaks (1949).

In this way, Balint intends to query Freud's (1905d) *perverse polymorph* child, the *autoerotic narcissistic* child. But, Balint says, the primary tendency of the child to think "I will always be loved, everywhere, in whatever way, without any effort on my part", which, of course, is the end goal of the passive love object, in fact belongs to the world of the child's ego, which has not yet worked out the differentiation between the ego and the external world, which is still completely narcissistic (due not to the child's perverse obstinacy nor to his innate badness).

In actual fact, Balint is suggesting, more or less implicitly, to replace the concept of primary narcissism with that of primary passive love. The child's narcissism derives, for Balint, from this thought: "If the world doesn't love me enough, I have to love and gratify myself". Consequently, we see how, for Balint, narcissism is always of a secondary nature. In fact, he insists on the difference between narcissism as a libidinal investment, that is, in which the person loves himself, and that in which the person does not take the outside world into consideration (totally or insufficiently).

But for Balint, if passive object love exists—which is, let us repeat, the primary aim of eroticism, libidinal love of the self—active object love also exists, in which, instead, we love and gratify our partner because he/she returns this with love and gratification. Both are closely linked. Commenting on the point raised by Freud in "On narcissism: an introduction"—"Here we may even venture to touch on the question of what makes it necessary at all for our mental life to pass beyond the limits of narcissism and to attach the libido to objects" (1914c, p. 85)—Balint declares that only the concept of active love for the object provides an explanation of this clinical description. Narcissistic love can never reach the goal of all the sexual drives: *to be loved, it is necessary to come into contact with the world and its objects.*

Before introducing what, in my opinion, is the most interesting essay, "On love and hate" (1952b), I believe a brief historic introduction is necessary.

It is not possible to tackle Balint's work on primary passive love, as I said above, without in fact first briefly mentioning Freud's work that he constantly referred to, by which I mean *Three Essays on the Theory of Sexuality*, which we have discussed at length in the paragraphs above. As we can see, Balint starts out from this essay, but then moves away from it, and not by a small margin.

Let us take as an example, by way of starting the discussion, the point in which, in "On love and hate", Balint discusses the concept of infantile omnipotence: "In fact 'omnipotence' never means a real feeling of power; on the contrary, a desperate and very precarious attempt at overcoming a feeling of helplessness and impotence" (Balint, 1952b, p. 357).

Balint begins to discuss the concept of omnipotence in order to better understand what he calls the difference between mature, or adult, love and primitive love, in which a timely and opportune gratification of all needs is of fundamental importance, due to the total dependence on the object. Or, according to another point of view, it is not so much the child, or the adult, who is avid, but their gratifications and object that are of absolute importance.

All the pre-genital or primitive—as we would call them today—object situations contain these three elements in various degrees: desperate dependence, denial of this dependence through omnipotence, and taking the object completely for granted and treating it as an object, a thing.

A false and little developed, or defective, control over reality underlies all these primitive relationships. This is why omnipotent, or avid, love is unstable and condemned to suffer infinite frustrations and transformations into hate. Hate, for Balint, is the ultimate remnant, the denial and defence against primitive object love. This means that we hate the people who do not love us and who refuse to collaborate despite our efforts to win their affection. We defend ourselves by raising barriers of hate. But hate needs a refusal of dependence, and the disparity between object and subject.

Kernberg, and the difference between the capacity to love and to maintain a relationship over time

Kernberg (1974b) stands out from other authors because he advocates an interesting approach, describing a continuum between falling in love and remaining in love or achieving a mature, loving relationship. In addition, he attempts an evaluation of the *couple* in normality and pathology. Kernberg believes that with mastery of both pre-oedipal and oedipal issues, the level of idealisation is based on the most realistic perception of the beloved, and takes into account shared values and aspirations. Moreover, he takes time to divide groups of people with different pathological personalities, who present more or less serious deficits regarding the possibility of falling in love and/or maintaining the love relationship. In the first place, he describes socially isolated people, with serious narcissistic disorders, who find it impossible to love. These people play with profound archaic phantasies of fusional desires, of incorporating with the other, of primitive omnipotence.

No real relationship can stand up to comparison with such original phantasies, and therefore no love is possible.

Then there is another group of people, always with narcissistic personalities, who, though, manage to develop some form of sexual or emotional relationship with the other. For these individuals, loving emotional involvement implies a tension towards the absolute that does not stand up to reality testing: the distress and suffering that result can be unbearable, and lead to forms of social and affective withdrawal that protect the individual from disasters following on from intimacy. In other words, for Kernberg, the level of intensity of the narcissistic pathology implies a difference in the capacity to love and to maintain a relationship over time. Acknowledgement of the need to be loved and to love encourages the start of some form of investment in the other, even if the intensity and instability of the primitive idealisations may risk ruining the intimacy gained with such difficulty.

Another group of people is represented by individuals positioned more towards the neuroses, who effectively possess the capacity of romantic idealisation. The unresolved issues of the oedipal events belong to this level, and risk compromising the loving relationships. Indeed, according to Kernberg, a relationship of adult, mature love is based on the elaboration of oedipal and pre-oedipal conflicts. In the more mature relationships, the romantic perceptions concerning the object of amorous investment correspond to the personal qualities of the loved one. For these people, idealisation is translated into excitement of a shared vision that is not a defensive solution or an ascetic renunciation but, instead, a capacity for integrating the creative energy generated by romantic passions into a progressive series of shared passions. This is the deep-seated force of libidinal energy directed towards an object, capable of corresponding, exchanging, and integrating expectations and ideals that belong to the nature of man's evolution.

In a word, Kernberg (1974b) believes that various aspects and levels of idealisation exist and that they belong to the experience of both being in love and successfully sustaining a long-lasting loving relationship. The most primitive level of idealisation characterises those individuals who frequently use splitting mechanisms but who are, nevertheless, capable of falling in love. These people present phantasies that are often very distant from the loved one's real qualities, and often just a small disappointment regarding their expectations is enough to drive them into a state of traumatic breakdown corresponding to the loss of their most intimate aspirations. Kernberg goes on to describe a level of idealisation at a more mature stage of personality development, which corresponds more to the reality of the loved object, but which is accompanied by strong inhibitions, suggesting incomplete resolutions of the oedipal conflicts. For this group of individuals, disappointments are part and parcel of the relationship's evolutionary progress, and intimacy with the loved one can continue, despite the disappointment, without having to relinquish the relationship.

To sum up, Kernberg postulates that, in knowing how to navigate one's own pre-oedipal and oedipal issues, one can arrive at a more realistic perception of the loved one while at the same time the original shared aspirations and ideal tensions can be preserved.

Bion, and love as a search for the absolute

For obvious reasons, this brief outline of the evolution of the concept of L (Love) and its relationship with H (Hate) and K (Knowledge) cannot be anything but a summary of Bion's thought in general. Standing for the first forms of pre-symbolic communication between mother and child, Bion's container–contained model and the concept of projective identification means that the child's most elementary fears of non-existence can be configured within a theoretical frame of fundamental representation and symbolism for analytic treatment, and has led to acknowledgement that the acting out in transference of our most-difficult-to-reach patients can be linked both to the child's original fears about dependence and to an alleged original incapacity on the part of the mother to provide an appropriate container for the child's fear of impending terror with regard to his early experiences of loss.

All this offers significant cues for understanding the anxiety of many patients about their dependence on being loved, a dependence that was profoundly shaken in the first months of life. Bion (1967) uses the term "nameless terror", or even "nameless dread", to refer to the very serious consequences deriving from the environment failing not only to take care of the child, ensuring a feeling of "continuity of existence", but also to help him find "a thought in search of a meaning", that is, internal coherence to his thoughts. In this way, Bion refers to the feelings experienced by the child when the mother appears incapable of metabolising the sensory information of anxiety that she has received from her child or, in other words, when the mother's capacity for reverie does not exist or is seriously defective.

L (Love) represents a useful psychoanalytic element for indicating, together with K and H, one of the passions or feelings, as well as, in the container–contained model, what connects or links between them the various elements of the Grid, like hate (see below).

In *Cogitations* (1992), Bion proffers enlightening words about love:

> A term like "love" cannot describe something even as well as the term "the love of God"—that at least makes an attempt to introduce an element that shows that it is not a discussion about something that is so simple as physical love known to the human animal. A lioness nuzzles and shows every sign of feelings of love and affection—if interpreted in human terms—for prey it has destroyed; but it is murderous love, the love that destroys the loved object. Such visual images may be used to talk about love, even what we imagine to be mature love, but there is some other love that is mature from an absolute standard. This other love, vaguely adumbrated, vaguely foreshadowed in human speech, is of an entirely different character; it is not simply a quantitative difference in the kind of love one animal has for another or which the baby has for the breast. It is the further extension to "absolute love", which cannot be described in the terms of sensuous reality or experience. For that there has to be a language of intra-sensuous and ultra-sensuous, something that lies outside the spectrum of sensuous experience and articulate language.
>
> (Bion, 1992, pp. 371–372)

In its turn, H (Hate) is a psychoanalytic element initially corresponding to the psychoanalytic object in Bion's thought; in more recent thinking, instead, it has the same relationship with the object as an atom with a molecule, that is, the elements are ideas and feelings representing abstractions, similar to letters for words, which are combined differently to represent all the possible theories of analytic work. In this case, Hate, Love, and Knowledge. It represents, together with love, one of the passions or emotions, and with K a dynamic link that by means of the container–contained mechanism binds the different categories of the Grid. In relation to classical theory, H should be the equivalent to the death instinct (Freud–Klein), while L would correspond to sexual instinct, and K to epistemophilic instinct or drive to knowledge.

K (Knowledge), instead, denotes the capacity to "know" something; it is not about what is already known, but about the propensity to know or to contain:

> "Knowledge" has no meaning unless it means that someone knows something, and this ... is an assertion of relationship, or of some part of a relationship. The term, "knowledge", I propose provisionally to employ to describe a state of mind indissolubly associated with a relationship between communicable awareness on the one hand, and the object of which the person feels thus aware, on the other.
>
> (Bion, 1992, p. 271)

Let us attempt a translation: K is therefore, together with L and H, a hypothesis that expresses a continuous and constant connection, conjunction, bond with L and H subordinate to K. For Bion, knowledge takes on and reaches a decidedly higher level of relevance and independence compared to any other psychoanalytic theorist or thinker. From a container–contained theory perspective, the level of K will depend on the capacity to sustain a container–contained relationship with the three elements involved: for example, a process that will eventually guarantee growth of the apparatus for thinking and of K, as well as the possibility of learning from experience, and integrating new knowledge, while remaining open at the same time, free from rigidity and ready for future assimilations. There is a progressive increase in the degree of sophistications to create new hypotheses that can form new systems of thought that in their turn can be continuously recombined.

Now, what does all this have to do with love? It can be understood if one realises that knowledge is not made up only of alpha-elements but of the ensemble of beta- and alpha-elements, a term that covers everything that the individual knows and does not know; emotional experiences and experiences that have not yet been experienced; psychic reality and external world; absolute and infinite; chaos; things in themselves; the ineffable unknown.

In these terms, we could say that, for Bion, love endows meaning; it finds a meaning for things that at times seem not to have one. And if this activity is specific to humankind, from another point of view, it is necessary to remember that one thing is to look for meaning (love?), the other is to find it, or to have it found. Every time we start out again from what we do not know, or think we do not know, but which we are longing for. For Bion, love is—we might say—a constant, and constantly surprising, search for the absolute. And here we may also see a clean break from Freud's concept of the relationship between love and genitality.

As I mentioned in the Introduction, to be loved means wanting to be seen and recognised for what we are in our innermost and most hidden depths; it is a striving towards the absolute in the request made to the loved one to understand us unconditionally, and an aspiration for reciprocity, or understanding the other, in the sense of taking him/her inside ourselves.

CHAPTER TWO

Ways of seeing: the role of vision

Remembrances of Marie A.

1

On a certain day in the blue-moon month of September
Beneath a young plum tree, quietly
I held her there, my quiet, pale beloved
In my arms just like a graceful dream.
And over us in the beautiful summer sky
There was a cloud on which my gaze rested
It was very white and so immensely high
And when I looked up, it had disappeared.

2

Since that day many, many months
Have quietly floated down and past.
No doubt the plum trees were chopped down
And you ask me: what's happened to my love?
So I answer you: I can't remember.
And still, of course, I know what you mean

But I honestly can't recollect her face
I just know: there was a time I kissed it.

3

And that kiss too I would have long forgotten
Had not the cloud been present there
That I still know and always will remember
It was so white and came from on high.
Perhaps those plum trees still bloom
And that woman now may have had her seventh child
But that cloud blossomed just a few minutes
And when I looked up, it had disappeared in the wind.

—Bertolt Brecht (1927)

The mother–child way of seeing

On the beach, a small child wanders away from his mother towards the water's edge. After a few uncertain steps, he swivels round towards her, looks at her intently, and says: "You watch me, ok?" Reassured, he moves off with greater determination towards the sea. Meanwhile, his mother never takes her eyes off her son for an instant. Every now and again, he turns around and makes sure that she is still watching him, that her eyes are still on him. He does not move far away, remaining within a safe distance, and starts playing with the water. His mother, obedient, moves closer, so as not to lose him from sight. Every now and again, they both make sure that they are still in contact.

A young patient comes to analysis after a long series of serious physical pathologies that a physician has finally linked together, hypothesising a psychosomatic component. Despite the affectionate presence of a united family, this young woman has repeatedly been left alone in moments of need, such as after car accidents, serious diagnoses, and debilitating illnesses. She is unable to explain this abrupt disappearance of her loved ones precisely when she needs them most: "They are like that; they can't look when something horrid happens".

One day, during a session, she says: "I feel relaxed here because I know that you're looking at me; even if you don't see me, you're always keeping an eye on me, and this is a new experience for me; you hold me together, you prevent me from falling to pieces. When I got here, I was all broken, but your way of looking at me is just what prevents me from doing myself further damage."

In both situations, the mother–child and analyst–patient pair were in mutual contact, in which the role of vision took centre stage. Being in contact with someone, really seeing them, means being completely connected to the feeling of being alive, both for the person looking and for the person looked at. This has more to do with the relationship that exists between these two people than with any other physiological aspect of the act of seeing. From this point of view, a level of non-verbal communication underpins the relational experience that I will attempt to describe in this chapter, investigating the ways of seeing and role of vision in the earliest stages of a child's development, and its origin starting from the object-mother in relation to two functions provided by the preverbal mother. I am referring to Winnicott's function of *holding* (1960) and to Bion's concept of *containing* (1962a).

Both terms refer to those aspects of the mother–child relationship that will subsequently lead to the development of the symbolic process via the process of separation. The relationship between maternal containing (a maternal *provision*) and mental containing (containing *in* the mind) can be described better by what Kenneth Wright calls *containing forms*: "These are patterned maternal responses to infant states which have the potential to become symbols if and when they are internalized by the infant" (Wright, 2009, p. 3).

In an important article of 2004, Ogden pointed out the fundamental difference, and at the same time the complementary nature, of these two concepts of Winnicott and Bion:

> Winnicott's concept of "holding" and Bion's idea of the "container-contained"—though often used interchangeably in the psychoanalytic literature—to my mind, each addresses quite different aspects of the same human experience and involves its own distinctive form of analytic thinking. … It must be borne in mind that the concepts of holding and the container–contained stand not in opposition to one another, but as two vantage points from which to view an emotional experience.
>
> (Ogden, 2004, p. 1349)

* * *

The importance of the impact of maternal holding on the emotional growth of the infant would be disputed by very few psychoanalysts. However, the significance to psychoanalytic theory of

Winnicott's concept of holding is far more subtle than this broad statement would suggest. Holding, for Winnicott, is an ontological concept that he uses to explore the specific qualities of the experience of being alive at different developmental stages as well as the changing intrapsychic–interpersonal means by which the sense of continuity of being is sustained over time.

(Ogden, 2004, p. 1350)

* * *

The earliest quality of aliveness generated in the context of a holding experience is aptly termed by Winnicott "going on being" (1956, p. 303), a phrase that is all verb, devoid of a subject. The phrase manages to convey the feeling of the movement of the experience of being alive at a time before the infant has become a subject.

(Ogden, 2004, p. 1350)

* * *

The mother's early holding of the infant represents an abrogation of herself in her unconscious effort to get out of the infant's way. Her unobtrusive presence provides a setting for the infant's constitution to begin to make itself evident, for the developmental tendencies to start to unfold, and for the infant to experience spontaneous movement and become the owner of the sensations that are appropriate to this early phase of life (Winnicott, 1956, p. 303).

(Ogden, 2004, p. 1351)

* * *

As is true of Winnicott's holding, Bion's (1962a, 1962b, 1970) container–contained is intimately linked with what is most important to his contribution to psychoanalysis. The idea of the container–contained addresses not what we think, but the way we think, that is, how we process lived experience and what occurs psychically when we are unable to do psychological work with that experience.

(Ogden, 2004, p. 1354)

Bion discussed the "container–contained" relationship in terms of a maternal process (the α function) that transforms the infant's raw experiences (the β elements) into a more manageable and contained form.

> The "container" is not a thing, but a process. It is the capacity for the unconscious psychological work of dreaming, operating in concert with the capacity for preconscious dreamlike thinking (reverie), and the capacity for more fully conscious secondary-process thinking. … The "contained", like the container, is not a static thing, but a living process that in health is continuously expanding and changing. The term refers to thoughts (in the broadest sense of the word) and feelings that are in the process of being derived from one's lived emotional experience. While conscious and preconscious thoughts and feelings constitute aspects of the contained, Bion's notion of the contained places primary emphasis on unconscious thoughts. The most elemental of thoughts constituting the contained are the raw "sense-impressions related to emotional experience" (Bion, 1962a, p. 17) which Bion calls "beta-elements" (1962a, p. 8).
>
> (Ogden, 2004, p. 1356)

* * *

> The metaphoric mother–infant relationship that Bion (1962a, 1962b) proposes is founded upon his own revision of Klein's concept of projective identification: the infant projects into the mother (who, in health, is in a state of rêverie) the emotional experience that he is unable to process on his own, given the rudimentary nature of his capacity for α-function. The mother does the unconscious psychological work of dreaming the infant's unbearable experience and makes it available to him in a form that he is able to utilize in dreaming his own experience.
>
> (Ogden, 2004, p. 1357)

* * *

Winnicott's holding and Bion's container–contained represent different analytic vertices from which to view the same analytic experience. Holding is concerned primarily with being and its relationship to time; the container–contained is centrally concerned with the processing (dreaming) of thoughts derived from lived emotional experience. Together they afford "stereoscopic" depth to the understanding of the emotional experiences that occur in the analytic setting.

(Ogden, 2004, p. 1362)

The other's way of seeing both objectivises and at the same time subjectivises, in an inexorable ambiguity, as Merleau-Ponty (1945, p. 146) explains so well when he says: "I live in the facial expressions of the other". Here, subject and object are in a state of reciprocal and reversible complementariness where the dialogue between the self and the "not-me" self (different from and opposed to the "other-than-me" object) becomes the basis for psychic development. In short, the preverbal maternal function, according to what has been stated above, consists in representing, mirroring, and containing the infant's psyche, and in shaping the outlines of his subjective nature, always in a psychic relational perspective. This is the analyst's work, too, constantly alternating between recognition of the patient's subjectivity and otherness and the task of supporting and protecting the patient's nascent subjectivity, that sense of self that is continually threatened by fragmentation.

Let me return to the two initial examples.

In the moment when the child says to his mother "watch me", he is asking to be supported in a process of separation and development, to be free to play with the sea without worrying about any eventual risks inherent in his game. His mother, drawn into the affair, or "into the game", shares his worries about the eventual risks of a too early detachment towards an unknown dimension, but at the same time promises to "keep an eye" on this separating process, to encourage it and at the same time protect it. It is a reciprocal pact that mother and child make to each other. It is a relationship of mutual subjectivisation (I recognise you as mother who has to keep an eye on me, and I recognise you as child that I must not lose sight of) and mutual objectivisation (you are the other, the object I must look at; you are the other, the object that has to look at me). I can become the "I" that I am completely only through you recognising me as that "I": when everything works adequately, both of them, mother and child, can grow and advance in the reciprocal stages of development.

In his article "Le Stade du Miroir", Lacan investigates the use of the mirror in different ways compared to those described by Winnicott. In Lacan's account, the baby feels joy (*jouissance*) about his reflection in the mirror, because it represents an external visual perfection that is beyond his motor grasp: "While reality precedes thought, it takes different forms according to the way the subject deals with it" (Lacan, 1953, p. 11). For Lacan, the mirror experience is the start of alienation from oneself, which is part of the human condition, whereas for Winnicott, for whom the baby's joy comes from the aliveness and accuracy of the mother's emotional reflection, the experience of mirroring is fundamental, underpinning the sense of self and protecting against the fragmentation to which the self is vulnerable. Winnicott describes this experience beautifully:

> What does the baby see when he or she looks at the mother's face? I am suggesting that, ordinarily, what the baby sees is himself or herself. In other words the mother is looking at the baby and what she looks like is related to what she sees there.
>
> (Winnicott, 1967, p. 112)

For Lacan, instead:

> The observation consists simply in the jubilant interest shown by the infant over eight months at the sight of his own image in a mirror. This interest is shown in games in which the child seems to be in endless ecstasy when it sees that movements in the mirror correspond to its own movements. ... We note that the image in the mirror is reversed, and we may see in this at least a metaphorical representation of the structural reversal we have demonstrated in the ego as the individual's psychical reality.
>
> (Lacan, 1953, p. 14)

So for Lacan, then, and the words he uses are equally beautiful, the mirror experience, which "has historical value as it marks a decisive turning-point in the mental development of the child" (Lacan, 1953, p. 14), is the start of an alienation from oneself, which is part of the human condition; it is an experience of the self inverted, mirrored, in fact, and the baby's joy is due to his imaginary triumph in anticipating a degree of muscular coordination that he has not yet actually achieved. The ego is built up by opposition in the mirror-reversal.

Furthermore, we always find the same sort of reversal, if we are on the look-out for it, in those dream images which represent the patient's ego in its characteristic rôle; that is, as dominated by the narcissistic conflict. So much is this so that we may regard this mirror-reversal as a prerequisite for such an interpretation.

(Lacan, 1953, p. 16)

For Lacan (1949), the narcissistic conflict dominates the child's mirroring experience, seen also through the mother's gaze that supports it. As he will say later on:

Here we see the ego, in its essential resistance to the elusive process of Becoming, to the variations of Desire. This illusion of unity, in which a human being is always looking forward to self-mastery, entails a constant danger of sliding back again into the chaos from which he started; it hangs over the abyss of a dizzy Assent in which one can perhaps see the very essence of Anxiety.

(Lacan, 1953, p. 15)

For Winnicott, instead, "in the early stages of the emotional development of the human infant a vital part is played by the environment which is in fact not yet separated off from the infant by the infant" (Winnicott, 1967, p. 144).

In the clinical vignette related above, there is no longer "the opposition between analyst as knowing subject and analysand as known subject, assuming the analyst's distance from a disenfranchised other" (Benjamin, 1998, p. 13), but recognition, on the patient's part, of the analyst's gaze. This also reveals the analyst's *subjectivity*, which "elevates the patient to the position of a subject who collaborates and knows" (Benjamin, 1998, p. 13).

"I feel relaxed because I know that you're looking at me", says the patient. This way of seeing holds together the fragmented pieces that she has brought to analysis with such great difficulty; it sees the wounds beyond the façade. The previous session she had brought this dream:

There was a girl doing bungee jumping from a very high bridge, but she smashed against a rock wall that was much too close. She was wearing a helmet, and you could see that she had hurt herself because blood was running everywhere. But she was smiling and acting as if nothing had happened. Terrified by all that blood, I woke up.

I shivered while listening to the dream, and an episode came into my mind of when, as a young girl, in a mountain refuge, I had seen a climber brought down on a stretcher after a fall. He was as white as a sheet and blood continued to drip from under the bandages covering his head. I should not have looked, but irresistibly, hidden behind my father's legs, I continued to stare at him. After long reflection, I commented:

> It's difficult to detach one's gaze from the wounds caused by the numerous accidents that have dotted your life. [She had previously told me that she had had two road accidents in which she had broken various bones, not to mention the numerous illnesses that had marked her young life.] However, I'm struck by your attempting to act as if nothing had happened, as if you were afraid of frightening whoever is looking at you.

In answer, I received detailed descriptions about how her parents, at the time of her road accidents, had not come to the hospital, leaving her alone to deal with the whole situation, and had showed themselves to be indifferent, as though "they had turned their eyes elsewhere". At the same time, my mother's words in the mountain refuge returned to mind: "Don't look, turn your face away". I reflected during the session, and added:

> You need someone to keep an eye on you during the descent, someone who will protect you from smashing against the rocks. On the other hand, you can never take your eyes off whoever has placed their trust in you during a climb or a pleasurable sporting activity that might be dangerous.

The two episodes I describe both contain the same emotional and empathetic drawing closer that stems from looking. When you begin to really look, not turning your face away to avoid suffering or distress, you assume mutual responsibility that transforms both parties. The patient, kept an eye on, began to reduce her dangerous behaviour, its libidinal excitement no longer compensating for the risk of destruction. I, the analyst, keeping my eyes on the patient, drew emotionally closer to her, coming into contact (or into *attunement*, as Daniel Stern (1985) would say) with her more fragile but also more adventurous parts. A long-ago sensation from my own childhood came to mind, a mixture of fear and excitement that has accompanied me ever since that moment, in the mountains but not only there.

Keeping an eye out and letting go; being close and allowing exploration of the external environment (separation). Containing the emotions that are there in a raw, potential state, still dormant but ready to become thoughts and vital actions.

Attunement, being in contact (on the mother's side) that Stern talks of, may be seen as something that facilitates mental development. The mother's, and the analyst's apposite, *resonating* answer—at the beginning felt as a response from the outside ("You [outside of me] watch me!")—possesses the potential for being perceived by the infant and by the patient as a container, within which he can cling on tight. When sustained, kept an eye on like this, experiences can be manipulated (playing with the sea, tackling increasingly steep climbs and descents) within a mental space that begins to develop. Naturally, it is necessary to distinguish between containing, which confirms the experience that the infant (or patient) is having through the capacity of the mother (or analyst) to identify herself with these experiences and be empathetic to them (which would be the process of reverie described by Bion—1957, 1962a, 1962b), and projective identification, in which the mother (or analyst) imposes her personal experiences, superimposing and modifying the child's (or patient's) subjectivity.

The artist's way of seeing

We can find a number of the considerations advanced above in these two paintings by John Singer Sargent (1856–1925), an American painter who lived most of his life in Europe and who was famous above all for his oils, although he was also a delicate and obsessive watercolour artist. In the first work, *Mrs Fiske Warren and Her Daughter Rachel* (1903, an oil on canvas in the Museum of Fine Arts, Boston; Figure 2), we see how the painter's gaze objectivises the scene, giving subjective space to the objects portrayed at the same time.

The mother looks the painter in the eyes with a firm, self-satisfied gaze. She is a beautiful woman, haughty and composed. She is being portrayed for who she is and for who she wants to appear to be. But in the objectivity of her portrait, Sargent paints something else about her character. Bolt upright in the armchair, the mother is flanked by her young daughter, leaning against the chair arm, who competes with her

Figure 2. *Mrs Fiske Warren (Gretchen Osgood) and Her Daughter Rachel* by John Singer Sargent, 1903, Museum of Fine Arts, Boston.

mother in beauty and noble bearing. The girl's eyes are not directed towards the painter but stare, melancholically, into space. Her hands are gently entwined with those of her mother, abandoned in her lap.

Seemingly objective, Sargent stages a little show, which powerfully restores the objects of the painting to their most intimate subjectivity: the mother does not seem to take much interest in her young daughter, who sadly observes this neglect with her gaze lost in space. Her position to one side appears to reflect the place she occupies in her mother's heart: an important element for her identity as a woman of high society. The daughter appears to be seen only by the painter: only Sargent's objective way of seeing notes her unhappiness, her being neglected, her not being central in the representation of the mother–daughter pair. In objectivising, this way of looking subjectivises the sitters in the portrayal.

The second painting, *Corfu: Lights and Shadows* (1909, a watercolour in the Museum of Fine Arts, Boston; Figure 3), instead, depicts a holiday house, a summer landscape, with the sea in the distance.

Figure 3. *Corfu: Lights and Shadows* by John Singer Sargent, 1909, Museum of Fine Arts, Boston.

Here, the painter's eyes have paused on a detail that transforms the whole watercolour: the shadows of the trees that surround the house and that are projected onto it. We do not see these trees; we guess at their presence only thanks to a delicate hint of freshness that we perceive through the midday haze. They seem to be moving as though there were a breath of wind. We would like to go inside the house, into its cool darkness, with the shutters closed. It is a landscape that the painter's gaze makes alive; he transforms raw emotions into profound thoughts within the spectator, who loses him- or herself in memories of Mediterranean summers, other cool houses in the hot heat of midday. The house, from object of the painting, becomes the receptacle of emotions and desires, libidinally invested by whoever is looking at it. It, too, seems to say: "You, look at me", and then allows you to come closer to it, making you part of its shade and its sun. We are in perfect harmony with the watercolour and its object.

Comment

In the stance I have chosen, being *in harmony with, in contact with, in attunement with* lies at the origin of non-verbal communication and reveals the relationship between forms and models that underlie the preverbal capacity to connect objects with emotional experiences. So it can be seen as the original relational mode between mother and child, and between analyst and patient. This mode provides the basic elements for the future development of the mind, and represents the imprint for subsequent loving investments. The mother and the analyst, in reformulating the child's and the patient's emotional and affective state (Winnicott's *going on being*), carry out a non-verbal representation that can later be transformed into complete thoughts, which by their very nature contain the imprint of the original desire of preverbal emotion, just like the holiday house preserves the painted imprint of the shadows of the leaves. As Winnicott says: "Feeling real is more than existing; it is finding a way to exist as oneself, and to relate to objects as oneself, and to have a self into which to retreat for relaxation" (1967, p. 117).

If, then, we want to turn to Bion, to comment on the above, in the experience of the loving investment there is not simply a quantitative difference compared to a type of experience or feeling or emotion that

one can have for other people. Rather, when talking about being in resonance with, in attunement with, it is more about:

> The further extension to "absolute love", which cannot be described
> in the terms of sensuous reality or experience. For that there has
> to be a language of intra-sensuous and ultra-sensuous, something
> that lies outside the spectrum of sensuous experience and articulate
> language.
>
> (Bion, 1992, pp. 371–372)

In other words, to love is also to look, to understand, to give meaning,
to find meaning, to recognise what the other is in a system of meanings
that restore reality and identity to the loved object, precisely because it
is seen, understood, taken within.

CHAPTER THREE

Nostalgia, or "something to love"*

Something to love

Something to love, some tree or flow'r,
Something to nurse in my lonely bow'r,
Some dog to follow, where'er I roam,
Some bird to warble my welcome home,
Some tame gazelle, or some gentle dove:
Something to love. Oh, something to love!

Something to love. Oh, let me see!
Something that's filled with a love for me;
Beloved by none, it is sad to live,
And 'tis sad to die and leave none to grieve;
And fond and true let the lov'd one prove,
Something to love. Oh, something to love!

—Thomas Haynes Bayly (1844)

---

*A version of this paper was previously published in 2010, for the 23rd Annual Conference of the European Psychoanalytic Federation (EPF) in London (25–28 March 2010), translated by Carla Bellucci.

In an old film by Louis Malle entitled *The Lovers* (*Les Amants*), with Jeanne Moreau and Jean-Marc Bory, a bored middle-class housewife with an ill-matched husband is quite unexpectedly struck by an *amour fou*, thanks to a young man met while on her way back home.

Rightly or wrongly, François Truffaut claimed that with this film Malle had dared to show on screen something never before attempted, an entire night of love. While the two lovers bask in their idyll in a beautiful landscape bathed in moonlight, the director had chosen Brahms' "Andante ma moderato" from his String Sextet in B-flat major Op. 18 to express the full flood of emotions during the long scene. Malle had perceived that this piece of music encapsulated a knot of erotic and sentimental feelings that were impossible to convey in words.

The clear, rational structure of the sonata perfectly matches Brahms' typically intense lyrical style. The "Andante" draws on an elementary musical form much loved by Brahms, the theme with variations. On the one hand, the solid D minor melody expresses ardent passion, and, on the other, a profound feeling of nostalgia for having already begun to regret lost happiness.

I am turning to music and film to introduce a rather complex concept, which occupies a central position in the representation of romantic passion, partly linked to what Freud termed narcissistic love. I intend to discuss what we might call the *romantic predisposition in favour of the sensual experience*.

We can say that the excessive element or the principle of repetition is one of the cornerstones of romantic passion. When in love, everything seems more beautiful, more attainable. Omnipotence reigns and previously apparently insurmountable limits of the self can be surpassed with ease. Nothing seems beautiful enough for the loved one, who, for a short time, succeeds in reaching, and exceeding, the ideal of the lover's ego, and in transferring part of this reflected light onto the lover. Plato, in the *Symposium*, has Socrates speak very profound words. After Aristophanes, it is his turn to hold forth about love. For Socrates, you love someone for their noble virtues:

> First, that Love is *of* something; second, that it is of something that he currently needs. (200e) … Didn't we agree that he loves what he needs and doesn't have? … It follows that Love needs beauty and doesn't have it? (201b) … Do you think that things that are good are also beautiful? … Then if Love is in need of beautiful things,

and good things are beautiful, he would be in need of good things? (201c) (p. 36). ... "But what could Love be?" I said. "A mortal?" "Far from it." "What then?" "Like those examples discussed earlier," she said, "he's between mortal and immortal." "What does that make him, Diotima?" "He is a great spirit, Socrates. Everything classed as a spirit falls between god and human." "What function do they have?" I asked. "They interpret and carry messages from humans to gods and from gods to humans. They convey prayers and sacrifices from humans, and commands and gifts in return for sacrifices from gods. Being intermediate between the other two, they fill the gap between them, and enable the universe to form an interconnected whole. They serve as the medium for all divination, for priestly expertise in sacrifice, ritual and spells, and for all prophecy and sorcery. Gods do not make direct contact with humans; they communicate and converse with humans (whether awake or asleep) entirely through the medium of spirits. Someone whose wisdom lies in these areas is a man of the spirit, while wisdom in other areas of expertise and craftsmanship makes one merely a mechanic. There are many spirits, of very different types, and one of them is Love" (202d–e–203a).

(Plato, *The Symposium*, 200e, 201b–c, 202d–e–203a; pp. 36, 38–39)

According to the Romantics, love is a yearning that cannot be fulfilled. Should such a desire be sated, its satisfaction would kill love, because one has what one seeks and love is the search for what one has not, as Diotima proclaimed: "First of all, he's [Love] always poor; far from being sensitive and beautiful, as is commonly supposed" (Plato, *The Symposium*, 203c; p. 39).

Following in Plato's footsteps, Freud, too, argues that love is driven by the search for an earlier condition. Since all later objects of attachment are imperfect substitutes for our original love objects, our sense of incompletion will continue to haunt us. This will condemn us to always look back. Desire longs for a sense of completeness that can never be achieved. We try to fill this lack, but the need remains insatiable and unfulfilled.

Excess, exaggeration, and infinite repetition (which is not, though, the compulsion to repeat) all arise from this insatiability. In a film of many years ago, *Last Year at Marienbad* (1961), by a director who has reflected much on love throughout his career, Alain Resnais, it is difficult to distinguish between truth and fiction, while the spatial and temporal relationships of the narrated events are blurred. Conversations and events are repeated in a number of different places in the chateau and, via a long series of tracking shots down corridors, the spectator is swept up into a mental stream of nostalgia that stylistically can only rely on repetition. In a similar manner, with the human psyche we assist at an inexhaustible repetition of words and gestures that should guarantee the unchanging continuity of our passion. Passion will last forever, for the whole night, for all the corridors in the chateau.

At the same time, though, the excess must remain unaltered, eternal. Passion does not survive the humdrum of daily life, and so it is not surprising that Brahms attempts to unite burning passion with intense yearning for something that will inevitably be lost. Sensual experience becomes something unique, unrepeatable, magical (to use the words often spoken by lovers). When it dies away, it leaves one bewildered, dumbfounded: "I thought that love would last for ever: I was wrong" (Auden, "Funeral Blues", 1938). How can passionate, romantic, eternally-the-same and never-changing love be wed to an adult perspective, in which the subject is capable of investing in the other while remaining himself at the same time, in which idealisation of the loved one and, consequently—as we have seen—of one's self, both respect and indeed reinforce the feeling of self, autonomy, and independence and allow the harmonious development of the individual?

In the Introduction, we have seen how *we fall ill if we cannot love*. But this love, to take up Kernberg's words, must be capable of allowing subjects to experience the excitement of romantic passion with the perceptions of the other, which illuminate instead of distort the other and oneself. Inevitable disappointments are compensated for by the pleasure of sharing with the other an expansion of our vital representation, in the most various contexts, in an infinite spatial and temporal combination, as *Last Year at Marienbad* shows so well. Adult love constantly brings new energy to the relationship, also because we need to love and be loved in order to live. We idealise our partner, but we also idealise love and, to a certain extent, reality. The transformation of the romantic passion and nostalgia we felt for the person we were when we loved also depends on our mature, adult ability to remain balanced between the irrepressible need to idealise and the capacity to accept the limitations of reality.

We want to be loved, known, and profoundly recognised in our most hidden intimate reality. We mirror ourselves in the loved one, we identify with him, we blend into him, but at the same time we accept that this, too, when all is said and done, is a thought, a desire, an idea that allows us to grow and be better, to overcome our limits and our inhibitions for being not so much fused together but instead autonomously independent in company with the other.

I would like to add one further detail about repetition in romantic love.

In "The emotion of amorousness and the principle of repetition" (a chapter in his 1963 book), Kurt Eissler points out how lovers tend to constantly repeat "I love you", or obsessively ask "Do you love me?", stressing, a shade ironically, that it is difficult to understand why an adult person has to constantly insist on repeating to the loved one something that he has already continually repeated and amply demonstrated with facts, or to ask for confirmation for something that has similarly passed the examination of reality an infinite number of times. He then adds: "There are strong forces in the psychic apparatus that work against an exclusive attachment. With each repetitive step in the state of amorousness, the image of the love object becomes more firmly attached to and integrated by the ego" (Eissler, 1963, p. 661).

Drawing on Freud, Eissler traces the need to be completely focused on the object of one's love, both for requesting and for offering declarations of love, back to the mobility of libidinal investments. We might say, also a shade ironically, that if love is blind, it is not, however, deaf and needs to hear repeated declarations as to its very existence.

I would now like to present part of a clinical case that illustrates the passage from illusion to disappointment and from disappointment to a necessary transformation for emotional growth.

Francesca and her cumbersome baggage

As an introduction to the case history of Francesca, I would like to quote Freud (1912d) on impotence:

> If the practising psycho-analyst asks himself on account of what disorder people most often come to him for help, he is bound to reply—disregarding the many forms of anxiety—that it is psychical

impotence ... I shall put forward the view that psychical impotence is much more widespread than is supposed, and that a certain amount of this behaviour does in fact characterize the love of civilized man ... We cannot escape the conclusion that the behaviour in love of men in the civilized world today bears the stamp altogether of psychical impotence ... I do not hesitate to make the two factors at work in psychical impotence in the strict sense—the factors of intense incestuous fixation in childhood and the frustration by reality in adolescence—responsible, too, for this extremely common characteristic of the love of civilized men.

(Freud, 1912d, pp. 179–184)

I remember very well how Francesca appeared at my door the first time: walking on tiptoe, trying to muffle the ticketing of her high heels—as I would continue to see her so many times during the course of her analysis. Dark glasses were hiding her face, and, at the same time, because of their size, were attracting attention. She seemed to be divided by two opposing trends: on the one hand, she did not want to intrude in the slightest; on the other, she did not want to give up her right to occupy some space. She was carrying bags and heavy briefcases that she deposited in the hall. I thought: "She is showing up burdened, weighed down by cumbersome baggage."

During the first interviews, she says: "The meaning of life has somehow escaped me. Most of all I don't understand what others want of me"; she repeats while going out.

But there is a more contingent reason than this sadness of hers that has prompted her to ask for an analysis: an unhappy love she cannot understand, that she cannot give up, the latest in a long series of affairs that have turned out badly.

I started an affair with this man last year. There was a very strong attraction between us and it became more and more palpable. He would hold my hand, caress me, kiss me, but always pretending nothing had happened, as though he was not truly interested. I know that he is still really attracted to me, but he doesn't want to have an affair with me at all, and I don't understand why. It is not the first time I find myself in such a situation. In my life I always seem to have encountered this kind of man; I could never understand what they wanted of me in the beginning, and why they no longer liked me afterwards.

In fact, Francesca's encounters with men over the years have been char-acterised by exhausting issues of understanding "what men wanted from her", and by attempts to establish relationships with unreliable, difficult, and often married people. Francesca's oedipal conflicts pre-vented her from enjoying a satisfying sentimental life and were fur-ther worsened by undermining her feminine self, arising from her early identification with a submissive, humiliated, and resentful mother.

What is striking in Francesca's story is her obstinate insistence on nursing for years the illusion that she could find space for a relation-ship with that man, despite the constant, obsessive presence of his wife. Why did Francesca not stop cherishing and pursuing a love that was so clearly unsatisfying and unacknowledged?

Francesca and the rabbit

During a session, faced with the umpteenth repetition of a situation of unmodifiable impotence and suffering with this man, I feel infected by impotence. I let my mind wander and strangely enough think of a funny story a friend of mine had told me many years before. The mem-ory brings a smile to my face and the clogged-up feeling of heaviness within me is dispelled. Suddenly, I realise how relevant the recollection actually is in the context of the session.

Analyst: "I have just thought of a story I believe has some relevance with what you are saying. A friend of mine who had a pet rabbit phoned me one day, laughing: 'You know what, yesterday it was snowing and when I got home my rabbit was out on the balcony, almost completely buried in the snow, and only his ears were sticking out!' Please for-give the somewhat comical and maybe also irreverent comparison, but in this situation, as in many similar ones, you make me think of this rabbit, a completely helpless being, unable to protect itself from the snowfall."

Francesca remains silent for a while, evidently struck and surprised by my reaction, which was, after all, so very different from my usual attitude of understanding and powerless, useless solidarity.

Francesca: "You mean that the rabbit was unable to protect itself from the snow, as I am, after all, unable to protect myself from this man's repeated refusals." A long pause. "But what exactly were you thinking, seeing that the rabbit can't protect itself from the snow?"

Analyst: "Well, I was thinking about that right now. Perhaps it is not equipped to recognise that it's cold and it has to find shelter."

Francesca: "I think that the rabbit would be better off under a roof, under a shelter. It's an image that strikes me and that I find quite to the point. I can see myself as a fearful and somewhat clueless rabbit that is unable to notice the cold and the snow. I have to learn to protect myself better from snowstorms as well."

I was the first to be amazed by my own remarks. Actually, my friend had told me: "The rabbit is a stupid animal, how can it fail to protect itself from the snow?" The episode had occurred at least fifteen years before, and it did not contain any element worth remembering so that it would stay in my mind. It really was an association that emerged quite unexpectedly, and it had undoubtedly been triggered by the comment on stupidity. I had never associated the adjective "stupid" with Francesca, also because she is undoubtedly a woman with a rare and keen mind. And yet the compulsive repetition of the experience of being rebuffed by that man had the exasperating obtuseness of someone who obstinately refuses to learn from experience.

Francesca: "Look, I think that the image of this helpless animal that remains so motionless and lets itself be buried by the snow reminds me very much of myself. It's not true that the snow doesn't bother me; the fact is I am incapable of seeking shelter." A long pause. "I clearly remember how my mother was helpless in front of my father. And I also clearly remember the icy feeling that paralysed me during their discussions."

There are two interesting elements in the rabbit story. The first, as I mentioned, is the revelation of the stupidity (the uselessness, maybe) of some of the patient's repeated behaviours. The other, more hidden, is grasping the chilling and paralysing power of the situation. "Why didn't the rabbit seek shelter?", Francesca immediately asked. And we, together with her: "Why can't she seek shelter from these repetitive freezing situations?"

The analyst's capacity for reverie in the presence of the patient's distressing elements is an indispensable component in the analytic relationship. Thanks to the projective identification reverie exchange with the patient, in the umpteenth repetition of Francesca's traumatic oedipal vicissitude I had caught a new, and apparently incomprehensible, but chilling narrative element. The story of the rabbit, motionless under the snowstorm, was very well suited to represent little Francesca in the paralysing identification with her mother confronted with her father's repeated accusations. At the same time, the episode appeared in my mind as incongruous and incomprehensible. In the *hic et nunc* of the transference, Francesca's not being aware of the aggressive and destructive character of the man she loved appeared incomprehensible. The image that had come to my mind and that I had exchanged with Francesca had allowed her to see herself involved in turn in an absurd event in the present. At the same time, my solidarity with today's Francesca had allowed her to make contact with her emotional experience of the past, by remembering for the first time the chilling and paralysing element of the vicissitude within a story that had been told many times before.

Comment

The relationship between love and the Oedipus complex was never fully resolved by Freud. He viewed the Oedipus complex as being at the heart of all human relationships, but we know that there is a delicate and fragile balance between oedipal desires and oedipal defeat. An oedipal defeat occurs, for example, when a father conveys to his daughter the message that he loves her, but cannot have a sexual relationship with her. She is both valued and admired by her father, but she is rejected and renounced as a partner. We can consider it a *necessary* oedipal defeat, necessary for the subsequent development of her future adult love investments. Yet, if the daughter is not admired and valued by her father, if she is unable to arouse the interest and admiration of her father and of her mother, if she cannot retain a deep sense of having been loved as a little girl, her oedipal desire cannot find a proper resolution. The longing for the oedipal conquest is a strong and powerful imprinting for the future development of the capacity to find a "good enough" love object in adult life. Destructive and rejecting oedipal experiences create major obstacles to the capacity for enjoying satisfactory love investments, and for experimenting with passion in adult life. Oedipal relationships are developmentally vital for understanding union and separateness, subjectivity and objectivity. Resolving the oedipal conflict entails understanding that a daughter cannot become her father's lover, and this will set her free in the future to find a companion outside her family.

Exclusion can be painful, but also positive. In Francesca's case, her father had established a perverse and compensatory relationship with his daughter, which had kept her imprisoned in the oedipal situation: as in her many dreams, she was imprisoned/hidden between two leaves of the door while spying unseen on the parental couple. This had been the chilling and paralysing element of the story: Francesca would escape into a dark corner to watch, unseen, the oedipal scene of her father and her mother together, a poor motionless rabbit in a snow-storm. She had never experienced exclusion, but, unfortunately for her, she was, instead, chosen by her father as a compensatory object for her mother's failures. With her boyfriend, she had then re-experienced the same destructive, *second choice* acceptance she had experienced with her father. As already pointed out by Freud:

> If we are to understand the love-objects chosen by our type as being above all mother-surrogates, then the formation of a series of them, which seems so flatly to contradict the condition of being faithful to one, can now also be understood. We have learnt from psycho-analysis in other examples that the notion of something irreplace-able, when it is active in the unconscious, frequently appears as broken up into an endless series: endless for the reason that every surrogate nevertheless fails to provide the desired satisfaction.
>
> (Freud, 1910h, p. 169)

At the end of her analysis, Francesca said: "I can't remain forever yearn-ing for something that is no longer there. I have finally understood that. I have also succeeded in making people close to me accept that it really did exist and that I didn't invent it (my love for this man). Now I understand, though, that I have different, new needs that the old struc-ture can no longer contain. So I feel ready to go out into the future."

Francesca was helped to continue the restoration of her old, origi-nal, internal structure, but also to develop and construct new build-ings, new life projects that could be used by her in the present and would be more consistent with the needs of the mature woman she has become, more functional to her well-being and therefore capable of allowing her to lead a better, more satisfying, and less self-destructive sentimental life.

The afterwardness, that is, the mode of belated understanding or ret-roactive attribution of/to the past to/in the present, the *Nachträglichkeit*, made it possible to reorganise the experiences that had not been inte-grated before. More than illuminating hidden truths of the past, this reorganisation allowed paralysed and frozen aspects of her emotional, relational, and love life to come back to life again.

To remain the prisoner of an investment that could not be satisfied was a makeshift solution. But: "Beloved by none, it is sad to live", the poet Thomas Haynes Bayly proclaims. So the close connection between the development of the analysis and the development of the emotional story recounted in the analytic relationship made it possible for the historical events to become narrative vicissitudes, and thus modify their plot line and transform Francesca's apparently unmodifiable repetition compulsion.

"I could not understand what these men wanted of me in the beginning", Francesca used to say at the beginning of her analysis. Now, no longer a rabbit covered with snow, she could understand and make herself understood by others. Yearning for a lost love remained within her as a warm, no longer icy, feeling. To have recognised and to have got others to acknowledge that she had been loved and had loved—a real, idealised love that was present as much in her interior reality as it was outside—encouraged the development of a feeling of nostalgia for the end of that love. As Bertolt Brecht says: "But I honestly can't recollect her face/I just know: there was a time I kissed it" (1927).

Yearning for her lost love was accompanied by satisfaction in having been capable of loving and being loved. Emerging from the frozen wastes of the repetition compulsion, she could begin to invest in people who were more attentive towards her and her needs, more in harmony with what she wanted and could offer. Meanwhile, the nostalgia remained as a faint, intangible warp for a new material, a new love to be lived with greater freedom.

CHAPTER FOUR

The unbearableness of being abandoned*

Cascando

1
why not merely the despaired of
occasion of
wordshed

is it not better abort than be barren

the hours after you are gone are so leaden
they will always start dragging too soon
the grapples clawing blindly the bed of want
bringing up the bones the old loves
sockets filled once with eyes like yours
all always is it better too soon than never
the black want splashing their faces

---

*Part of the case of Alessandra was published in the *Romanian Journal of Psychoanalysis*, VIII, no. 2 (2015), translated by Carla Bellucci.

saying again nine days never floated the loved
nor nine months
nor nine lives

2
saying again
if you do not teach me I shall not learn
saying again there is a last
even of last times
last times of begging
last times of loving
of knowing not knowing pretending
a last even of last times of saying
if you do not love me I shall not be loved
if I do not love you I shall not love

the churn of stale words in the heart again
love love love thud of the old plunger
pestling the unalterable
whey of words
terrified again
of not loving
of loving and not you
of being loved and not by you
of knowing not knowing pretending
pretending
I and all the others that will love you
if they love you

3
unless they love you

—Samuel Beckett (1936)

As I anticipated in the Introduction, many authors attribute another role
to love in addition to that of re-finding (the object of early love investment), even if re-finding continues to be an essential prerequisite for the
loving experience. Many authors point out the therapeutic "strength"
of love, which enriches the self and brings with it hopes that the loved

person can heal the wound originally inflicted by a not-good-enough primary object.

Yet analysts are all too familiar with patients who ask for help after a love relationship ends. And we might say, quite openly, that the events narrated do not present anything particularly unique or exceptional, and yet, along with Tolstoy, we can say that every unhappy love story is something unique and exceptional, both for the person who lives it and for the person who assists and shares it. Both men and women who ask for help to find a way out of the suffering of love, caused by a lost or impossible love, are burdened by a great weight of suffering that goes far beyond the loss suffered. Perhaps they are people who have built their whole world, their interests, and above all, more than anything else, their self-esteem and their sense of identity on the love of which they were the object. The loved person becomes the representative and interpreter of the part for love of their internal psychic structure. The end of their relationship leads to heightened anger and aggression, directed at times towards the love object who has left them, and at times—and these are the patients we generally see—towards themselves.

We have seen how idealising the loved person is essential in the love relationship.

Ethel Person (1988) has emphasised how this process can be much more protracted than is commonly believed. Idealising the loved person, or the relationship with the loved person, may alter over time but it will not necessarily expire. In an attempt to protect the ego, prolonged idealisation can even be more important, thanks to the sensation of loving, than the original passion or the loss of the object of this passion. In some cases, being abandoned is just not a possible option; it is totally unacceptable to the ego. The parts of the self that were loved through the projective identification of the loved one are those involved here. The loved one seemed to offer a reassuring and familiar relationship that was, at the same time, surprisingly new. The part of the self placed in the loved person cannot be successfully recovered and so persists in the other, lost to the ego forever. As Beckett says:

> a last even of last times of saying
> if you do not love me I shall not be loved
> if I do not love you I shall not love.

When abandoned by the loved one, the possibility for loving again, and for being loved, is lost. What the loved person, by means of projective identification, had imagined around the parts of the self and placed well inside himself are lost forever. Every time one of my patients suffered a disappointment in love, a profound and penetrating narcissistic wound, she lived it as a bitter and total rejection, complete with a somatic-psychic self, and she saw herself in the mirror as deformed, fat, huge. The rejected self becomes a horrible self, in response to this rejection. Rejection removes the filter that transformed the self into something good and beautiful and thus reverts to the original rejection of the self. "He/she doesn't want me, or no longer wants me", and so "inevitably I become deficient in what he/she saw in me".

The subjective state of the projective identification disappears and becomes undeniable reality, which is deformed for others but not for the person living it, just as though it were reflected by a deforming mirror.

Joseph Sandler (1976a) advanced another psychoanalytic explanation that complements the first. The concept of internal object, or internal representation of parts of the self, is very useful in these situations. Internal objects are, in fact, loved as much as external objects; indeed, these internal objects are often exteriorised onto others, who become the unconscious representatives of the internal love objects. When the other, the object of this exteriorisation, evades this investment, the internal objects lose all their value. Initially, before knowing the other, these objects had a value but as soon as the subject is deprived of the external love object, he also loses the internal love objects. When one is abandoned by the object of one's love, what one loses, apart from the object, is an aspect of one's self, complementary to the object. Mourning for the loss of the loved object is thus doubled: in addition to the object, one also loses those aspects of the self that were originally projected onto the object. A good part of the mourning process lies precisely in the narcissistic process of recovering the lost objects of the self. The myth of Apollo and Daphne, recounted in the Introduction, is a good example of a possibility for a positive working through and a transferal of the trust and expectations that the lost love took away forever on to other aspects of the self.

Therefore, it is clear that when originally, in the first phases of life, or in infancy or even in early adolescence, the subject suffered traumatic elements of loss or devaluation of the self, the process of recovering and re-appropriating the lost parts of the self is much more laborious and demanding.

In perfect, unknowing harmony with Apollo, one of my patients, in the months after he had been left by his girlfriend, phantasised about being a victorious commander in past battles. These phantasies took up much of his time and a great deal of space in his mind, and even if their invasion of his mental space riled him considerably, they acted as true therapeutic elements in restoring the processes of self-esteem that had been so traumatically interrupted.

Another of my patients, several years after the end of a relationship, when she had already created a family, had children and an interesting job, dreamt, on the occasion of an important step in her career, that she was in her ex-boyfriend's house, where he lived with his new partner, and had blocked his toilet with her prestigious, newly won certificate. She had woken from this dream with the feeling that "justice had been done!" That achievement had shown her not only how much she was worth, and therefore how much he had lost, but also that she could now allow herself to do what, at a conscious level, and in the past, she had never allowed herself to do, and that is to cause him harm and insult him, angrily, for the psychological injury he had inflicted on her self-esteem.

Dreams like these are fairly common, even years after a love affair ends and it has truly been brought to a conclusion, demonstrating that in the unconscious the narcissistic aspect of being abandoned—that is, the wound or the loss of those parts of the self that were entrusted to the other—is more profound than the real, external loss of the love object itself.

Alessandra, prisoner of shame

When Alessandra started her analysis with me, she was a very attractive woman, apparently unconstrained and self-confident. She telephoned to ask for an analysis on 1 September, immediately after she had returned from her holidays: over the summer, her husband had asked her for a separation, plunging her into profound depressive anxiety. Due to an obstinate form of bulimia, after numerous diets had failed, her dietician had already recommended that she undergo psychoanalytic treatment, but she only decided to contact me after her husband asked her for a separation, even though she had lost a lot of weight again in the meantime.

Alessandra had had a serious traumatic experience in pre-adolescence: in six months, she had lost her father and her brother, and was thus alone, the prisoner of a mother devastated by grief, but committed to denying it and mindful only of her daughter's physical well-being, particularly regarding food, about which she took especial care. At home, the child Alessandra could not say a word about these two deaths.

Now Alessandra immediately became bulimic again, thanks to the failure of her marriage and her husband leaving her.

Eating disorders have never been easy to define nor to cure, and the dizzying increase of these pathologies in recent years has made the complexity of their symptoms and the huge number of their possible meanings more and more evident. People who suffer from such disorders feel they have no efficient way of communicating with the outside world. They live their state of desertion in profound shame and solitude, often aggravated by repressing either the traumatic event itself or the emotional consequences of it. The concrete and non-verbal way in which these patients act forces them into a repetition compulsion that is extremely difficult to break (Diena, 2004, pp. 80–81).

For Alessandra, the shame and distress provoked by her obesity, which revealed to the whole world the suffering caused by being deserted, massively and negatively characterised any possibility for recovering her self-esteem and those objects of the self lost when abandoned.

We know that the analytic experience is not just about helping patients to understand the nature of their problems, but that it mainly involves helping them to overcome their suffering, anxiety, and the taxing problematic relationships that have caused so many difficulties in their lives.

However, it is a common experience for every analyst to feel how, in some patients, the development of insight and understanding remains exclusively on an intellectual and conscious level and, however fundamental and important for them, never goes beyond this level; it never succeeds in becoming a real, transforming and changing experience in their lives. In other words, these patients seem incapable of making a really transformative use of the analytic process; they are incapable of using the understanding developed in analysis to trigger any significant change in their lives. Rigid fixations, an apparent incapacity to change, and impasses that seem to block the analyst and patient are all issues that every analyst risks encountering in their clinical work and that are capable of throwing the daily analytic process into a state of crisis.

These impasses are well known with eating disorders, and the situation with Alessandra was no different.

When Alessandra started her descent

I remember very well when Alessandra started her descent. She had been stuck "up there" for many months, almost two years. "Up there", to be clear, refers to her weight of almost one hundred kilos (two hundred and twenty pounds/nearly sixteen stone), which she now permanently weighed. We were—patient and analyst—both desperate in the same way. Alessandra appeared to have changed a lot in her character and in her personality. However, despite all the analytical interpretations and constructions we had shared; despite the agreement we had exhaustingly reached together about the precocious traumatic aetiology of her eating disorders, and of her identification of the representational metaphor of her obesity as a concrete, somatic defence against the investment drives as both subject and libidinal object; despite every symbolic transformation achieved step after slow step during her long years of analysis, from the thing to the thought, from the acting out to the feeling, and to the thought; despite all this and much more, her body would triumph unscathed and majestic in its obesity.

On the other hand, many elements revealed an exhaustion and fatigue that were no longer bearable on a physical level. Alessandra had developed a particularly painful tendinitis in her foot, due to being overweight, which prevented her from walking; due to eating constantly and in a disorderly way, she had got a gastric ulcer; she suffered from a particular form of insomnia, always thanks to the quantity of food eaten in the evenings; without mentioning her respiratory and cardiac difficulties strictly linked to her obesity. She had, in fact, recently suffered from asthmatic bronchitis, due, according to the lung specialist, to a diminished respiratory capacity caused by an excessive dilation of her diaphragm; her glycaemic levels had risen alarmingly and her blood pressure was often way above the accepted norm. Not to speak of her cholesterol levels.

The early death of her father—a smoker, hypertensive, and overweight—from a myocardial heart attack greatly worried Alessandra, who feared she herself would suffer a repeat of such a dramatic event.

I, too, was worried about the physical consequences of such prolonged and excessive obesity. The sessions often resembled medical bulletins; every day a new crack appeared, renewed confirmation of her body's difficulty in dealing with such huge dimensions. Alessandra now weighed fifty kilos (one hundred and ten pounds/nearly eight stone) more than when she had begun analysis.

The only thing that was clear to me, and with which Alessandra agreed, was the fact that if she did not lose weight, it could only mean that psychologically she was not yet ready to do so. Terrifying fears persisted on an unconscious level about rediscovering the sexuality that would have implied a new libidinal object investment and a new possible exposure to another trauma of being abandoned.

I was reflecting and suggesting during a session that maybe she was afraid of terminating the analysis and of being abandoned by the analyst, and that her failure to lose weight perhaps corresponded to a wish to continue the analysis forever, thus postponing the resolution of those somatic elements that seemed to physically hinder her every possible movement. Alessandra would nod, but did not seem persuaded; instead, she repeatedly confirmed her wish to terminate the analysis as soon as possible, that she could no longer afford it, and that it was not bringing any change to her life. Her protests often ended with her declaring that the analysis had really helped with one thing, and that was her relationship with her children. In this, she felt truly supported and helped every day by the analyst. I would diligently put everything on record, but could not find any element to hitch on to. On the other hand, her regular attendance, constant presence, and punctuality were all signs that seemed, instead, to suggest a strong desire to continue with the therapy, especially when compared to her behaviour of the early years, when she often used to skip sessions or arrive late. She now paid correctly, too, and on time—despite repeated protests about how much it cost—again quite different to the early years. In a word, numerous signs pointed to an extreme dependence on and need for the analysis, and profound expectations in the transformative aspects of the therapy of words on the somatic issues. Now her body was frequently ill, and there were no more of those triumphant elements of the narcissistic somatic self that characterised the first years of her analysis. This is why we must pay particular attention to psycho-sensorial elements and not just the strictly verbal ones that emerge during the session.

Betty Joseph, in 1985, stressed that:

> If we work only with the part that is verbalized, we do not really take into account the object relationships being acted out in the transference (p. 158). ... I have tried to discuss how the way in which our patients communicate their problems to us is frequently beyond their individual associations and beyond their words, and can often only be gauged by means of the countertransference. These are some of the points that I think we need to consider under the rubric of the total situations which are transferred from the past.
>
> (Joseph, 1985, p. 167)

Faithful to these theoretical lines, which I follow and which guide my interventions, I would exhaustedly ask myself what I was not seeing, and what I was not hearing.

One day, Alessandra began a session particularly nervous and tense, and confessed: "I'm afraid I can no longer go back. I'm afraid that my body has got used to this weight, and that I can no longer find in myself that stimulus to try to go back, to descend." It was not the first time she had said something like this; on the contrary, she would say it quite often. I felt physically stuck on that spot as well, as if stiffened. But this time, I caught myself thinking of something else. I was thinking of that time when during a climb I had remained stuck on the face of the mountain, and I had told myself: "I can no longer go down". My daughter, who was beside me, had patiently shown me where to pass and waited for me a little higher up. I would always think of my daughter, who had just left to go abroad for a long period of time—and needed my support, as I had needed hers then. These thoughts suddenly became clear and intelligible vis-à-vis the daughter/patient I had right in front of me. Alessandra had shown me where to catch hold on the face of the mountain in order to cope with a very difficult passage. And, in turn, she needed my help and my support in that moment. I answered: "Maybe you are telling me that for the first time in this moment you are realising that you really need help in order to get over a difficult passage you cannot cope with on your own." "Yes", she answered, "I feel exactly like that; I feel you should help me, because I can't make it by myself."

When expounding the concept of the "unthought known", Bollas (1987) emphasised the importance of the mental process of evocation by which information begins to emerge from the deepest parts of the self. Ogden (1989), too, describes these countertransference sensations, referring to what he calls the "autistic-contiguous mode" of the experience:

> More specific to the autistic-contiguous mode of experience is countertransference experience in which bodily sensations dominate.... Very frequently the countertransference experience is associated with skin sensations such as feelings of warmth and coldness as well as tingling, numbness, and an exaggerated sensitivity to skin impressions like the tightness of one's tie or one's shoes.
>
> (Ogden, 1989, p. 44)

The psycho-sensorial basis that asserts itself in the countertransference in the presence of unrepresentable traumatic areas is reactivated in the significant interactions between patient and analyst (Gammaro Moroni, 2003).

I was at a loss as an analyst in that moment, and risked being stuck there for a long while, incapable of descending. My daughter/patient was showing me something to catch hold of: she needed my help. If we remember Alessandra's exasperated narcissism, her difficulty in asking for help and in really resorting to others, her confidence in her own resilience (ability to survive in extreme conditions), her making her happiness depend upon "being thin and passing exams", we can truly understand that in that moment she was really asking me to help her lose weight, because she was not able to do it by herself, with her own strength alone.

What did it mean? Alessandra had often started and also successfully completed a number of diets, always with an attitude of challenge and disdain towards the analyst, who would deal with *unreal* psychical elements, that is, things that had nothing to do with her reality as a woman who was a bit overweight and was perfectly able to lose weight by herself, if only she had wanted to.

Unfortunately, the smallest narcissistic wound would be enough to drive her once more to find refuge in food, the only real source of consolation and satisfaction in the face of disappointment. Now she was telling me that she was no longer able to do something useful on her own. And I, through the imagery of a mother/daughter relationship, could understand how to offer her real help, capable of supporting her in a difficult choice, like that of starting to lose weight after all these extra kilos. As I had understood that I had to offer concrete help to my daughter during her experience abroad, so I could understand that I had to consider Alessandra's excessive weight like a person in a foreign country, requiring a great deal of support in order to restore the lost equilibrium.

At her next session, Alessandra begins by saying:

> I had a dream. I was on top of a mountain, it was winter, and there was snow all around. We were very high, I was not alone, I was feeling quite well, all my friends, my old friends were with me, you were there too, I believe, and we were all staying in this refuge protected by rocks. I knew that it couldn't last forever, that I had to go down, go back to the valley, but I didn't know how to. All the others could ski, and so they put on their skis and began to descend while I leaned out over the void and postponed the descent, although I was feeling somewhat uneasy. Then a little girl arrived, who could ski, and she told me to keep calm, to ski behind her and that we would go safely down one bend after the other. I trusted her, she had somehow been sent by you, or she was you, I don't know exactly, because you were beside me as well. She could ski and I could trust her, but then I decided to wait all the same and went back to the refuge.

I told her:

> It seems to me that with this dream you are referring to yesterday's session. You picture yourself on top of a mountain from which you don't know how to descend, as you were saying yesterday that you have gained too much weight and were afraid you couldn't lose it by yourself. But you are not alone, there are many friends with you and also your analyst. However everybody but you seems to possess the necessary skills to ski down the slope, so you are forced to remain isolated on the top of the mountain. To go down you have to rely on somebody who is more skilled although younger than you, like the little girl in your dream.

I am attracted by the thought that she could be my daughter, whom I had evoked within myself to help me in our previous session. Maybe something really had been unconsciously transmitted about how to find those indispensable elements for getting out of a stalemate, or narcissistic impasse.

Alessandra portrays her situation at a narcissistic level very well. Shut up and isolated on the peak of a mountain, she is not able to come down because she is not adequately equipped with the skills everybody else has; she illustrates a narcissistic impasse that is difficult to escape from. She could put her trust in someone younger than her, but she prefers to wait, and turns back to take refuge in an impervious but safe place. I tell her so:

> At a narcissistic level it is very difficult for you to come out of a situation in which you took refuge a long time ago, and it seems clear that what is frightening you more than anything else is the very descent, which the others in your dream all seem, instead, able to manage.

The next time Alessandra says:

> I had a very strange dream. I was at the seaside and absolutely had to dive into the water and reach the other side of the bay. I was on a pier and a person was waiting for me on the other side. I had to dive in, but I was terrified; I was frightened of diving; in actual fact, I hate diving. The shore I was on seemed very safe, but I knew that there was nothing for it because something very threatening was arriving that I absolutely had to escape from, by diving. I dived in but at this point, who knows why, I was in a car and the windows were closed, and so I was trapped. I felt I was going to die. Then from the other side the person waiting for me was actually me, myself, looking on at the car sinking and you were right next to me. And therefore I understood that the person drowning was not really me if I could see myself alive and well next to you on the shore. Then I got out of the car all the same, I don't know how, because I was also the person who should have dived in, and I understood that I had been saved because I had taken off this scuba-diving mask that had prevented me from breathing. The mask floated near the shoreline and it was really gruesome because it had strands of skin attached to it; it was obvious that I had had to tear at my flesh to get it off me. But I was safe. In the dream, I felt terribly anxious but at the same time very relieved.

I comment:

> It seems to me that in the dream you represented the conflict you are living extremely well, between the fear of leaving a safe shore, even if only temporarily and for a short time, and the need to tackle the passage towards the other side, a change that you can no longer postpone because, as the dream says, you have absolutely got to escape a danger that is threatening you even if the shore seems safe at the moment. The sinking car seems to me to be an allusion to the future anxiety-inducing loss of the welcoming safety of the analytic car. Besides, you see me next to you on the other side of the bay, therefore you know you will not be alone. The main problem is that for you the loss of the mask exemplifies a lacerating event, in which you risk tearing off strands of your skin. The mask alludes to a false self, which you know you must abandon before you can make that crossing, before you can descend the mountain. There you have to trust a person younger than you, but more expert; here you have to tear off the mask you have been wearing for so long that it has become a second skin for you.

Alessandra:

> I feel exactly like that, I feel I absolutely have to lose weight, that I can't see my face anymore because I'm so fat, but that I don't want to discover that I am no longer able to slim down and go back to how I was before, that I am frightened, terrified of not being able to succeed, and that, yes, I need help.

She loses a remarkable amount of weight, but soon begins to put it on again. A few weeks pass. During a fight with her ex-husband, he tells her: "You who have drowned in your fat…"

It hurts, and cannot be denied. She has a dream in which the words "fatness", "anxiety", and "loneliness" are repeated endlessly. During the session, she says: "I see that as soon as I feel hurt I eat in order not to feel anything. But now this dream makes it clear that, even inside myself, that fatness is the result of the anxiety produced by my loneliness. Please, help me."

A particular period begins. Alessandra appears determined to slim down, fully aware of the huge effort it will cost her to lose all those kilos.

Was the living room empty or full?

One year before the end of the analysis, Alessandra brought a dream. She finds herself in her living room at home and there is a coffin in the middle of the room. Her father is in it, but she is not upset. She understands that *it is high time* (she actually said this) to move this cumbersome presence. And she tries to find in the wardrobe/bookcase at the far end of the room a door in which to fit the coffin. Associations went in the direction of the affects she was feeling. There is no surprise in her father's death, rather the acknowledgement of the inconvenience, the mess that this object is still producing in the middle of the room. The room represents her mind, the coffin is her dead father who has not yet been moved into an area of her mind so as not to keep on cluttering her internal space. The words *fatness, anxiety,* and *loneliness* come up again. She thought that she had not been able to find a space to mourn and bury her father. She thought that the loneliness she had experienced for the sudden loss of her father and her brother had made her terribly anxious, that she could not share and give vent to her distress, especially with her mother, who was lost in her grief and in her anger for the survivor. Fatness had been her way of stifling this unbearable sorrow.

> I could not bear feeling miserable. Every time I felt as if everything was going to collapse. I felt alone, unable to cope with the abyss that was opening under my feet. I see that everything began then, when I had to shove everything back in, because there was nothing else to do. Now that I live in a very different situation, I understand that it has been very difficult to go back down, to accept feeling miserable without risking to fall again into the abyss.

Comment

Alessandra's transformation process is worth reflecting on.

In one of my earlier works (Diena, 2008), I postulated that transformative processes strong enough to break the traumatising chain can be developed only by making the early traumatic experience relevant again in the transference.

In my opinion, with these words of hers as recorded above, Alessandra perfectly represents this aspect. That is, she is highlighting the acquired skill of differentiating the transferential and countertransferential elements in the present analytic situation from her past experiences. In the analysis, there has been a transferential and countertransferential change. The analyst has been able to perceive the patient as a daughter needing help, and the patient has relied on a mother who could help her. The experience of the abyss, shared by both, has made it possible for the patient to achieve the emotional change necessary to produce a real psychic transformation.

Betty Joseph suggested that psychic change is not "just an end, a final state, but is always going on in treatment and that we as analysts need to be able to find and follow the 'moment-to-moment' changes in our patients" (1986, p. 192). By getting fat, Alessandra would take refuge higher and higher up the mountain, until she could not get any higher, and her persistent weight increase would perfectly reflect the metaphoric sense of this movement, the taking up of an extreme defensive position.

But at the same time, the motionless Alessandra on the top of the mountain would mirror the motionless analyst during her climb, a stalemate for both which would appear as the sign of a protracted and suffering impotence constantly at risk of collapsing and falling into the abyss. It is interesting to point out in Alessandra's condition the aspect of the stalemate, or eternal checkmate; this continuous sensation of eternity without movement, hovering over a dangerous and terrifying emptiness. Change implies modifying one's own equilibrium and moving towards more risky positions, positions that are that much more risky if we are capable of understanding that a gaping abyss lies below them; that is, underlying them lies the risk of a catastrophic collapse of one's defences and equilibrium. Only the analyst's understanding and actual sharing of this abyss, this *void* of symbolic representation, made it possible for the patient to finally get over it and at last go through the affective, representational, and symbolic emptiness of her past unresolved traumatic experiences.

In that moment, as in many other infinite moments during the analysis, the analyst had *lent* the patient her own capacity for creative imagining. She had responded—emotionally—to Alessandra's difficulties, making them resound within her and producing an imaginative answer that opened up a whole new relational world based on listening and dialogue, completely different from the one experienced with her mother, crushed by her grief and her own problems.

One day, a few weeks before the end of the analysis, a very excited Alessandra arrived in my studio. In her office, she had seen a little bird smashing against the window of her balcony trying to get away from a big, threatening pigeon. Moved to pity, she had opened the window and saved the poor little bird, stroking its feathers.

> Poor thing, its heart was beating wildly and in the beginning it couldn't manage to feel safe in my hands. It made me think of myself, of my early years in analysis. I would run away from threatening, dangerous situations and often smash against windowpanes, knocking myself out. You would take me in your arms—metaphorically speaking—but I couldn't relax, I would remain mistrustful and frightened, thinking that I could have saved myself only if I had flown again. It took me a long time to accept your help.

I would like to conclude by quoting a last comment from Alessandra and comparing it to a final comment written by Harold Boris, in a paper of 1984:

> But it is the analyst's quiet tolerance of the muddle and uncertainty, of the gradualness of approximations, of error and apology that makes possible for the patient to simply *come to be* … The capacity for both parties to the analysis to manage the *presence of the absence of certainty* is what, more I think than anything, to be or not be the conducive factor.
>
> (Boris, 1984, p. 441)

Unaware of being on the same wavelength as Boris, towards the end of the analysis Alessandra was sharing her thoughts with me:

> I can solve parts of my problems only by coping with a tiny bit at a time. I can't solve everything at once. Life is a continuous process of partial transformations and we have to accept this fragmentation of the solutions we are presented with. I chose to let my husband go away from within me, also as a presence to hate. Considering the way I was—always striving for perfection (to be always slim and to do well in my exams), and this was sheer bliss—it has been a superhuman effort.

CHAPTER FIVE

Fatal love

Blessed Longing

Tell it none, except the wise
(Lest the rabble cry, for shame!),
Living beings I will prize
Who but long for death by flame.

Cooling, after loving-night
When you passed your life-seed on,
Alien feeling will alight
When the candle's gleaming, calm.

Now no more are you surrounded
In the night by shadow-net;
Rather, new desire unbounded
Rends you, that you may beget.

Freedom from long effort granted,
Flown, you're held here fast, illumed,
And at last, by light enchanted,
Butterfly, you'll be consumed.

And until you learn the best,
This: Die, and become!
You are but a sullen guest,
Earth is dull and glum.

Height will reeds of cane fulfil,
Worlds the sweeter grow!
From my able writing quill
Let endearment flow.

—Johann Wolfgang von Goethe (1819)

In his beautiful book, *Love in the Western World*, Denis de Rougemont ponders on how literature and poetry are full of tales of unhappy or fatal love stories, those that are:

> frowned upon and doomed by life itself. What stirs lyrical poets to their finest flights is neither the delight of the senses nor the fruitful contentment of the settled couple; not the satisfaction of love, but its *passion*. And passion means suffering. There we have the fundamental fact.
>
> (De Rougemont, 1939, p. 15)

Let us also recall Tolstoy's beautiful incipit to *Anna Karenina* (1877): "Happy families are all alike; every unhappy family is unhappy in its own way". This is a provocative beginning because "every unhappy family is unhappy in its own way" implies that the story that Tolstoy is about to unfold is unique and exceptional. De Rougemont, on the contrary, sustains throughout his book that a typically Western way of feeling, desiring, experiencing, and representing love exists that is inextricably linked with death, so that amorous passion finds relief only in death, in love-death, the German *Liebestod*. In love-passion (Stendhal, 1822), instead, the obstacle creates the adventure, the plot of the story.

"Happy love has no history" (De Rougemont, 1939, p. 15); happiness cannot be narrated. Years ago, when organising a cycle of films about love with a group of colleagues, we racked our brains to come up with a film that portrayed a happy love story. But to no avail. If there are any, we just could not remember them. For Denis de Rougemont, the archetype of all literature about love is the medieval myth of Tristan and Isolde. According to his interpretation, though, Tristan and Isolde, lovers *par excellence*, do not in actual fact love each other:

> *What they love is love and being in love.* They fall in love with *love*, not with a concrete person. They love, but not one another. They love to love love more than the object of love, to love passion for its own sake … What they need is not one another's presence, but one another's absence. Thus the partings of the lovers are dictated by their passion itself, and by the love they bestow on their passion rather than on its satisfaction or on its living object.
>
> (De Rougemont, 1939, p. 41)

Stendhal too, in *Love* (1822), describes love as a feeling that annuls every distance; you cannot protect yourself against it. The key word for Stendhal is *crystallisation*:

> At the salt mines of Salzburg, they throw a leafless wintry bough into one of the abandoned workings. Two or three months later they haul it out covered with a shining deposit of crystals. The smallest twig, no bigger than a tom-tit's claw, is studded with a galaxy of scintillating diamonds. The original branch is no longer recognizable.
>
> (Stendhal, 1822, p. 45)

The same thing happens with love; it establishes itself in our psyche and ramifies its presence as extensively as possible. Passionate love implies total subservience to love, which makes any other interest impossible. As Goethe, above, says:

> Freedom from long effort granted,
> Flown, you're held here fast, illumed,
> And at last, by light enchanted,
> Butterfly, you'll be consumed.

"My lords, if you would hear a high tale of love and of death"—so starts one of the versions of Tristan and Isolde (Joseph Bédier, 1902–1905). "Where does the spell come from?" wonders De Rougemont, as it lures the reader into a trap of thrilling expectations spun by the narrative illusion and by the pact between love and death, a fatal love that kindles the most profound resonance within us. By passion, we do not mean what makes us suffer but what thrills us to the very core. Be that as it may, in literature, the passion of love equates to perpetual unhappiness. But it is paradoxical that man desires passion and unhappiness just so long as he does not have to confess that he desires them as such: "The pleasure of love lasts but a moment/The grief of love lasts a lifetime" as a famous French song of 1784 by Jean-Paul-Égide Martini goes.

In De Rougemont's book, the romance of Tristan and Isolde becomes a myth essential for conveying the deeply obscure and unspeakable fact that passion is linked with death:

> A myth is needed to express the dark and unmentionable fact that passion is linked with death and involves the destruction of anyone yielding himself up to it with all his strength. For we have wanted to preserve passion and we cherish the unhappiness that it brings with it … The myth *expresses* those realities to the extent exacted by our instinct, but it also veils them to the extent that broad daylight and reason might imperil them.
>
> (De Rougemont, 1939, p. 21)

In other words, Tristan and Isolde do not love each other; what they love is love, the state itself of loving, and the lovers' separation is therefore brought about by their passion and by the love they feel for this passion, rather than for its satisfaction and for its object. The obstacle to passion therefore becomes the very object of passion.

We sometimes find these concepts in our clinical work too. The symbiotic love of infancy, the fusionality lost forever, can never be regained in the same way in adulthood. A yearning for utter, phantasised happiness remains; for a passion that is fuelled by literature and myth, as we have seen above, and as De Rougemont very perceptively reveals. But this yearning for fatal love does not stand the test of reality. Both perception and interpretation of the loved one coincide, in a dangerous shift away from the real context. The passion for love-passion surpasses the amorous passion itself, necessitating a search for ever new obstacles to achieving normal, everyday happiness. Fatal love is experienced as the only possible form of love, and is often an impossible love. A phrase frequently repeated by these patients at the end of their passionate affairs is interesting to note: "But how on earth could I have fallen in love with such a person? How could I?"

Elisabetta was so beautiful

Elisabetta is beautiful, very sophisticated, and elegant. In our first encounters, she says that she has been racked with anxiety for the last few weeks because she is afraid something awful is going to happen that she is unable to prevent. Her impotence in front of what she feels is inevitable torments her and completely occupies her mind, to the point that she can no longer run her own life. The story she tells resembles a bit of fiction and is difficult to believe. Terror of this imminent collapse, which led her to ask for help, was triggered by her husband's problems. He is a Mafia boss, on a probational system of semi-liberty. (One of the reforms in the Italian prison system allows an offender to leave prison every morning and return to it to sleep there every night. It can be obtained after several years of a prison sentence, on the positive appraisal of the examining magistrate.)

Elisabetta and her husband have been together for several years, and have a daughter. Now, however, Elisabetta feels the ground opening up beneath her. She is the first to realise how precarious their future plans were but, despite that, she continues to express unrealisable requests and to demand illusory life prospects.

Elisabetta:

> I'm here because I'm consumed with worry about my husband. He does things he shouldn't do and I go mad every time I hear about them. He drives without a licence, because they took it away, and I can't make him understand that if they ever stop him he risks real trouble. He, too, should realise that he's acting dangerously.

The dangerous things her husband has been doing were quite something else, but Elisabetta cannot talk about that; she is only able to talk about what she knows and is closest to, what she can see is clearly illegal.

Elisabetta seems unable to go beyond the simplest descriptive narrative dimension as though, in a certain way, this sums up and contains the explicative psychic elements, or, in other words, already possesses a meaning, a sense in and of itself. But this meaning lacks any significance in her internal and also relational dimension. It is all "totally crazy", to use her pet expression. This total craziness reveals the initial traumatic element and the subsequent consequences to her psychic apparatus. In Bionian terms, this is the *collapse* of *meaning*, or the *breakdown of tracking the "felt meaning"* (the attacks the self makes on links between thoughts, between thoughts and feelings, or among thoughts, feelings, and action. The attacks on linking processes ensure the collapse of meaning; Bion, 1962a). In other words, the failure, the lack of trust in the capacity of the good interiorised objects to offer adequate protection against traumas one may have suffered. This is "totally crazy" for Elisabetta: absurd, incredible, and therefore alien, not of this world.

I would like to single out this expression "Look, it's totally crazy!" and pinpoint its literal meaning. It certainly was crazy, that is, there was something quite bizarre about it all, but it was not worked through at the level of mental representations, and the expression remained as a handhold that nobody, until then, seemed to have paid any attention to. Although intelligent and sophisticated, Elisabetta was not capable, in a Bionian sense, of using the alpha functions in the most extreme traumatic situations and transforming the raw sense-data, and the raw emotional data, or the beta-elements, which are very concrete, into alpha-elements (Bion, 1962a, 1962b). By this, I mean those elements of experience that can be linked up together in conscious and unconscious thought processes.

Her narration of their love story in the past, and of its development in the present, proceeds meanwhile during analysis, in all its "totally crazy" details. After only a few years, the couple's situation changed dramatically: an arrest warrant was issued for her husband for belonging to an organised crime syndicate; he went underground and she joined him. "You know the film *GoodFellas* by Martin Scorsese? My life was exactly like that! I was so out of it, but just so out of it I couldn't think. I thought we had escaped to some remote island. Then I got pregnant: it was the happiest time in my life." (She really said this!)

She did not worry about the future at all, except to plan—along with her parents—their flight to Brazil once the baby was born. This idyll was brusquely interrupted by the Italian police, who burst into their refuge at dawn, machine-gun to hand. At that sight, Elisabetta, eight months' pregnant, went into labour and had to be transported urgently to hospital. There she gave birth, under police guard.

When Elisabetta told me this last story—in her normal neutral tone of a person who, after all, does not realise the enormity of the trauma—I reacted violently. Intent on following her story, I began to cough uncontrolledly, for almost five minutes, to my great embarrassment. I was pervaded by a feeling of great unease and at the same time awareness that I was dealing with a phenomenon that escaped any possibility I had of controlling it.

Sandler (1976b) says that the analyst perceives his or her countertransferential reactions only after such reactions have been acted out. Through coughing, I had attempted to violently expel the shock triggered by this story which, with equal violence (the violence of indifference), had been deposited within me. Elisabetta had projected inside me the traumatic/emotional aspect of the event surrounding her labour, which she had been unable to perceive. I think that, at the same time, in doing that, both the experience of her daughter's delivery and birth was reactivated and her own psychic birth was represented, a rebirth prefigured as a violent expulsion. In recounting this birth, she had had to deal with the unbearable aspects of her narration; this unbearableness had been repressed, as had often happened with those who had had anything to do with her on an affective and/or therapeutic level, and even, in my case, had been expelled in a violent way. At the same time, though, this expulsion by coughing did indeed also represent a violent psychic birth of a newborn part of her. Technically speaking, what had occurred was what today would be called enactment; interaction that reflects what occurs in the relationship between patient and analyst, and which distinctly underlines especially the analyst's participation in the analytic process (Sandler & Sandler, 1978; Schafer, 1977). In particular, the enactment refers primarily to the externalisation of traumatic elements from the past.

Elisabetta takes refuge in a state of increasing abulia, interspersed with visits to the maximum security prison in which her husband is held. As soon as he is allowed out of prison, they immediately begin to live together again, and before long he is put on probation. At this point, Elisabetta arrives in my counselling room. She is distraught and terrified.

In our early encounters, I was generally worried and anxious; in my turn, I felt a growing despair and urgency, a certain fatality waiting in the wings. Elisabetta was literally going to pieces, and was looking for an adequate container that could halt the "breakdown of tracking the 'felt meaning'" (Bion, 1962a), that could function where she was no longer. The urgency lay right there, in finding what Anzieu (1985) calls a *psychic envelope* that could allow the recovery of an "apparatus for thinking", and make the impossible possible (or perhaps I should say impossible the possible?).

Elisabetta becomes more and more agitated and cannot glimpse any possibility for the future. I think this lack of future prospects also mirrors the lack of perspective in our encounters, but I am unable to propose a precise enough therapeutic object. I cannot understand where to place this enormous quantity of material. I feel I need more time to digest it all. In actual fact, something did happen, although Elisabetta had nothing to do with it. One day I receive a harrowing phone call: "They've just killed my husband!" Sobbing into the receiver, Elisabetta tells me that they had just shot her husband, killing him as he was returning to prison.

Unravelling this story (so unusual in the calm, welcoming consulting room) represented for Elisabetta her first attempt at sharing a psychic reality. Every patient in analysis, in telling her story, is in fact also a witness to the events of which she was a part. The analyst, with his presence of participating listener, has to transform the truth contained in this internal reality into a shared truth, helping to create a psychic space in which it is possible to share not only memories, but also desires, hopes, and legitimate instinctual expectations, thus making them thinkable and communicable. In other words, the analyst must be a witness of this internal truth, which sometimes has never been told, or even thought.

But for Elisabetta, these truths were dangerous in and of themselves; an expression of unbearable emotions. The emotions felt by the analyst in listening to her story could therefore be used in analysis to communicate a willingness to circulate affects (Di Benedetto, 2001), and to allow the passage from narration to shared story.

Elisabetta's anxiety, which had pushed her to ask for help, was a sign—one of the first—of normality, of perception of an unendurable situation. Her husband's murder, though, introduced a new element. Now the consulting room seems to have been invaded by a body that is alien to the atmosphere of the analysis itself; alien due to its analytic impenetrability. It was all about a Mafia settling of scores; it seemed like a film noir that was not even very original. And this lack of any seemingly criminal originality allowed an illusion of normality to be created around the event. What on earth could I, analyst, do?

This chapter describes the impact of an external/material reality at the limits of the believable of an apparently normal patient, with her common desires, who found herself, though, in the middle of events that were quite beyond her capacity of containing. An exaggerated and excessive love story, with an excess of reality that made the narration and listening unbearable, had taken the place of good sense, of common sense in its particular meaning of a sense that is common to more than one person, a sense used for the recognition of a fact by more than one observer (the sense-data) as used by Bion (1966).

I have called it fatal love or impossible love. Elisabetta fell in love with a man, who obviously abounded with more than usual charisma, and who was able in some way to offer her what she was looking for. Various factors contributed to furthering this exceptionally exaggerated attachment.

When I discussed romantic love, in Chapter Three, I referred to the fact that romantic passion is based on the element of excess, or the concept of repetition.

Elisabetta needed to feel safe, to receive confirmation, to feel welcome, and to be listened to. Paradoxically, in her normal life, in her apparently happy childhood, these had been lacking, thanks to her parents' excessive narcissism. Instead, the all-consuming, absolute passion that she felt for this man, and that he felt for her, seemed to repair the original affective deficit of her childhood. The shared experience of fleeing and going underground with him—such an unusual and excessive thing to do—confirmed the attachment (of him to her and of her to him) that Elisabetta needed.

Her first dreams in analysis all unfolded around his murder. For Elisabetta, the start of analysis inexorably coincided not only with a violent birth but also with violent deaths, for which she could find no guilty culprit. At times, it was a road accident, the event so feared by her at the beginning; at times, her husband was the killer, at times the victim. Through her obsessively repeated dreams, the inevitability of what had happened—her husband's murder—slowly emerged in her psychic reality. The impossible nature of the event merged and blended with the impossibility of love; Eros and Thanatos went hand in hand. The passion of love existed only as a passion resulting in death.

To myself, I thought that this death did not represent only her murdered husband but also a part of her self, exposed in the past so many times to the risk of dying in the real context and in constant equilibrium with death in her psychic reality. The duel between Eros and Thanatos had in fact showed itself on many dangerous, but also very exciting, occasions in her life, before the fatal encounter.

Often after having recounted a dream, Elisabetta would remain silent, waiting for an interpretative comment from the analyst in place of her own, and, at the request for associations about the material she had brought, would answer: "I don't know; it doesn't say anything to me".

From her dreams, incomplete, denied, or repressed mental representations emerged, so the analyst had to carry out part of the mental work in place of the patient. The analyst's reverie was fundamental, but required much caution. Elisabetta's world was light years from mine, and I knew that I would have to descend into the hell that had been her life for the past years so that she, in her turn, would be able to make contact with those things that had happened to another person. Elisabetta continues to repeat: "It's true, why on earth didn't I think about it? And yet I'm so removed from these things, at times it feels as though they happened to someone else."

I recalled one of Bion's fundamental concepts: it is necessary to transform the *Absolute Truth about Reality* downwards to finite, tolerable, personal, and later, objective meaning. The analyst's listening to the infinite and inexpressible Absolute Truth requires a process of transformation into mentalisable, tolerable, and meaningful aspects and is helped by the patient's irrepressible need to come to terms with the normal, factual truth of external reality.

So the analysis continued in that way, in a constant swaying between construction and reconstruction, between transference and narration, in a perpetual dialectics between inside and out.

Elisabetta begins to talk about her childhood and adolescence. She remembers how she used to get so bored as a child, the long afternoons spent alone; her mother who was never there. Slowly the family picture begins to fill up with episodes and events that help to restore characters to people and to remove them from a flat background where they had had no relations with the patient's inner world. Elisabetta described herself as a silent, studious little girl. The happiest moments were the evenings when her parents went out and the girls stayed at home with her grandmother: "We ate bread and milky coffee; I was really happy then".

But here we must interrupt Elisabetta's story for a moment, to give voice to one of the analyst's. That identical phrase was one that my mother often repeated when talking about her grandmother, who always used to welcome her back home after school with a smile and with bread and milky coffee: "I was really happy then". My mother was a woman of great common sense. She had been orphaned when very young and had then been caught up in the war and in the racial persecutions of the 1920s. That phrase—"grandma's bread and milky coffee: I was really happy then"—had been one of her very rare allusions to her childhood, as though the subsequent traumas had swept every other memory away. It was curious to hear the same words from Elisabetta. They aroused the same feeling of pity that I felt when my mother used to say them, "I was really happy then". With everything that that implied... All the horrors that were to come... (The war and all that followed...).

In *Within a Budding Grove* (1919), the third volume of *Remembrance of Things Past*, Marcel Proust, too, describes his deepest feelings of being safe:

> I knew, when I was with my grandmother, that, however great the misery that there was in me, it would be received by her with a pity still more vast; that everything that was mine, my cares, my wishes, would be, in my grandmother, supported upon a desire to save and prolong my life stronger than was my own; and my thoughts were continued in her without having to undergo any deflection, since they passed from my mind into hers without change of atmosphere or of personality.
>
> (Proust, 1919, part I, p. 344)

Proust connects his feeling of being safe and secure to being with his grandmother. Winnicott (1960) calls this "a sense of being held", in other words a sense of being inside something good, a safe place which itself expresses an idea of being inside something *safe and good*. If this sanctuary, this sense of being inside something secure, is lost, the individual feels that he is forever falling. If the inner meaning is lost, a sense of internal incoherence and fragmentation is felt.

After almost three years of analysis, Elisabetta recounts:

> One day I was invited to a party of young people who I didn't know very well. That was the only time in my life that I have ever felt so terribly uncomfortable. I don't know what it was that went wrong. I remember that the girls were all older than me; I was obviously out of place, but I didn't realise. I remember that the girls all had pearls and Gucci scarves around their necks; I felt very young and completely left out. So there, that was a truly horrible moment in my life.

I have two emotional movements. The first, still, was of discomfort. I think: "But goodness me! And all the rest? Going underground, your daughter born in those conditions, your husband killed… and yet it is parties with the wrong dress that are so terribly awful."

But then, at the same time, a similar memory floats up from my past: a party I had gone to, wearing a red and grey tartan skirt and a twin-set, as they were called then. The other girls were wearing evening dresses—black, blue, low cut—and danced with the boys; they were all older than me. Excruciating embarrassment still vivid in my memory. A moment that is still "truly horrible" many years later. I could understand the humiliation, the out-of-place adolescent that Elisabetta had felt herself to be.

Milky coffee and a Gucci scarf were the only two episodes in this long analysis that were common to my life. They were two openings, between her and me, two channels of communication.

Let me be clear, I never said anything about this to her; at the time, it was not customary and even now I would not say anything of the sort. But they helped me to feel her a little less alien, to live her experience as a little less bizarre, and, once more, reinforced my perception that something really horrible must have happened to catapult such a normal person into such an absurd life. A flickering of pity for the milky coffee, sympathy for the Gucci scarves. It was more than she had ever received in all these past years.

For example, her description of how she slept was quite shocking; this, too, was an image of an alien that was far removed from the well-groomed, elegant patient who appeared by day in the session. Elisabetta slept in a chair, and never for more than one or two hours consecutively. She often used to get up to eat, almost without noticing, shouting inarticulately, as her daughter or her occasional lover would tell her. During the night, she smoked ten, twenty cigarettes; this, too, in a state of semi-consciousness. The light was always on because she was terrified of the dark. I was struck by these images, which in their turn had slipped into the sessions, *en passant*, "as a matter of fact".

And in this case too, my amazement had transmitted to Elisabetta an awareness of the bizarre nature of the event, which before, apparently, she had not felt. This waking up terrified in the night, or better remaining half-awake gripped by nocturnal anxieties, recalled Bion's concept of *nameless dread*, terror without a name (1967). This term—nameless dread—refers to the very serious consequences deriving from the environment failing not only to take care of the child, ensuring a feeling of "continuity of existence", but also to help him find "a thought in search of a meaning", that is, internal coherence to his thoughts. It refers to the feelings experienced by the child when the mother appears incapable of metabolising the sensory information of anxiety that she has received from her child or, in other words, when the mother's capacity for reverie does not exist or is seriously defective.

Slowly, as normality was conveyed—nothing said, everything osmotically transferred—thanks to the analyst's sustained capacity for reverie and metabolising anxieties, Elisabetta began to sleep for longer periods and without interruption. This restoration of waking–sleeping patterns, which implied a recovery of life rhythms closer to those of other human beings, more than anything else showed me how far she had emerged from a destructive narcissistic isolation in which the most basic rules of life had been totally ignored.

The monster from the sea

During the fifth year of analysis, Elisabetta brings this fundamental dream:

> I'm lying in the sun on a beach. It's very pleasant; the sun is hot and the sea calm. Suddenly a monster comes out of the sea and walks towards me. Terrified, I watch it getting closer, paralysed by fear and unable to move. The monster gets closer, but goes past me, apparently unaware of my presence.

Elisabetta wakes up, still terrified, and asks herself: "Who was that monster? Where did it come from? And where did it go?"

I would like to share some theoretical considerations that I made partly in the session (a few) but mostly here and there, during the course of this analysis, that were extremely helpful for metabolising this dream.

When Freud again takes up his discussion of trauma in *Beyond the Pleasure Principle* (1920g), he states that:

> We describe as "traumatic" any excitations from outside which are powerful enough to break through the protective shield. It seems to me that the concept of trauma necessarily implies a connection of

this kind with a breach in an otherwise efficacious barrier against stimuli. Such an event as an external trauma is bound to provoke a disturbance on a large scale in the functioning of the organism's energy and to set in motion every possible defensive measure.

(Freud, 1920g, p. 29)

* * *

We may, I think, tentatively venture to regard the common traumatic neurosis as a consequence of an extensive breach being made in the protective shield against stimuli.

(Freud, 1920g, p. 31; author's italics)

And in a previous passage, when illustrating the living vesicle of living substances, he asserts that:

Its outermost surface ceases to have the structure proper to living matter, becomes to some degree inorganic and thenceforward functions as a special envelope or membrane resistant to stimuli.

(Freud, 1920g, p. 27)

Freud insists greatly on the need for this membrane: "*Protection against stimuli* is an almost more important function for the living organism than *reception of stimuli*" (Freud, 1920g, p. 27).

I believe it is correct to state that by 1920 protection against stimuli and reception of stimuli were already closely connected. In traumatic events, a receptor, capable of functioning as an element of reception and metaboliser of stimuli, is fundamental in the process of protecting the mind from excessive, paralysing stimuli. We are in the area that will subsequently lead us to Winnicott's "good-enough mother" (1965) and to Bion's "container–contained" (1962a). In other words, we can say that when the mind is subjected to excessive stimuli in trauma the protective shield may suffer an irreparable breach; a traumatic event requires an enormous amount of mental work because the capacity of the mind to react to the process of the stimuli is overcharged and interrupted in its normal functioning. In Bionian terms, we can say that the alpha function remains overwhelmed and is incapable of containing and digesting the quantity of stimuli it is subjected to, until it collapses. Breakdown of the alpha function produces chaotic, fragmentary, unrecognisable sensations in a normally functioning mind, or, as Bion would say, it produces beta-elements. Therefore, the relationship between trauma and mental functioning is much closer than we are normally able to perceive. The trauma springs from those mental functions essential to its understanding, creating a vicious circle of rejection and repetition, repetition and rejection.

But let us return to Elisabetta's dream. If we think about the protective shield of her mind, the dream content of the beach, the sun, and calm sea would all appear to be excellent mental representations. Suddenly a monster shatters this continuity and peace. What does this monster represent? While it is important to understand this, I believe that, first of all, it is essential to draw Elisabetta's attention to the breach the monster made in the tranquillity of the landscape.

Analyst: "It seems to me that the first basic element of the dream is your surprise that monstrous parts—which lead an autonomous life alongside your person—are escaping your inner world."

I think back to how in the first years of analysis Elisabetta was unable to recognise the monstrous horror inherent in some of her experiences, and I think that this dream was the first to represent this monstrosity, this not being aware of the violence of the senseless reality she had been living.

So what did this monster represent? Was something exiting the scene? Monstrous parental objects? Monstrous identificatory representations of the self? Or, and also, transformed representations of events that had actually happened? In the interpretation of dreams, their meanings expand as they are gradually linked up to each other, thanks to the breakdown of those dynamic shields that prevent any contact among the emotional experiences.

I attempt to recover the material reality: "Perhaps this monster who ignores you may have something to do with some of the things you have told me about."

Elisabetta coughs at length: "It's true, I always try and get rid of it. I could have died, in many situations. It's a miracle that the monster went past me without seeing me. But it wasn't my fault." This time it is the patient who coughs, not the analyst, as though the analyst had re-deposited once more inside the patient the shock of a story that she had initially tried to expel.

A second phase in Elisabetta's life begins. She feels relaxed and happy. She speaks of her relationship with her husband, of the time they were together. And here, too, with amazement: "How on earth did I put up with him? He was terribly jealous; he didn't let me go out in the evenings; I never had a holiday because I didn't feel as though I could go away while he was in prison. And then he couldn't hang out with my friends, he was different, you understand, and so we were always alone."

The consulting room fills with an infinite number of people: friends, sister, nephews and nieces. Every day there is a new story about one of her friends. I comment: "When you talked about your husband keeping you imprisoned at home, you were also talking about an aspect of your self bound up and prisoner of habits and bonds that you could not separate from."

Elisabetta: "I realise that in the past I didn't have any alternative. I thought I had lots, and in fact I did; I could do exactly what I wanted, but if inside yourself you are unable to move, you can't do it."—Pause—"I think that I was also incredibly unlucky in my life because if I hadn't run into certain situations, certain things wouldn't have happened to me."

This is a huge change for a woman who, despite everything that had happened to her, continues to say that she is so lucky. This marked a huge shift in Elisabetta's psychic structure. It was an important renunciation of her past narcissistic isolation.

One day, towards the end of the analysis, she blurts out:

> I haven't had a proper boyfriend, after my husband, because I was so shocked not only by his death but also by my life with him. [Long silence.] But I also had the most frightful family! My parents never did anything to help me! They were light years away from my life. And from my problems. After all, I was only twenty! At most my father spoke about his job, and did that for the whole of his life. There were never any discussions, explanations, sharing, critical analyses, reasoning. There were only rigid stances. He really doesn't believe in anything. His ideas come simply from the fact that the Communists want to take his money away. My mother even less; really zero. Zero reasoning, zero critical stances, zero life analysis. She only wanted to know if I needed something: "Do you need anything?" I always said no, and they were happy. I was with a Mafia boss, and they said nothing!

Elisabetta is coming to terms with her past again, in all senses. I believe that she has continued to go over and re-go over her story, trying to understand—in the sense of accepting and introjecting—that her father and mother had gaps, deficits, and had been unable to help her because they were not capable. It is difficult to accept; for Elisabetta, it is difficult to shatter the image of the powerful and always successful father. It means relinquishing the ideal image that her parents had projected onto her, and coming to terms with how things really stood. She also reassesses her husband, and his violent Mafia killer side now powerfully emerges, alongside the romantic, heroic image of the early period. I think that Elisabetta never had many opportunities, as I had thought about her husband ten years earlier. I think that her father, with his histrionic personality, had pushed his daughter's rich and vital creativity into a corner.

The inexorable nature of Elisabetta's life, expressed with great vividness through the numerous dramatic events that starred it, also revealed a defensive aspect, worked out during childhood. The long-drawn-out processes of splitting and denial that were constantly brought into play by the patient were also an expression of her family culture, both a paternal and a maternal legacy, thanks to an extraordinary mixture of defensive closures and denials by both parents. The impossibility to work through the traumatic aspects had allowed an extensive defensive system to develop, directed, on the one hand, at denying the event and, on the other, at denying the possibility for that same event to leave identifiable psychic traces. The resulting narcissistic closure had produced a serious reduction of subsequent opportunities for growth, for working through, and above all for developing relational trust.

The obsessive repetition of some dreams and the returning to mind at different times of past incidents allowed the narrative events to be inscribed in the analyst's mind; they could then slowly be developed along shared and therefore comprehensible paths. Once the logical-causal connections of the stories were slowly restored, the search could then ignore the traumatic causes of Elisabetta's story and broaden out to include both the possibility to psychically work through them in a less rigid and violent way, and the analysis of the consequences on her psychic reality and on her internal defensive organisation.

Our last sessions clearly represented the conflict between the resistances in abandoning consolidated and rigid mental representations and the need to experiment with different solutions. The transformation from the need to understand to the desire to be understood, to the relief in understanding in order to be able to make free autonomous choices, characterised the final stages of this analysis.

Comment

In Bion's theory, the way in which the analyst's mind aesthetically grasps reality is fundamental. How the analyst's mind works, how it is able, through reverie, to transform the patient's emotions (and the absence of emotions) is a fundamental variable of the analysis. The images that the analyst associates during the sessions are extremely significant. First, the milky coffee and then the tartan skirt and the Gucci scarf were two images that helped connect me to a shared aesthetic dimension—to a nostalgia (milky coffee) and to a humiliation (the tartan skirt) that made a "totally crazy" story human and that gave it back to the patient—rather than to "stories that had happened to another". There was a feeling of being "at-one-ment" (to use Bion's words, 1965, p. 163) in that moment that allowed the initial state of circular ambiguity between patient and analyst to be overcome, in which the immoral and dramatic aspects of the factual story blurred together in the lack of a container where the contents remained suspended and undigested because of their enormity and unbearableness.

Fatal love cannot stand up to everyday frustrations. Fatal love yearns for the absolute, for infinity without time. On returning, through the analytic process, to a shared temporal state, to the before and to the after of a coherent and logical narration, Elisabetta gave up this type of passion, relinquishing at the same time any compensation for what she had never had in childhood, in exchange for a daily life full of interests, relationships, and also passions—small, normal, human passions.

CHAPTER SIX

Transference love: "There really was absolutely nothing to be done..."

Amors par force vos demeine!
Combien durra vostre folie?
Trop avez mené ceste vie.
(Love by force dominates you!/How long will your folly last?/
Too long you have been leading this life.)
—Chrétien De Troyes (twelfth to thirteenth century),
"The Poetical Romances of Tristan", p. 111

As many authors affirm, the analytic setting provides the environment that allows us to study the nature of love in all its many forms. The transference and countertransference are the natural objects of study for all these types of love. As Kernberg (1995) postulates:

The main difference between the original oedipal situation and transference love is the possibility, under optimal circumstances, of fully exploring in the transference the unconscious determinants of the oedipal situation, the full exploration of oedipal conflicts in a gradual conscious integration of infantile sexuality into the adult ego as part of analytic work.

(Kernberg, 1995, p. 1137)

Kernberg's 1994 article—"Love in the analytic setting" (reprinted as chapter seven in Kernberg, 1995)—is also particularly clear and exhaustive about the topic in question, and I will cite it on a number of occasions.

Working through transference love entails working through the renouncing and mourning that generally accompany any resolution of the oedipal situation, as well as learning that such work will mark the permanent traits of all future love relationships (Bergmann, 1987). This does not mean that all future love stories will resemble the oedipal situation exclusively, but rather that this, as we have already seen in earlier chapters, will influence the forming of new experiences: "The finding of an object is in fact a *re-finding* of it" (Freud, 1905d, p. 222).

However, according to Balint (1960), *"Die Objektfindung"* in the original, a beautifully concise expression, was translated rather clumsily into English as "the finding of an object". He writes:

> I wish to make two remarks about the otherwise excellent English translation. The last sentence which has real beauty in German: "Die Objektfindung ist eigentlich eine Wiederfindung", in English is a pale rendition of the forceful and categorical original. Although not quite correct, a somewhat freer—and to my mind truer—translation would run as follows: "All object discovery is in fact a rediscovery."
>
> (Balint, 1960, p. 7)

The difference between *finding* and *discovering* is, to my mind, rather interesting, and concerns creativity. Winnicott underlines the paradox that "the baby creates the object but the object was there waiting to be created" (Winnicott, 1971, p. 89).

In optimal circumstances, the experience of regression and analytic dependence, the nature of the "what if..." of the analytic situation implicit in the contract should encourage the development of unrequited love. The lack of reciprocity in transference love prevents (or should prevent!) its transformation into a proper love story. Analysis of transference love describes all the usual components of the normal process of falling in love: projection onto another person, the analyst, of the mature aspects of the ego's ideal; the ambivalent relationship with the oedipal objects; and the defences against perverse infantile desires and their development. All this leads to the "sublimated integration" (Kernberg, 1974b, p. 750) of sexual desires, even if only briefly and fleetingly.

By definition, transference love is a subspecies of neurotic love, in that it is unrequited love *par excellence*. Transference love betrays its neurotic components in its intensity, in its inflexibility, and in its obstinate persistence. At the other end of the scale, a complete lack of loving or affectionate feelings towards the analyst may signal the expression of a strong defence against an unmentionable oedipal relationship, or a narcissistic Kohut-style transference, in which the oedipal developments are blocked and coerced. Patients who have suffered sexual traumas, especially victims of incest, may try to seduce the analyst, and their requests, as we will see in the case of Gianmarco, can sometimes dominate the transference for a very long time. Identifying with the aggressor plays a very important role and requires careful analysis of the angry resentment the patient feels as a result of the analyst not responding to his sexual requests, before the patient can feel relief and gratitude thanks to the analytic setting being maintained.

The neurotic aspects of transference love are evident not only in the intensification of erotic desires with regard to the unrequited love, but also in the normal infantile narcissistic desire to be loved. Rather than in the active adult love for the analyst, they are revealed in the desire for sexual intimacy as an expression of desires for symbiosis or for pre-oedipal dependence and dependence in general. And I should like to emphasise the importance of this last aspect, in the overall intensification of sexualised idealisation as a defence against aggressive impulses. Even the most intense erotic transference usually abates when the patient manages to shift his desires onto more realistic opportunities and satisfy his sexual feelings outside the analytic context.

When analysing transference love, it is obviously essential to bear the countertransference in mind, although much more has been written about the aggressive countertransference than the erotic one. The general opinion of experts (among them Gabbard (1995), who has written a great deal about setting violations by the analyst) maintains that the most intense erotic countertransference and consequent violations of the setting, with acting out, occur when the analyst (of either sex) presents strong, unresolved, narcissistic traits.

In general terms, it is useful to know how to distinguish in the patient the differences between what can appear as intense erotic manifestations and his pure and simple desire to be loved by the analyst. This is a fundamental difference that calls for considerable expertise from the analyst, who at times risks taking fright at the sheer reality of the investment placed in him by the patient, and thus may miss the underlying dynamics. Wanting to be the object of the analyst's desire is a common phantasy for many patients, and finds its origin in the earliest desires for fusion with the mother.

It is important to analyse not only the patient's defences against the erotic transference but also the nature of these transference phantasies. The desire for a sexual relationship with the analyst can, for example, mask an aggressive transference, a desire for revenge for the humiliation stemming from dependence on the analytic situation, the rejection of abandonment, and so on. The analyst must be capable of exploring transference love without being placed in the condition of acting out either a rejection or a seductive approach. Listen and give back. Listening and giving back are the initial basic elements in these situations. Interpreting will come later, after an attentive "listening to listening", to use Haydée Faimberg's words (1981, p. 19). By which I mean listening to what the patient, in an obvious transference state, may have understood of the analyst's interventions about it.

The patient's experience of the analyst's rejection, as confirmation of the prohibitions against oedipal desires, should also be explored. As the patient's emotional growth gradually develops during analysis, some free expressions of transference love and oedipal and pre-oedipal desire may be manifested that shed light on the extent to which the patient has opened up and is overcoming his own inhibitions, consequently allowing himself to experience encouraging results and sexual and affective relationships in the outside world that are more gratifying than in the past. In general, it can be said that the more satisfying the analyst's own personal affective and/or sexual life, the freer the analyst will be to help the patient resolve the inhibitions and limitations of transference love.

In fact, we often assist at events that are the opposite of setting violations, in other words strong refusals to perceive the patient's affective and loving investments towards the analyst and, as a result, incomprehension and blind spots arise concerning the positive developments of a repressed and clandestine sexuality and affection. If the analyst also contributes to the clandestine nature of the transference feelings, then we shall have a state of repetition of the old infantile issues in the countertransference.

The erotic transference: theoretical considerations

The erotic transference is not a rare occurrence during analysis and indicates an intricate clinical node, full of difficult problems to understand and to place in the correct developmental perspective. As De Masi states so well:

> It is not easy to distinguish between these … mental states, nor is it simple to define their limits with respect to other analytical phenomena. The erotic transference … seems to be a sort of frontier zone, interposed between and contiguous to many clinical experiences, rather than an isolated clinical fact in itself.
>
> (De Masi, 1988, p. 78)

As a topic, the erotic transference dates back a long time and coincides with the birth of psychoanalysis. A partial indication about the importance of the erotic transference comes from Freud, who treated it in an organic way in "Observations on transference-love" of 1915. Here, Freud very clearly expresses the concept that transference love is an attempt by the patient to detach himself from what will later be called infant dependency transference, as he tries "to destroy the doctor's authority" (Freud, 1915a, p. 163). This analytic event does not constitute, though, only an expression of resistance but is potentially rich in development:

> It is, therefore, just as disastrous for the analysis if the patient's craving for love is gratified as if it is suppressed. The course the analyst must pursue is neither of these; it is one for which there is no model in real life. He must take care not to steer away from the transference-love, or to repulse it or to make it distasteful to the patient; but he must just as resolutely withhold any response to it. He must keep firm hold of the transference-love, but treat it as something unreal, as a situation which has to be gone through in the treatment and traced back to its unconscious origins and which must assist in bringing all that is most deeply hidden in the patient's erotic life into her consciousness and therefore under her control.
>
> (Freud, 1915a, p. 166)

In an earlier passage, he says:

> I shall state it as a fundamental principle that the patient's need
> and longing should be allowed to persist in her, in order that they
> may serve as forces impelling her to do work and to make changes,
> and that we must beware of appeasing those forces by means of
> surrogates.
>
> (Freud, 1915a, p. 165)

With these words, he suggests that the loving profferings should
either be set gently to one side or, on the contrary, accepted, but only
platonically.

Freud, therefore, postulates that it is important to keep the erotic
transference alive with the aim of revealing its infantile roots. He
advises treating love as something "that … is lacking to a high degree
in a regard for reality" (Freud, 1915a, p. 169): something decidedly difficult, he adds, when:

> There is, it is true, one class of women with whom this attempt
> to preserve the erotic transference for the purposes of analytic
> work without satisfying it will not succeed. These are women of
> elemental passionateness who tolerate no surrogates, who refuse
> to accept the psychical in place of the material, who, in the poet's
> words, are accessible only to "the logic of soup, with dumplings for
> arguments". With such people one has the choice between return-
> ing their love or else bringing down upon oneself the full enmity of
> a woman scorned.
>
> (Freud, 1915a, pp. 166–167)

Forced to oscillate between Scylla and Charybdis, between gratification
and frustration, the analyst must bind himself tightly to his own analytic skill so that he is not seduced by the patient's sirens (Hill, 1994).

For Freud, "lacking to a high degree in a regard for reality" implies that
this love story will repeat, almost stereotypically, the patient's experience of the past and of his childhood: his love would not be, at a final
count, destined for the analyst:

> But this is the essential character of every state of being in
> love. There is no such state which does not reproduce infantile

prototypes. It is precisely from this infantile determination that it receives its compulsive character, verging as it does on the pathological. Transference-love has perhaps a degree less of freedom than the love which appears in ordinary life and is called normal; it displays its dependence on the infantile pattern more clearly and is less adaptable and capable of modification; but that is all, and not what is essential.

(Freud, 1915a, p. 168)

Which love, he wonders, in the moment in which we are struck by it, does not repeat the past? In concluding his paper, Freud ends by asking himself if love for the analyst really can be considered "lacking to a high degree in a regard for reality" and, respectful of the extraordinary nature of this analytic event, at this point suspends his investigation, writing:

Let us sum up, therefore. We have no right to dispute that the state of being in love which makes its appearance in the course of analytic treatment has the character of a "genuine" love. If it seems so lacking in normality, this is sufficiently explained by the fact that being in love in ordinary life, outside analysis, is also more similar to abnormal than to normal mental phenomena. Nevertheless, transference-love is characterized by certain features which ensure it a special position.

(Freud, 1915a, p. 168)

So Freud swings between two poles: is transference love a defence against a relationship of dependence or is it a real analytic relationship? Is the eroticisation a compulsion to repeat the past, a defence against the new, or, instead, a powerful new analytic bond ("forces impelling her to do work and to make changes"; Freud, 1915a, p. 165), a push, then, towards the new? Confirmation that this is a new and real relationship is endorsed by the fact that if we attempt, through our interpretations, to take the patient back to the past, we often succeed only in wounding him when, after defending himself for years from affectionate experiences, he now impetuously turns to us.

Blum (1973) describes the erotic transference that we often come across in our most critically ill patients (such as Gianmarco, below), defining it as a tenacious and uncontrollable request for sexual gratification. As we shall see in the following case, in the eroticised transference

the patient is profoundly convinced that the sexual act, or a loving relationship with the analyst, represents the final phase of his therapy, as
well as being an indispensable element towards his recovery.

Schafer maintains that "Freud was indecisive in this respect", as he
seeks "to clarify the relationship between relived experience and new
experience within the interpreted transferences, for the question of what
in these transferences is real, artificial, and mere stereotyped repetition
has not yet been satisfactorily settled" (1977, p. 336). He believes that
for Freud the differences are more to do with quantity than any essential substance, and that transference love is as genuine as normal love.
Patients do not readily accept that their loves are unreal. We could say,
along with Gabbard, that "love is both real in the sense that it involves
a unique current relationship and unreal, or displaced, in the sense that
it has elements of past object relationships that have been internalized
and then reactivated in the analytic dyad" (1996, p. 35).

De Masi (1988), examining the nature of "love" and "sexuality" in
transference love, highlights the discontinuity among the idealisation,
erotisation, and sexuality that characterise different modes of the erotic
transference, with opposing clinical results.

Bolognini (1994) has proposed a classification that includes various
types of transference: erotised, loving, and affectionate. The loving and
affectionate transferences are placed at opposing poles of the continuum compared to the eroticised transference, and the type of love that
the patient manifests in the transference resembles the forms of love
that the patient manifests in his real life.

Here, too, I would like to present part of a clinical case in which I
found myself searching, with great difficulty, for that indispensable
equilibrium between real and unreal, in that transitional state that
Schafer and Gabbard describe so beautifully.

Gianmarco and his struggle to survive

At the time of our first sessions, Gianmarco was about thirty years old.
He is a big, tall man, weighing more than a hundred kilos (two hundred
and twenty pounds/nearly sixteen stone) with an inexpressive face,
low voice, and monotonous way of talking. He is seriously depressive,
bi-polar, and ill since adolescence. He lives with his family. His mother
suffers from grave psychotic depression, which appeared shortly after
she got married and for which she has been hospitalised on numerous

occasions. Of his childhood, Gianmarco remembers long afternoons spent playing silently next to his mother, constrained to bed due to her depressed state and often under the effect of strong psychotherapeutic drugs. Nuns also used to sit at her bedside, reciting their rosaries, and Gianmarco remembers this constant chanting as a calming accompaniment to his solitary games. He spent the weekends, instead, out and about with his father, a lively, vital man, who took him to play football or on a tour of the bars, or to watch matches.

When he was seventeen, on a school trip, he unexpectedly collapsed. Dressed up as a girl, for a masked party one evening, he suffered hallucinations in which he thought they were changing his sex. This episode disappeared by itself, without giving rise to any undue worry in his family, so that he was not seen by any specialist. During the next school year, though, while listening in a lesson of religion about a child who had been beatified, he thought they were talking about him. He spent the next lessons in a growing state of confusion, which this time necessitated hospitalisation.

Apparently, there were no more psychotic episodes until he was twenty, when he was again admitted to hospital.

From that moment onwards, Gianmarco progressively worsened. Once, he was surprised naked along the motorway while he was trying to get to St Peter's in Rome on foot. Another time, he was saved from the railway tracks, again naked, and again while he was attempting to reach the pope.

At home, Gianmarco was put into the double bed with his mother, and his father moved to his son's room. The two, mother and son, were considered to be on the same level, and looked after by the same psychiatrist. In actual fact, the family preferred to entrust Gianmarco with looking after his mother, now in the grips of a chronic persecutory delusion and particularly difficult to manage.

Gianmarco's analysis would also be long and difficult. It initially progressed thanks to Gianmarco's almost religious faith in the therapeutic possibilities of analysis. Although severely depressed, Gianmarco is in his own way also a funny and vital man. One day, for example, he told me how, on talking to a priest who had asked him why—given his strong religious convictions—he had not chosen to be ordained, he had replied, pointing to the crucifix: "Father, when one has risen so high, there is nowhere else to aspire to", alluding to his delusions in which he believed he was Jesus Christ.

We can divide his analysis into three phases. The first can undoubtedly be called the phase of survival. Indeed, at the beginning, we had to tackle the psychic suffering that his preceding therapists had fled from. This enormously weighty burden, which Gianmarco felt constantly invaded by and which literally robbed him of breath thanks to the effort needed to sustain it, stemmed from his early experience of physical and psychic annihilation that he had suffered in the long periods spent by his sick, inert mother. This massive identification with a lifeless and almost dead maternal object was at the base of his sufferings. Borgogno (1999) talks of these patients having the persistent impression that their mother and analyst love death and want them dead.

So the early phase was monopolised by actions aimed at reassuring the analyst about the unquestionable changes that were occurring thanks to the analysis. This movement was due to the desire to keep the analyst alive, something he had not been able to do (psychically) with his mother. In reassuring me, Gianmarco attempted to guarantee my presence and thus make sure that the analysis continued. He was in fact afraid that in my turn, like all his previous therapists, I would succumb to his depression and declare it impossible to effect any therapy.

Due to long years passed alongside his sick mother, Gianmarco had developed an extreme sensitivity to the moods of others. He did everything possible to liven me up, desperate about any possible contagion of his depression. Indeed, it would slowly emerge how, when little, he was convinced he was to blame for his mother's illness, and that he should pay for this. In this early phase of analysis, lasting about four years, Gianmarco did something that I have never come across in any other patient: he began to dream about the analyst with remarkable frequency, to the extent that we can safely say that for at least half his analysis I was present in every one of his dreams.

I only realised very late that I had become *the woman of his dreams* in all senses. In this stage, the analyst represented a different environment, more stable and autonomous in comparison to those experienced previously. I would like to recall his constant expression from these years: "There's absolutely nothing to be done…", to indicate the insurmountable difficulties that he encountered in every attempt at autonomous movement.

Gradually, thanks to the presence of an analyst who could be the object of solid investment and apparently uncontaminable with his own destructivity, Gianmarco could begin to deal not so much with the object so phantastically damaged or actually destroyed by him, but with the damage that this absent and everlastingly sick object-mother had done to his own self. And bit by bit, his anger at his family—who had placed him at his mother's sick-bed and thus made him responsible for managing situations that were quite beyond his control—also emerged.

This second phase of his analysis—focused on his self, and no longer on the analyst—was characterised by the need to understand and work through the delusional experiences of the years preceding analysis, above all the story of the blessed child. Now we were dealing with a livelier patient who was more interested in the world around him. He was able to lead a normal life, and started going round with his old friends again and working with interest and dedication, although he was still unable to develop an autonomous plan for a family or job.

At the same time, in analysis, he continued to repeat and to work through once more the memories of the episodes from his adolescence and early adulthood, until at a certain point he had to give up the phantasy that these delusional experiences might have had a basis in reality. First recovering Gianmarco's delusion, then working through it, and finally letting it go were hugely significant analytic experiences.

In fact, under my eyes, his delusion unravelled and slowly faded as its defensive aim subsided: "I don't need to believe I'm God any more in order to overcome my feeling of non-existence, nor to immolate myself as Christ on the Cross: I'm no longer interested in martyrdom", he said to me one day.

The third and final phase of his analysis was characterised by both of us becoming aware of the profoundly intense investment in the figure of the analyst. The huge amount of progress made did not, however, modify the patient's basic depressive state. Gianmarco continued to worry that I would dismiss him, and also started to get anxious about an endless and timeless repetition of the analysis, similar to keeping watch alongside his sick mother. He began to dream about the analyst again: he desperately wanted to arouse my interest, much more than ever before. He started reading, going to concerts and conferences, and to the cinema. Bit by bit, he lost almost forty kilos (eighty-eight pounds/almost six and a half stone), and was beginning to become an interesting man, much more so than in previous years. When the time came to tackle the issue about concluding the analysis, he collapsed. He became ill with a whole series of gastric and intestinal disorders, culminating in an eversion of the anus, which required hospitalisation. He finally began to accept that the analysis should reach a conclusion, which, besides, was something he himself wanted, because in the meanwhile the travelling needed to come to sessions was beginning to take its toll, plus he needed more time for work. Then, for at least a year, he brought the most distressing dreams. He went into a supermarket and found it empty, the shelves bare of all products; he went fishing and the lake too was empty, no fish. He feared the end of analysis as the loss of every possibility for sustenance. But we can also say that he feared losing the analyst as the only investment of his life, the only asset won up to that moment. He hoped to be able to see me still once the analysis was finished, as he had succeeded in making himself interesting during the analysis itself. Here, too, there was a very slow working through of the separation, eased by recognising the transformations that had occurred during these years. Gianmarco had succeeded in his goal: to arouse the interest of a depressed mother/analyst. He had looked after the object and had also looked after his self. And in looking after the object, he had been able to free himself of its destructive and deadly presence. His recurrent expression was important in this sense: from "There's absolutely nothing to be done…", it now became "There really was absolutely nothing to be done…", as he said one day, alluding to his newly gained recognition of how difficult it had been for him to grow up in that sort of family environment.

The lake and no fish

When Gianmarco recounted his dream about the lake with absolutely no fish in it, he made an interesting psychic operation. One of the transforming elements of the last phase of his analysis lay in recovering one of his passions as a boy, fly fishing to be precise, that he had done with his father.

Now I must confess to knowing absolutely nothing about fishing, a sport I have never done nor even seen done. Well then, for long sessions Gianmarco described and made this sport extremely interesting to me, with astute expositions, funny memories, and expert explanations about how to do it, in case I might have wanted to have a go. So we could say that he had also taught me to fish, with all the necessary equipment and skills.

Therefore, the lake totally lacking in fish represented something more than a supermarket with empty shelves. It was also a relational space that had suddenly been emptied of its contents, fish and fishing that had kept us company over the last years, had aroused my curiosity and interest, and had awakened in him memories of an active and lively past full of a creativity and ingenuity that had seemed totally lost at the beginning. They were the tools for interesting the analyst, engaging her attention beyond the clinical aspect and the setting. Gianmarco was transformed and, busy trying to please the analyst, had drawn up from his interior those elements that he believed he had lost for ever, for which "There really was absolutely nothing to be done...". Now, instead, with the approaching conclusion of the analysis, the lake/container of thoughts was suddenly emptied, transforming into a well lacking contents and food for the mind. Gianmarco risked dying of hunger because he was losing the object of his love, which affectionately nourished him. An old Chinese proverb came to my mind that President Mao used to quote often, which goes more or less like this: "If you give a man a fish, he will eat today, but teach a man to fish and he will eat forever."

I reflected that it was Gianmarco who had taught me to fish, and who had helped me to help him, arousing my interest in him and allowing him to feel affection for me. My work, therefore, lay in allowing him to look for other lakes, richer in fish, whose capture he had showed me he was capable of. And so he would not have lost the analyst love object, but would have transformed it into an affective proto-experience that would have given him confirmation of his virility and strength that right from the beginning had seemed so very shaky.

And so it happened. Gianmarco met a woman with whom he had a long love story that he told me about in detail, just as he had told me in such detail about fly fishing. He had hooked another fish and this time it was a fish that he could hook.

Comment

The type of transference love I have described above corresponds to a painful state of emotional exaltation that blends together the loss of the object and a possible fusional union with it. To quote De Masi again:

> Since this kind of total request seems to express an exasperated return to primary needs, we can assume that those patients who have already suffered from interferences in their first experiences of

dependence are more sensitive to an insufficient or distorted emotional response on the part of the analyst.

(De Masi, 1988, p. 92)

As the story of Gianmarco and his mother illustrates so well.

This combination of tender affection and nostalgia appears quite often in some patients when, in difficult moments, they remain attached to the analysis, phantasising the gentle, ideal, and constant presence of the analyst. These patients bring to analysis a precarious equilibrium between an idealised condition and

> *a fear of a breakdown that has already been experienced.* It is a fear of the original agony which caused the defence organization which the patient displays as an illness syndrome.
>
> (Winnicott, 1974, p. 104; italics in the original)

Their search for a new life is very fittingly defined by Winnicott as "going on being" (1956, p. 303). Our problem as analysts, then, lies in not dismissing the patient's illusions while, at the same time, not colluding with their unrealistic expectations. These experiences of love in the transference in fact contain a potential capacity for development that must be sustained, as Pontalis (1977) so rightly asserts, as a "sustained illusion".

So we must keep in mind that the request for idealised, dreamy fusion ("the ecstatic mind" that Fachinelli, 1989, talks about) represents a preliminary passage for arriving at a capacity for satisfying relationships with the outside world or, to remain with our clinical case, for learning to fish trout from the lake, without having to depend on the analyst/supermarket for his own affective nourishment.

CHAPTER SEVEN

Maternal love: "Flowing-over-at-oneness" (F. Tustin)

> Some say good night—at night—
> I say good night by day—
> Good bye—the Going utter me—
> Good night, I still reply—
>
> For parting, that is night,
> And presence, simply dawn—
> Itself, the purple on the hight
> Denominated morn.
>
> —Emily Dickinson, "Poem F586" (1863)

Down the centuries, philosophers, writers, and artists have drawn our attention to the fact that the subjective experience of time is often in stark contrast to time as an external, chronological phenomenon. Internal psychological time and external chronological time rarely coincide, and the experience of an analysis—with its constant alternating of subjective and objective, internal and external elements—can develop within, and thanks to, this contrast. In their relationships with the analyst, patients reproduce their own subjective experience of the passing of time, creating a characteristic and special temporality in the transference that is unique to every patient.

In the psychoanalytic literature, the representation and deformation of temporal linearity has been the object of much reflection, starting with Freud. In almost all his works, he shows his interest and pays much attention to time, describing a temporality of psychic reality that does not follow the traditional, linear sequences of chronological time. Already in *The Interpretation of Dreams* (1900a), Freud speaks of "shattered time" in psychoanalytic conceptualisation and a "timelessness of the unconscious", representing the psychic apparatus as "caught in the double vectorisation tending towards the future, now towards the past, in the pure present of dreaming" (Green, 2002, p. 11). But it is with the elaboration of the concept of *Nachträglichkeit* (in French: *après coup*; Freud, 1914c, 1937d)—according to which the events of the past are revised only at a later date, and in the light of the present—that Freud seems to break every traditional notion of time as a linear and sequential system. This re-transcribing of the past, this creating of a meaningful past, allows the invention of the present to be constructed.

In taking up Freud's notion that perceptions of time that differ from chronological ones can exist in the unconscious, Marie Bonaparte (1940) traces this dyscrasia back to the eternal conflict between the pleasure principle and the reality principle.

G. Abraham (1976) presents an interesting discussion about the interdependence and interchangeability between space and time in the Freudian unconscious, suggesting that there may be points in common with Einstein's theory of relativity, in the sense that time and space are considered also by Freud as relative and variable. Lack of space prevents mentioning all the literature on this topic, but among the most recent and relevant studies, we can cite Laplanche & Pontalis (1983), Sabbadini (1989), Rose (1997), Green (2002), Bell (2006), Faimberg (2007), and Perelberg (2008).

The capacity for perceiving oneself as a subject exists in the flow of time (Winnicott's "going on being" that we discussed in Chapter Two), with a precise direction, from the past to the future (the physical concept of the *arrow of time*, according to which all physical processes are symmetrical compared to time). This ability implies that one has reached an important stage in the maturing process of emotional life. It unites the capacity/possibility to experience mourning and to endure loss. In the absence of such a facility, we witness the construction of an illusory, compensatory world where the passing of time ceases to be a shared reality.

Alice, and murdered time

Alice comes to analysis for an anxiety and depersonalisation crisis that has struck her a short time before. A curious episode triggered it: while she was reaching to see the time on her wristwatch, she realised that she had lost it. The watch had been a present from her grandmother, and Alice had remained paralysed with terror for the whole day because she felt that she had lost a time that she would never again recover.

Alice's mother died when Alice was still very young, but as she states at the beginning of analysis: "For me this doesn't mean anything because I've always known, and I don't have any particular feelings about it."

She has an ageless face, "like an old lady", as she says. She tells me that when she looks at photos of her childhood she is always surprised by her appearance: "It looks as though I got suddenly old, though staying a little girl."

From the very beginning of Alice's extremely long analysis, I realised that her life was extraordinarily slow, almost at a standstill. She moved and spoke slowly because she was afraid that any movement would precipitate the collapse that had brought her to analysis. Time, for her, seemed to have painfully come to a halt, and transformed into an illusory time in which she could flee those aspects of reality that she could not manage to deal with.

Alice immediately told me that she was very anxious because she was afraid she was going to lose her boyfriend, since she found it very difficult to make a move and get involved in any sort of project. When this love story did in fact finish, for almost two years I was an impotent witness to her incessant and extremely painful despair at being abandoned.

One day, quite unexpectedly, during an interminable soliloquy about how empty and desperate her life was without this man, I was surprised to find myself whispering under my breath: "Stop… Stop all this suffering…".

Alice broke off astounded, and as for me, I was quite at a loss: I had not realised that I had spoken out loud. Both of us burst out laughing. Alice said: "Well then, if even the analyst can't take any more…". To which I added: "It means we've really touched bottom…".

It was not yet the bottom, but it was an empathic moment of sharing, exasperated by the eternal immutability of the experience of being abandoned, which was repeated at every single opportunity. I finally realised that it was a prototype: the prototype of all losses, that of the mother. In those two years in analysis, Alice had finally managed to have a mother who paradoxically could understand the sufferings her daughter had endured when she had died.

On seeing me in my turn confused and impotent in front of her prolonged suffering, Alice had succeeded in finally making contact with her feelings of confusion and impotence endured during all those long years of her childhood following the death of her mother. The confusion and humiliation stemming from this loss were what had to be tackled first. Until we succeeded together in making contact and in fully understanding the humiliating experience really suffered in those years we would not have been able to tackle the later confusion and finally the pain for that loss, and the nostalgia.

After almost four years of analysis, memories and a desire to remember finally began to emerge. Her shame at school, her desire that no one should know she was an orphan—"what a horrible word" she said—her love for her grandmothers and her anger that neither of them understood, because they were old, and above all because they were not her mother.

Alice dreamt extensively, especially in the first years of analysis. They were rich and fantastic dreams, often resembling fairy tales. They were peopled with little elves, gnomes, talking animals, extraordinary flowers… She had one dream a great deal, either by itself or as a beginning to other dreams: there was one episode (which varied from time to time) where as she witnessed it, she would be thinking "Now I'm going to change the story"; the dream changed and turned back to repeat the episode, modified in the light of what she had learned the first time. It was her absolutely characteristic way of dreaming; the dreams were cadenced by time, act 1, act 2, act 3, and so on. And above all she seemed able to go back in the dream and re-write the plot; then dream of being in the present, and go back to the past, but only for a moment, in order to change the details of the story to then move into the future. She wanted to be able to re-write the script of her past, becoming the author and no longer the passive victim of her fate.

Alice came into my life at a particular moment: my children were still small, and I was just a few years older than her mother when she died.

The time element therefore developed from the beginning as though we were both involved in a dimension of seductive and contagious timelessness, caught in the dimension that Frances Tustin defines as "flowing-over-at-oneness", the process by which the illusion of "primal unity" is maintained (Tustin, 1981, p. 80): in other words, flowing harmoniously together.

One day, in the second year of analysis, she brings a dream that suddenly enlightens me. It is one of her favourite dreamlike fairy tales, in which a large rabbit rushes busily around, talking all the time and continually retracing his steps. "It's five o'clock in the dream" adds Alice at a certain point, rather incongruously. And then I suddenly understand: it is of course the Mad Hatter and his world, where it is always five o'clock!

> "When the Queen bawled out, 'He's murdering the time! Off with his head!'" ... "And ever since that," the Hatter went on in a mournful tone, "he won't do a thing I ask! It's always six o'clock now." ... "It's always tea-time, and we've no time to wash the things between whiles."
>
> (Carroll, 1865, pp. 186–187)

Alice was a prisoner of time like her namesake in the book. When her mother died, time, for her, stood still, halted in an unreal dimension, where everything carries on as though in a fairy tale and, as in fairy tales, is not really true.

As I said before, there is something very special in the representation of time in analysis. Time presents itself both as the creation of our minds, and as an independent event to which we must submit. For Alice, the passing of time had been experienced as a permanent threat of an imminent catastrophe, a catastrophic collapse that could be avoided only by creating a fantastic universe, one without time, where nothing would apparently change. But precisely this a-temporal illusion brought with it the terror of never developing, never succeeding in escaping a time created illusorily, just like her literary homonym.

The circle is not round

I would now like to relate a fragment from a session in the fourth year of Alice's analysis. It is interesting because it illustrates a moment in a dimension of altered and alienating time (although simultaneously a familiar and comforting "psychic retreat"; Steiner, 1993) apparently destined to be prolonged into infinity. An external element was unexpectedly introduced into this moment that broke the suspended, timeless, and enchanted atmosphere that had been shared up to that point with the analyst.

Alice: "Yesterday I saw a film that I absolutely loved, *Before the Rain*. It's a very dramatic film, in three episodes, about the war in the Balkans."—Pause—"It tells how people try to escape the horrors of war but despite themselves are always drawn back deeper into them. I felt it was about myself, perhaps it was the fragmentary way the story was told, so many people who never meet, all with awful and incomplete stories. Perhaps I'm like that too, fragments of a story that are never connected up to each other."

Analyst: "What do you mean by that?"

Alice: "Well, actually, it irritated me, that aspect of the film, all that putting off and postponing: I never understood how the single stories finished. It's a circular film where the first episode corresponds with the end of the film, with the last episode. Perhaps it wants to say that everyone was swept up into the war and there was no possibility for escaping it."

Analyst: "I must say that I'm very struck by your words. One aspect of the film, as you say, is precisely its circular nature, a strong portrayal of everything, in which the characters meet in different places and times. No one seems to disappear, in the film."

I fall silent, thoughtful. I feel a bit irritated by her comment, irrationally, quite without reason. Alice is a sophisticated cinema-goer and the circular structure of the film is very evident, as she says. My and her irritation have to do with something else.

Analyst: "Did it bring anything particular to mind?"

Alice: "Well, now you ask, yes, the dreams I had at the beginning of my analysis, do you remember, they were like that too—chap 1, chap 2, and so on—except that then I could go back and re-write them if they were too upsetting."

At this point, a scene from the film comes to mind in which the words "Time never dies. The circle is not round" appear quite clearly on a wall. The circular nature of the film is only apparent, there are small dyscrasias, different details. Perhaps the story never repeats itself in the same way.

Analyst: "Perhaps it upsets you to think that it is not possible to go back in reality and re-write the unpleasant episodes, that time does not wait and nothing can be removed."

Alice is silent for a long while and then starts crying, and says: "As a child I always used to hope that it wasn't true, that at a certain point I would have found out that my mum wasn't dead, that they'd just been horrid, and that in actual fact she had only left, but then she would have returned. For years, I nurtured the illusion that she wasn't dead, that it was a secret between me and her, that all I had to do was wait for her!"

Comment

The film in question, *Before the Rain* by Milcho Manchevski (1994), begins with the phrase "It is the time just before the rain" from the poem also by Manchevski that he places at the start of the film. It beautifully transmits the oppressive sense of expectation that pervades the air just before a storm. "Time never dies. The circle is not round" says one of the characters soon afterwards, placing Alice suddenly in front of a simple truth, an "unthought known" (Bollas, 1987): time inexorably passes; the story is never repeated. The ambiguities, the bizarre temporal paradoxes in the film allow Alice to meet on the screen not so much her own biographical events as her particular defensive and narrative behaviours.

Together, we understood that it was not the fact itself (the loss of her mother) that we could alter but our interpretation of the event. During the analysis, Alice had been able to re-live with the analyst the fundamental experience of sharing her phantasy world, repeating the projective illusion of having a child who listens to fairy tales told by a mother. Winnicott (1987) talks of a "third area" (or transitional space or intermediate area), in other words an area of illusion, of playing, and of culture:

> The third part of the life of a human being, a part that we cannot ignore, an intermediate area of experiencing, to which inner reality and external life both contribute. It is an area which is not challenged, because no claim is made on its behalf except that it shall exist as a resting-place for the individual engaged in the perpetual human task of keeping inner and outer reality separate yet inter-related.
>
> (Winnicott, 1953, p. 89)

But some hold on reality remains, however, as Pontalis (1977) points out when discussing the "illusion sustained", alluding to that dimension of psychic life that has to be maintained and expanded by the analytic work in order to guarantee good mental functioning.

During this analysis, I had to think the unthinkable, in temporal and consequential terms, together with this patient: that a mother could die. The crux of this analysis lay in the logical inconceivableness of such an experience, the unthought known: in other words, that it was possible for such an essential thing as a mother to die and yet, despite this, life could continue.

Alice: "The only way for staying faithful to her memory, to the little that remained, was to halt everything. Nothing could exist after her death, absolutely nothing, not deep inside myself anyway." To continue with or to pick up life again meant definitively burying her mother and betraying what little remained: her memory within. The experience of her mother's death had remained in deadlock for many years, following the fate of traumatic experiences that remain at a level of experience that is neither conscious, nor repressed, because it cannot be thought. However, its very presence—even though unexpressed and without a voice because it was deprived of any possibility of being represented—had hindered the natural development of any representations. The only way for representing the loss was to freeze everything.

The motif of the circle's imperfection—the story does not repeat, or at least, not completely—recurs several times in the film (to which Alice often returned during her analysis, continuing to be angry at my not wanting to accept the circularity of the narrative events). As in Alice's story, the succession of images, with which the director attempted to represent the inexorable ambiguity of the representation of death, was probably more important than the way they linked up together.

Alice, too, had understood, during analysis, that if we pretend that something that has happened has not happened, we risk infinitely modifying every other real event and slowly place ourselves outside the natural flow of time (time does not wait). But her mother's untimely death, and the ensuing family tragedy, really did signify a temporal break, an anomalous event: "Mothers don't die when their children are so small", said Alice.

The war (represented in the film) is also a temporal break that interrupts the lifetimes of populations, but at the same time it is a historic and political element present since the dawn of time. All things eternally return but not necessarily in the same way. It is possible for the story not to repeat itself. And so even Alice's circle could finally be closed. At the end of analysis, Alice accepted her mother's death: from here, she could start to let time flow once more.

We know that people incapable of relinquishing their "false beliefs" (a belief based on denial) (Britton, 1998, p. 13) are also incapable of giving up their lost objects. Relinquishing one's beliefs means activating the mourning process. Likewise, the capacity to experience mourning and to bear loss implies being capable of understanding oneself as a subject inserted into a temporal dimension, in full flow, in the making.

At times, when trapped by terrible feelings of pain and loss, obliged to think the unthinkable, in other words what one does not want to think, one takes refuge in a system of phantasies that are given the status of real facts. But, as in Alice's case, these phantasies or false beliefs become unbearable in the end in the process of reconstruction, or the *après coup*.

When a reconstruction fails the reality test, the defensive phantasy that had created it can be abandoned, in the same way in which a lost object is let go through continually discovering its disappearance. This is, in short, the process of working through mourning in analysis, which always accompanies a recovery of that time and that space that were subsequently developed after the loss of the object, in a world, in an external reality, that one preferred to believe was not consequential.

I would like to add a literary aside to this clinical vignette, the heart-rending account by Amos Oz of his mother's suicide in *A Tale of Love and Darkness*. The guiding thread through the book is the dramatic suicide of Oz's mother in 1952, when Amos was thirteen, a suicide announced from the very beginning and that ends only on the very last page.

The story unfolds between constant leaps forwards and backwards, between the distant past, the recent past, and the present, between reflections and anecdotes. But the last sentence, literally Oz's epitaph, goes like this, exactly what Alice might have said:

> I have hardly ever spoken about my mother till now, till I came to write these pages. Not with my father, or my wife, or my children or with anybody else. ... My mother decided to sleep fully dressed and to make quite sure that she didn't wake up again to spend an agonized night in the kitchen she poured herself a glass of tea from the vacuum flask that her sister had left by her bedside, waited for it to cool down a little, and when she drank it she took her sleeping pills. If I had been there with her in that room overlooking the

back yard in Haya and Tsvi's flat at that moment, at half past eight or a quarter to nine on that Saturday evening, I would certainly have tried my hardest to explain to her why she mustn't. And if I did not succeed I would have done everything possible to stir her compassion, to make her take pity on her only child. I would have cried and I would have pleaded without any shame and I would have hugged her knees, I might even have pretended to faint or I might have hit and scratched myself till the blood flowed as I had seen her do in moments of despair. Or I would have attacked her like a murderer, I would have smashed a vase over her head without hesitation. Or hit her with the iron that stood on a shelf in a corner of the room. Or taken advantage of her weakness to lie on top of her and tie her hands behind her back, and taken away all those pills and tablets and sachets and solutions and potions and syrups of hers and destroyed the lot of them. But I was not allowed to be there. I was not even allowed to go to her funeral. My mother fell asleep and this time she slept with no nightmares, she had no insomnia, in the early hours she threw up and fell asleep again, still fully dressed, … she paid no attention to them, or to the specialist from whom she had heard that the psyche is the worst enemy of the body, and she did not wake up in the morning either, or even when the day grew brighter…

(Oz, 2003, pp. 506, 516–517)

Alice, too, used to tell me that if she could have, if only it would have been possible for her, she would have done everything to keep her mother alive, narratively speaking. But her narrative skill was not so powerful, and had lost the primary object of her love. From that moment, every other investment became suspect, at risk of a circular repetition of a story without time. The story that had in fact happened in the past can be re-presented only if we do not succeed in finding the wristwatch lost at the start of analysis, whose hands—ticking slowly along—find themselves marking the time of another, new story, if we know how to listen to it and narrate it. In accepting the initial fusion, the "flowing-over-at-oneness" or flowing harmoniously together, the analyst had finally allowed the separation to take place. The film, seen together but read in different ways, had created an intermediate space where other investments became possible even after the primary investment had been lost forever.

CHAPTER EIGHT

Love in old age*

The Heart asks Pleasure—first—
And then—excuse from Pain—
And then—those little Anodynes
That deaden suffering—

And then—to go to sleep—
And then—if it should be
The will of it's Inquisitor
The privilege to die—

—Emily Dickinson, "Poem F588" (1863)

Psychoanalysis or psychotherapy in old age can be a fascinating experience for both the therapist and the patient, an experience allowing the patient to reconstruct his internal vicissitudes so that during the last years of his existence he can give an overall significance to the whole of his life.

---

*An earlier version of most of this chapter was previously published on the EPF website (www.epf-fep.eu), translated by Carla Bellucci.

At seventy, the Oedipus complex manifests and represents itself with the same strength and passion of youth, while mental and emotional functioning do not, on the whole, seem to differ from the analysis of younger persons. Old people, too, have an unconscious, conflicts, desires, the compulsion to repeat, defence mechanisms, and so on, and, therefore, the ways in which therapy functions—in its common aspects regarding the work on transference and countertransference, drives and defences, as well as repetition compulsions, the fusion between Eros and Thanatos—do not differ so much from what takes place at a less advanced age.

What are the motivations that lead an elderly person to ask for analysis or therapy, and why take such patients into therapy? Naturally these therapies must be adjusted to a different time schedule, as regards both the overall duration and times of the setting, which must take into account the needs of an elderly person, with all the difficulties that might arise at a certain age.

Thanks to my not vast but fairly good experience, I feel I can say that the main reason that leads these people to ask for an analysis or therapeutic support is certainly the need, at least at the end of their lives, to get to grips with those vicissitudes whose solution or identification they have always managed to postpone in one way or another. Being close to the end of their lives makes them more or less consciously wish to be able to give an overall meaning to their internal emotional and personal history by tackling those very difficulties that they have preferred to avoid adequately investigating. Why all this courage so late in life? Sometimes they feel the need to find an ultimate meaning, meaningfulness, for vicissitudes that have lost much of their instinctual urge or for expectations that have long exhausted their external persecutory character, even if they still show up in their internal world.

Above all, it is the feared and more-often-than-not suffered illnesses that bring urgency and intensity to the wish for being concretely helped. The anxiety of dying with much "unfinished business", which up to a certain point had not been a problem, leaves them feeling unhappy and unsatisfied, to the point of desiring the therapeutic relationship that—often—they had already experienced in their youth or, rather, had wanted to experience but had postponed in different moments of their lives. Quinodoz argues that:

> It is difficult to give up our place without first having found it, to leave life without first feeling that we have actually lived, to close

our internal life-history without first having made it into a "whole
history", one that belongs to us.

(Quinodoz, 2009, p. 774)

Growing old does not simply mean letting the years go by, but, above
all, sorting out all the events that have taken place so far. For example,
some people sort out their possessions; others write their biography,
perhaps to leave it to their grandchildren; others arrange their books, or
their photographs, or films. All of them, in this way, wish to survive in
the memory of those who remain and, in therapy, in the memory of the
therapist, who thus becomes a sort of executor of all those passions and
desires that failed to develop in life. Therefore, the analyst is, as usual,
a witness, but also an avenger of the wrongs suffered, of petty or great
injustices, of the betrayals of the past, of jealousies among siblings, of the
desertions of parents, and the more recent abandonments of spouses.

Love in old age presents itself in many ways. Sometimes it is an acute
and persistent longing for what one has lost, for what could not be developed due to defences and anxieties and resistances towards instinctual
aspects that at the time seemed to be intolerable. Sometimes, instead, it
is the claiming of a right that had been inhibited and denied for a long
time, the right to be recognised in one's ability to love and be loved,
a right that has been stifled by a repressive education or by political,
social, or economic reasons. Sometimes it is a painful longing for something that was there but has been long lost, widowhoods that are still
unbearable, that have not been replaced by other forms of affection, or
even parents' deaths that are still intolerable, decades after the event.

One is often confronted with the resurfacing of suppressed memories, split aspects, memories that distance makes it possible to put, at
last, in the right perspective. Therapy often takes the form of compensation, the final recognition of an identity that has been stifled and suppressed for too long. After so many years, it is odd to see the persistence
of narcissistic wounds. Often jealousy towards siblings, or fierce envy
resurfaces; sometimes the feelings that were once originated by parents
or siblings are projected on to one's children. Memories that were too
painful to be remembered sometimes re-emerge in a completely unexpected way, both for the patient and the analyst.

From a technical point of view, I can say that it is particularly important
in the treatment of the elderly to pay attention to the present moment.
Historical reconstruction appears to be useful only and exclusively if it

can be signified in the present time, especially if one can capture those feelings, those moods that have been constantly mortified, suppressed, and denied. With the elderly, it is vital to capture the present, the instant, the moment.

To stop, or capture, or define the moment is always important in analysis. However, in the history of psychoanalysis and in analytic treatment has it not perhaps always been central to value the experiences of the past and how these play a key role in determining the development of future vicissitudes? And, therefore, that it is the past experiences that give shape and substance to the present, which is thus always at risk of becoming a prisoner of an endless repetition of the traumatic events of the past? Is the historical reconstruction of primitive childhood vicissitudes not perhaps central in analytic treatment? Is remembering, repeating, and working through not perhaps the favourite plot in an analysis, the one that is repeated most in its however endless personal variations? Perhaps with the elderly this central element is forgotten, neglected?

The present time—the here, the now—is the moment when we live our lives.

Peter Fonagy, in "Memory and therapeutic action", stresses that:

> The only way we can know what goes on in our patient's mind, what might have happened to them, is how they are with us in the transference [and I would add, in the present moment]. ... Therapeutic action lies in the conscious elaboration of preconscious relationship representations, principally through the analyst's attention to the transference.
>
> (Fonagy, 1999, pp. 216, 217)

Therefore, the past experiences recounted by the patient acquire a meaning only in the light of the present, that is, when they are recalled and repeated in the present time, in the here and now of the analytic session. And in the analysis, between the patient and the analyst, there is the problem of looking for the most appropriate word for exactly expressing the mood, the fears, anxieties, and desperations, but also the hopes, desires, and excitements of a time past that resurface and come alive again through the narration and the recalling as if they were taking place again in that very moment. Not the story, not the plot, but the perception, the emotional experience that had accompanied them. And if, as often happens, these very perceptions, these emotional experiences have been repressed, suppressed, denied, and isolated within a single word, if defensive barriers have been built against these feelings and perceptions, even if they then re-emerge in the analysis, in the present time, in the instant, in the here and now, that instant can sometimes be misunderstood or wrongly defined. When that happens, the emotional vicissitude that accompanies that particular word will not be fully captured and the analyst will miss the opportunity to help the patient find a meaning, in the *après coup*, in retrospectively recalling the conflicts and anxieties that had blocked his development and his ability to live in the present. The analyst gives a temporal shape to experience thanks to his ability to modulate—through careful and empathic listening—the vicissitudes of the past by restoring to them a meaning in the present.

Perhaps more than other patients, elderly patients need the analyst to find their vicissitudes interesting, so that they themselves can attribute importance to them. Among them all, it is the love vicissitudes of the past and the hopes of love in the present that most need to be taken care of and recognised.

By acknowledging that one has loved and been loved, the elderly manage to make peace with the idea of their more or less imminent death. The love that is reactivated in the transference experience, as a possibility of being loved by the analyst, and to love him, as it was in the past, brings reconciliation with life and, ultimately, with death.

In Bach's "St John Passion", the Evangelist says that when Jesus had committed whom he loved most, his mother, to John, he prepared, being serene, to go towards death.

And, together with John, we can say: "And after committing his most precious memories to the analyst, he prepared, being serene, to go towards death."

Giovanna

Giovanna is getting on in years. She has already lived much of her life and also had time to undertake analysis and psychotherapy. Both helped her to a certain extent, but she is not well now. As I said in the Introduction, a person's conscious or unconscious reason for asking for help at a certain age concerns the death anxiety, which is obviously more specific at this age than at a younger one.

I do not intend to talk about Giovanna's analysis here, but to report a session in which the libidinal elements, mixed with the oedipal ones of the past, resurfaced, as in other moments during the analysis.

Giovanna has never married nor had a love relationship important enough to make her want to live together with her lover. Smart, brilliant, well read, pleasant-looking, she does not like to be in the limelight, to expose herself too much, although, because of her culture, rank, and vivacious character, she has often been talked about, certainly more than she would have liked.

The session deals with a trivial, irrelevant episode Giovanna would never have considered, which, however, was picked up by the analyst who gave a meaning to it that would help signify many other elements of Giovanna's past.

Giovanna arrives irritated, a bit down, annoyed. She does not know how to define her mood. She feels, she says: "As if she were going to an elephants' graveyard: you know what elephants' graveyards are, don't you? Those places where you go to die."

Analyst: "Do you feel like an elephant, then?"

Giovanna: "Well, yes a bit. There isn't much more left to do than dying."

I remain silent for a while, and then I ask her how long she has been feeling like this.

Giovanna: "I've been feeling like this for a while, without much desire to live, without anybody now who needs me. Yesterday I saw X and spent the day with him."

X is a long-time love of hers, with whom she has had a love affair for years, with ups and downs, that never turned into anything more lasting or binding, but remained a warm and tender friendship. Now X is very old, and ill too, and Giovanna had fantasised that if he had married her, she would have received an economic benefit (by inheriting his pension as his widow), without damaging anyone, since he had no heirs.

I was puzzled by this fantasy. She was referring to something weird, also because she certainly has no financial difficulties. I was thinking of the desire for a compensation for what she had not experienced as far as love is concerned, for what she had missed, but I remained silent. She tells me instead that she had talked about it with him yesterday, and she is happy she did. However he was embarrassed and upset and answered: "You know, I thought of marriage in other terms." Then they dropped the topic and neither of them mentioned it again.

Analyst: "It seems to me that the term 'elephant' could have another meaning. You feel you behaved just like an elephant yesterday, in a rather tactless way."

It is a face-to-face session and the patient regularly uses the objects on my desk to represent constructions, which we interpret. Today she has put many barriers between me and herself, many strong bulwarks. I point this out to her.

Analyst: "The topic seems to embarrass you a lot."

Giovanna: "Well, for sure I wasn't pleased." Suddenly she becomes very animated and lively: "However, what annoyed me most is that he didn't think of me at all, of how I would feel. He always seems so loving and careful and helpful, but he didn't even bother to ask me why I was asking, how I would feel, how I would feel after his answer. He made me remember an episode of the past: once I gave him a record, a rare record, which had a certain meaning for me, and he was so absent-minded, although he seemed pleased. Then one day we were at some common friends and they played that very record, and I pointed out to him that it is like his record, and he says 'no, it is the very same record, I gave it to them'. And he just did not understand that it was something you don't do, it was unforgivable. And then, even worse, there had been a situation in which I was very exposed, and he had to assess me, a competitive exam, and he just talked all the time to a colleague of his and never paid any attention to me, without realising that it was important for me, and it was so annoying."

Analyst: "Really unforgivable. But now that I think of it, it seems to me that maybe the thought is not so much that you have been awkward, but that he had the tact of an elephant, and that you were so angry and sorry and annoyed as to think that you might as well die, in his peers' graveyard."

Giovanna: "Well, yes. He has always been like that, someone who takes care of others but from a distance; he actually only takes care of himself; he has never married, he has never had any women, but myself, a life very much like this, a narcissistic, closed life, and, in the end, you are right, a tactless life."

In the meantime, while she was talking, she had removed all the barriers on the desk and had turned them into a sort of "royal road" with columns and borders.

I point this out to her and add that, although many years have gone by, her pride seems to have remained intact and lively, and that she seems to think that he should have married her many years before.

She nods, satisfied, and says: "Yes, I'm happy I asked him now. He behaved badly, because of the way he answered me. After all, I'm happy I asked him."

Comment

In my opinion, this short clinical vignette contains everything that I have said above about our absolute need to remain focused, that is, not to miss the emotion, the vicissitudes of the present moment. The barriers that Giovanna was bit by bit erecting on my desk as she spoke evoked a defensive bulwark raised to protect herself from what she was recounting, which made her feel both ashamed and proud. Her sentimental life had mainly been governed by an imperative need to protect her autonomy and independence. She was also permeated by a strong oedipal bond that had done much to damage her affective experiences. Having been the preferred child of an important and much loved father had, on the one hand, "raised the bar" for any other pretender—who could never stand up to comparison with the father figure—while at the same time undermining her self-esteem. Indeed, instead of psychically protecting her and preparing the ground for future replacement objects, unconditional paternal love had, in fact, crippled her, leading her to think that anything she had constructed by herself was not worthy of merit. She was often caustic, both with herself and with her loved ones, demanding much but expecting little in return. What she was, her most intimate identity, seemed fictitious to her, not resulting from her gifts and skills but from the luck of the draw, or rather, from having been her father's favourite.

Analysis with a younger person had been useful for her. It was not a relationship of equals, and she had felt sufficiently protected narcissistically by her experiences and skills, superior thanks to her age. At the same time, she had allowed herself to accept a certain affective reciprocity from the analytic relationship, precisely because it was outside the competitive or seductive aspects that had compromised her earlier therapeutic experiences. These previous experiences had also been marked by the prejudice of having "tricked" the analyst, of having successfully sidetracked him away from her real needs. Now, this late "confession/request" of marriage/love laid her bare and exposed her needs, which were not so much economic as affective, revealing how they had been brushed aside then and many other times in her life. There was a certain urgency in all this, mixed with fear of losing her autonomy and independence.

As in Francesca's case, she still harboured an impelling need to remember that she had been loved and had loved, despite the ensuing refusals and denials she had suffered.

The analyst became the witness of these old loves, and also a new object to invest in. In fact, the analyst, too, was loved and in some way

became part of the patient's affective panorama. This assuaged anxieties and placated old disregarded needs of the past.

The attentive, participating analyst who would not be "tricked"
could soothe old wounds and allow the course of the patient's still long
life to begin again, with increased confidence in herself and her capacities for loving and being loved.

Filippo

Filippo is over seventy. In the past, he too was in treatment for a few
years because of depressive anxiety disorders. He was satisfied with
the results of psychotherapy that allowed him to overcome some phobias about travelling, especially travelling for pleasure and relaxation.
Now he comes for a consultation because of a state of indefinite mal-
aise: "A vague dissatisfaction… I am no longer the person I used to be,
I find less pleasure in doing things, I move around less and less and
with increasing difficulty. I seem to be back where I was many years ago
when I undertook my first analysis."

He is obviously uncertain about the possibilities of being helped.
"Maybe it's too late for me now and I have to put up with this way
of living, after all most of my life is behind me and I don't think I can
change. I have been like this for so many years, how can I make a turn-
around now?" On the other hand: "I don't want to resign myself to
living in such a limited way for a long time. Both my mother and my
father lived to be over ninety in very good health, therefore I have at
least twenty years ahead of me and I would like to live them in a more
positive mood."

Again, I do not intend to discuss in detail Filippo's short analysis
(which lasted three years), but only to mention, here as well, the libidinal
and love aspects that were unsettling him.

Filippo has always lived a double life. He has had a relationship with
another woman for years without his wife knowing anything about it.
He talks right away about these aspects of his love life. They have been
a standard feature of his life, ever since he got married. A few months
after the marriage, he realised that:

> I had made a great mistake. I liked my wife very much, however
> she is not the woman to spend a lifetime with. For me, she has
> something bothersome, something irritating, even if she is neither
> a bothersome nor irritating woman. But every time she speaks,

everything she says is so commonplace, she has such an impenetrable dullness, she does a lot of voluntary work but always in the realm of the obvious, and I get so bored with her. We share nothing; nothing of what she says interests me. In order to spend some time with her on holiday I always have to have other people around, friends or relatives, otherwise I can't bear it. Whereas with Chiara, I feel great. She has not been the first: right after my marriage, I had a long love affair with a woman I liked very much; however, after a few years she realised that I would never leave my wife, so she ended our relationship. It was a pity because we were very much in love.

On the other hand, Chiara, whom he met shortly afterwards, accepted without too many problems her situation of mistress. They have always had a very good sexual harmony, besides an excellent intellectual understanding, and both are continuing now they are elderly (they are the same age). Now, however, Filippo feels uneasy. What would happen to this double life of his if he died?

Filippo:

> I wouldn't want to find myself in embarrassing situations, do you understand? That's why, every time I sleep out, I get into a state; once it was different; now I'm afraid to be found out, not that my wife wants to find out or that she suspects; she is the kind of person who says "I see this, then it's not true", that is, she is someone who defends herself a lot against unpleasant things, and pretends not to see them even when they are under her nose; on the other hand, I have no intention whatsoever of displeasing her; I really love her, but what can I do if I can't stand her?

Analyst: "Are you afraid of ending up like the priest Fra Alberto, who lay 'sundry times' in the arms of a woman and was imprisoned for it?" (Giovanni Bocaccio, *The Decameron*, "Fourth Day, Second Story", 1353.)

Filippo:

> Exactly! My problem has always been that I want to do certain things, but I can't stand the idea that what I do may have unpleasant consequences for others. But then, I always feel my freedom is at risk, and I don't seem able to do what I want. Now the consequence

of this mood of mine has become worse: I'm counting the nights I manage to spend with Chiara, and this year they have been fewer than ten, very few. She is complaining about it; she would like to spend more time with me, and so would I, but I'm frightened, I get real phobias. When we leave I sweat all over, I'm in a real state, and the moment I decide to go back or even not to leave any more, I immediately calm down. But the result is that in the end I feel depressed, a coward, one who is not able to do even the smallest part of what he wants. And then I seem not to feel like doing anything, I seem not to be interested in anything. In other words, I feel almost inert; I who have always been on the move. Do you think that these phobias will pass and that I will be able to spend some nights out again?

Analyst: "Why are you talking about phobias? You don't seem phobic to me. You travel a lot on business, many times a week, and you sleep out. The problem you are bringing here, and that makes you so upset now seems to be this double life that continues without any solution, when in actual fact you would be perfectly capable of making your own choices."

Then Filippo turns to talking about the family life of his childhood, about how much he feared his father's sudden scenes and how much he wished never to make him lose control. "This is why I have never felt really free to make my choices—he says—I hate scenes, above all the shouting, losing control. I always say I want to be *maitre de moi même*, this is my motto."

I point out that it must be particularly distressing for him to be so much at the mercy of an emotionality he does not approve of, to be constantly deprived of the freedom of choice.

Filippo: "I have always tried to please everyone, to make others happy. More than anything, I didn't want them to protest against me. I have been lucky, but now I'm worried about this mood of mine."

It seems to me that Filippo is going through a serious narcissistic crisis. His defences, which have allowed him to continue undeterred in his life, though with great attention for the feelings of others, are crumbling. Here, too, an old oedipal phantasm is returning, the castrating father he thought he had defeated and buried a long time ago.

I tell him that he seems still young to me and above all very vital, and that exactly his being worried about the fewer nights spent with Chiara seems to be a clear sign of the passions agitating him, an expression of a vitality and libidinal desire that are certainly present.

This intervention has an explosive effect: the next time he arrives with a very clear, very pleasant erotic dream. Perhaps the dream is about the analyst, maybe about Chiara, maybe about yet another woman. He points out that he has not had an erotic dream for many years.

I interpret it literally: "There is an eroticism that can be desired and dreamt of, and it has surfaced again after the first sessions." I prefer not to hint at transference interpretations although, with Fonagy (1999), I believe this libidinal response has been triggered precisely by the renewed interest of the analyst in him. However, this libido is immediately connected with the old oedipal struggle: can he stay with Chiara? Or must he always and constantly fear his wife/mother and not allow himself to outdo his father with not one but two women?

The analysis proceeds, and Filippo little by little retrieves his confidence, and also that particular tendency to secretly break the rules that had always characterised him and saved him from his parent's rigidity and strictness. He goes on working, always successfully, and abandons any idea of retiring early. He sees Chiara regularly and begins to think of her; he buys her unexpected gifts; he thinks about how he can remain close to her even when he will be no longer there, all without unsettling his wife and marriage—as usual.

In the middle of the analysis, he brings a significant dream:

> He is in a tunnel and there are threatening presences that are grabbing him by his jacket; he frees himself with difficulty with a blow similar to a tennis backhand. He comes out of the tunnel but somebody is still following him down an alley. So he turns, stops running away, tackles this person and knocks him down, with a blow.

I comment that he thinks everybody seems to be grabbing him by his jacket, that is, urging him to do things, and that he seems to want to come out of this tunnel which apparently has no way out. His secret invention is the backhand, that is, a way to reverse his prospects. It is the only way for him to come out of the tunnel (of death? of the end of his life?) and fight successfully and out in the open against both internal and external persecutory aspects.

Filippo seems to fully agree with this interpretation. He also says that Chiara has pretentions she should not have; after all, she had always known she was only his mistress and that he would never leave his wife. On the other hand, his wife has to accept the fact that he needs to have the freedom he cannot experience with her. If he does not achieve this now, at this point in his life, when will he be able to?

The backhand in the dream is a reversal of perspective: not what he is supposed to do to satisfy his women and their needs, but what they should do in order to give him more freedom.

The search for freedom seems to be a desire long postponed that he can now pursue a bit more intensely. Freedom, above all, from the internal persecutory aspects he had always underestimated.

From this moment on, there is a turning point in his love life. He spends much more time with Chiara and with her friends and relatives, and finds his wife less bothersome, managing to build up an acceptable family life with her. So, in a certain way, it is as if they lived separately, although in fact they are not and are, indeed, spending much more time together, and of better quality, than in the past. The feelings of guilt have vanished. He often allows himself brief but frequent holidays with Chiara, and he is no longer worried about his possible departure. If it should happen—he says—that would no longer be his business, obviously.

When the analysis is over, he finds himself *maître de soi même* again, however with a more mature self and no longer suffering from old castration complexes.

Comment

I realise that to comment on this snippet of analysis involves tackling moral aspects that other clinical comments might well have ignored. It would be easy to label Filippo an egoist from the point of view of love, a person who "wants his cake and eats it", but here we are addressing the situation from the point of view of his psychic equilibrium, asking ourselves what it might be, bearing in mind his moral and libidinal needs.

The freedom that Filippo has always hankered after in his life, what he calls "being *maître de soi même*", has been ignored for too long. His never-completely-resolved dependence on paternal judgement, mixed with fear of his father's angry outbursts, revealed castration anxieties that had been circumvented at various times during his life, by resorting to some kind of psychic avoidance.

At this point, late in life, he once again felt impotent and gripped by those persecutory (or castrating) threats so well described in his dream. His backhand at tennis allowed him—once out of the tunnel (of death? of impotence?)—to reverse his future prospects. Here, too, the transferential event was essential in reviving those characteristics of libidinal object investment that had seemed burnt out or exhausted.

By means of the transference, he had regained confidence in his amorous possibilities and capacities; once again, he felt himself to be interesting to someone, the possible object of libidinal interest (on the part of the analyst) and capable of new libidinal investments (always the analyst). This made him realise to what extent his freedom of movement and opportunities for investment had narrowed over the years.

What had seemed an excess of abundance (two women!) had shown itself to be a lack of liberty and autonomy; exactly what he had feared all his life.

Now advanced in years, this curtailment of his independence had replayed his failure at separating in late adolescence and his incapacity to make himself truly autonomous. Now, with the passing of years, the idea of death—even if it appeared to be pretty remote in his thoughts, thanks to his strong physical makeup and good family genetic prospects—seemed intolerable to withstand without having first resolved this problem of regaining his freedom, especially his libidinal liberty. An excess in the sense of duty, a sadistic and persecutory superego risked ruining the last years of his life, just like an illness. The analysis had "cured" him, restoring the balance between his ego and superego and re-establishing the correct distance between his two women.

CHAPTER NINE

Making choices; not making choices

Full many a glorious morning I have seen
Flatter the mountain-tops with sovereign eye,
Kissing with golden face the meadows green,
Gilding pale streams with heavenly alchemy;
Anon permit the basest clouds to ride
With ugly rack on his celestial face,
And from the forlorn world his visage hide,
Stealing unseen to west with this disgrace:
Even so my sun one early morn did shine,
With all-triumphant splendour on my brow;
But, out! Alack! He was but one hour mine,
The region cloud hath mask'd him from me now.
Yet him for this my love no whit disdaineth;
Suns of the world may stain when heaven's sun staineth.
—Shakespeare, "Sonnet 33" (1595–1600)

One morning, Emma came out of her house. She looked first right, then left. She paused on the threshold. Where was it she had to go? What was the best way to get there? Right or left? It suddenly struck her that she did not know. And she could not decide. Which of the two streets was best? And where would her choice lead her?

I actually dreamt this opening paragraph, clearly referencing Emma Bovary. As Flaubert relates, when talking of his heroine:

> From that moment on, her existence was little more than a tissue of lies, in which she swathed her love, as if behind a veil, to hide it from view.

> It was a necessity, an obsession, a pleasure, to the extent that, if she said she had walked yesterday along the right-hand side of the street, it actually meant she had walked along the left-hand side.
>
> (Flaubert, 1857, p. 252)

I am turning to Madame Bovary because, as I suggested in the Introduction, it is undoubtedly a literary classic in the annals of passion, a romantic model illustrating the inexorable nature of adultery. Madame Bovary can only be a victim of her unavoidable choices. For Flaubert, her suicide is the logical consequence of the web of lies she could no longer extricate herself from and of the extinction of her desires and illusions, which could not withstand comparison with reality.

Adultery and infidelity are complex matters. In analysis, we sometimes see patients filled with anxiety because they cannot decide between two loves; however, in actual fact, it is much more common to see patients who have been betrayed and are unable to make rhyme or reason of it, incapable of either pardoning or leaving the unfaithful partner. It is much easier to hate than to make peace with each other. Hating does not require sacrifices or compromises. The first desire, the first instinct of the betrayed partner is to leave, to break it all off, to nullify the original investment.

To this end, the narcissistic protection of the rejected ego—whose trust placed in the other is what has, above all, been betrayed—appears to be stronger than the libidinal object investment. It is better to lose the love object that has dashed your expectations and deceived your ideals than to undertake a long and painful journey of reflection on past events, on what was said and done together, on the responsibilities underlying the unfaithful behaviour, and on the unconscious complicity in not having wanted to see or understand what was going on. Something, in the amorous fine-tuning, went wrong. Something, in the harmonious development of the relationship, stopped beating in unison and took a different path. The suffering endured is unbearable. The person you want to find refuge and consolation in is precisely the one who has betrayed and deceived you, the last person on earth you could turn to.

With the act of betrayal, everything in your life seems to alter: relationships with friends, with family, and at work.

Mothers take to their beds and cry their eyes out all day long, regardless of their children. Husbands phantasise terrible vendettas, completely foreign to their normal mild and tranquil natures. The betrayed attacks; the betrayer marshals his/her defences. Making the peace, reciprocal understanding, pardon asked for and granted all seem quite out of the question. Relentless blame, ghosts of chastisement, the impossibility to make amends are the only paths possible, archaic representations of crimes and punishments, of primitive, implacable superegos.

In Theodore Fontane's novel *Effi Briest*, the author condemns Effi first to being disowned and then to an early death. A stifling sense of duty forcefully imbues the novel in many places, as the moral element infringed by infidelity.

Like *Madame Bovary* and *Anna Karenina*, *Effi Briest* illustrates the myth of nineteenth-century middle-class marriage, which harbours boredom and marital misunderstanding, the woman's subjugation, a desperate search for passion, and the adulterer's blame and requisite atonement. All three heroines die, since death is the only possible conclusion to an impossible passion.

But let us pause for a moment on the title of this chapter "Making choices; not making choices". Well, as analysts, we know all too well that the concept of choice is an illusory one. What man does in fact succeed in attaining is the capacity to grasp the many opportunities that fate reserves for him and offers him during his life. But often, he is not even capable of seeing them, nor of realising the huge variety of chances and occasions that life presents along its way. Analysis— when it works—transforms these destinies and makes patients capable of libidinally investing in those objects that may otherwise not have been perceived. In common parlance, we call this "making choices", fully knowing, though, that they are not proper choices but simply the activating of libidinal impulses that are otherwise repressed or denied.

Shakespeare's sonnet at the beginning of this chapter describes delicately but precisely through the metaphor of the sun how the state of mind of people who have been betrayed, and who then succeed in working through the infidelity in a mature manner, alters. The poet proceeds from "glorious morning I have seen/Flatter the mountain-tops with sovereign eye"—in other words, the dawn of the perfect love story, when the "sun one early morn did shine,/With all-triumphant splendour on my brow"—to the discovery of the infidelity, when "Alack! He was but one hour mine,/The region cloud hath mask'd him from me now": now there is no sun of love to so brilliantly illuminate and excite the ego. But, wait a minute, one can pardon and the mass of clouds, the darkening of life that ensues from being betrayed, can be overcome: "Yet him for this my love no whit disdaineth;/Suns of the world may stain when heaven's sun staineth". The message is clear: do not lose your trust in love, or rather in the opportunity for either new encounters or for restoring trust in the betrayed love, because there is a profound difference between the earthly and celestial suns, that is between Absolute love and the everyday matters that nurture its progress.

We now come to the clinical development of these all too common problems. Among the many that have reached my consulting room, I have singled out two that share the uncommon characteristic of arriving at the same time and presenting many similarities. However, they concluded very differently, due to the different personality structures of the two people involved.

I will call them Emma—Emma 1 and Emma 2—even if they were not, in the story, adulterers, but victims of adultery. Besides, as I have mentioned above, it is much more common to have patients who suffer adultery rather than those who perpetrate it, because there is an incomparable degree of suffering between those who are betrayed and those who betray.

Emma 1

Emma 1 is a young woman, married now for several years to a man she describes as "beautiful, really handsome" and with whom she has a young daughter. She has an interesting job and quite a good relationship with her own family. She came to ask for help because she has recently discovered that her husband has been betraying her, and for some time, probably quite a long time. It took her a long while to make this discovery: small details that did not match up, distractions, repeated absences supposedly for work but lacking any further explanations. And a sort of bad feeling that was difficult to define after several years of being happily married, with shared projects brought to conclusion, and reciprocal support in work difficulties and important planning decisions. They also enjoyed excellent co-parenting of a much desired and loved little girl, doted on by her father. Worthy of note in Emma's family history is that her father died when she was nineteen, which had strong repercussions on the family's economic and affective life. Emma 1 got her degree, therefore, while she was also working; she had a difficult life, but became a "strong person", as she herself says, proud of her independence.

This was not the first time her husband had been unfaithful. As soon as they were married, when she was pregnant, her husband had gone to work abroad and had had quite an important love affair at that time that she had discovered by chance. She had cried desperately, he had excused himself and had sworn that it would never ever happen again, and yet now, five years later, she finds herself in the same situation. What upsets her most, now as then, is her husband's repeated attempts at denying every single thing about his infidelity, or, to be more explicit, the parallel story that he has with another woman. This has led Emma 1 to check his diaries and mobile phones; to compare times and dates; to doubt herself and also what appeared obvious. Her husband denies everything, always.

It emerges during analysis that this pleasant, amusing, loving man who had made her feel desired and important, who had given her serenity and joy after the difficult period spent when living alone—proudly doing so but also forced to making "necessity a virtue"—has always been a person who loves telling lies, whether they are necessary or not. A "serial adulterer" we called him after a while. Emma 1 knew, but preferred not to realise on a conscious level, that he had been unfaithful to her many times after the first; that he was a person who did not know how to be alone; that every time he went away for work—even for a short period—he started up a story with another woman; that, in short, he had been cheating on her the whole time and the only way she could bear him was by denying it all to herself, but she could not really live with him in those circumstances. She spent some time in analysis. He returned home, but his affair with the other woman did not stop. At that point, she understood that she could stand it no longer. All trust in their relationship was irreparably damaged, and that feeling of being loved and desirable, of being indispensable for him, was shaken to the very core. If he lied in that way, always and despite everything, if she could no longer hide the truth from herself, she felt as though she was returning to the difficult life of her younger years, forced to get by alone, without help from anyone.

Analysis helped her to leave him, to understand that she felt stronger and more secure alone. Emma 1 had a good capacity for mending and a good defence system. She suffered, especially for her daughter, but could not accept such blatant polygamy, especially accompanied as it was by never-ending denials. Her husband—eternal spoilt adolescent— had to put up with the situation. He tried to get back with her in various ways, but all to no avail. Every time he slipped back into his old ways and repeated behaviour of shameless deception.

Emma 1 chose to go right rather than left or, simply, during analysis, had she come to understand the real nature of what she was up against regardless of her own deepest needs and her needs for illusion? I believe this to be true and that her decision to leave her husband was an obligatory path, rather than a true choice, taken in order to protect herself and her daughter from a situation that had become unbearable once it had become explicit. The analyst had accompanied her along this path without any preconceived ideas about leaving or continuing this union. In this way, for both of them, the repeated discoveries of her husband's continual and almost infantile lies were shown up to be humiliating and in the end completely unacceptable. However, as Shakespeare says, this did not stop the sun from shining in the sky. The patient was able to meet other men and accept their courtship, discovering that she could also be an attractive woman in other people's eyes, and not only in those of her ex-husband.

Emma 2

Emma 2 arrived asking for help in the same week as Emma 1, and for a problem that, at first listening, appeared absolutely identical. She was even more or less the same age, as was her son. I got ready to listen, with all the "negative capability" I had at my disposition. Very soon, though, it was clear that Emma 2's story, while similar in its material and factual substance, played out in a profoundly different way in her internal psychic reality.

Emma 2 is very beautiful and sophisticated, financially much better off than Emma 1, and has a closer relationship with her family of origin. On paper, it looks as though her contractual power is stronger and more stable, but in actual fact it turned out not to be so in the real world. Emma 2 also lost her father when she was twenty and then found herself, together with her mother and twin sister, running the family business. Despite being a flourishing concern providing economic well-being during their infancy, the firm slipped into an inexorable decline at her father's death. The word "inexorable" would in fact characterise the whole of Emma 2's analysis.

The presence of a twin sister in this patient's life greatly reassures me, compared to the apprehension that I immediately felt, quite unlike my meeting with Emma 1.

Emma 2 has not lived in straitened circumstances but in constant battles with creditors and suppliers, and with a mother worn out by the whole situation, who tends to ask her daughters for both material and moral help. For Emma, too, it was vital for her to leave home and escape this claustrophobic family situation and she soon succeeded in building up a rewarding and interesting work life. She got married young to an affectionate kind man and everything seemed to be going well.

But, as we have already seen on many occasions, the external material situation does not necessarily correspond to the internal psychic reality, especially when passion is at play.

Emma 2 unexpectedly falls in love with another man and, despite all her senses telling her not to get involved, that her husband is much better, and that the new family that has welcomed her in has a lot to offer in the way of repairing her unhappy adolescence, she leaves her husband and gets together with this new man. They get married and have a baby, but Emma does not find the peace and serenity that she had enjoyed with her previous husband. Instead, she comes up against something entirely new.

Apparently, this man relentlessly undermines her self-confidence and self-esteem. Slowly, he convinces her that she is inadequate, distracted, incapable. He even belittles her physical appearance, saying she is now dowdy and quite different from the woman he had married.

The patient who comes to me is a woman devastated by suffering, by having put herself with her own hands in exactly the same situation she had fled from when young. She no longer works because the child is too small, and she depends economically on her husband, who is forever criticising her, also because she does not know how she could maintain herself alone and, the last straw, she suspects he is being unfaithful. Again for Emma 2 it was the details, the inconsistencies, his unexplainable absences that aroused her suspicions. Emma tackled her husband and he, too, denied everything, sustaining that it was just a figment of her imagination, and thus further undermining her self-esteem. Emma stoops to tailing him and catches him red-handed, but once again her husband defends himself, making her feel like some sort of visionary who aspires to invent reality. Emma increasingly comes across as a pre-ordained victim.

Her husband appears to be a pervert; he enjoys creating problems for her. Emma 2 is desperate. She knows she is right, but feels she is at the mercy of this man. Her sister and mother can offer no help, and on this occasion we discover in analysis that Emma's father had, in his turn, been a serial adulterer and that her mother had borne it all, for her children's sake and for her economic dependence.

Unlike Emma 1, Emma 2's husband does not lie because he is immature but because he is sadistic. He replaces an absurd and unacceptable reality with the truth of a desire "that disguises itself" as the "the desire to know" (Aulagnier, 1967) according to the pervert's ability to "invent reality" through denial and splitting. Indeed, I suspect that he is a serious pervert, also thanks to other details that Emma told me, and that he found in her the perfect victim.

Denial and defiance are the basic strategies of the perverse universe. The desire for knowing coupled with transgressing dominates this world, but it is a world in which acting out and action perpetually replace the elaboration of thought. The pervert believes he is free, but in actual fact he is subject to the most rigid rule, in which the imperative "Cum, baby, cum!" allows no leeway. The pervert sees the other as a body, an object from which to extract pleasure, and is ravaged by the urgency of possessing it. The pervert's psychic scenario is dominated by extreme symbolism, and by a similarly extreme erotic poverty. External reality is incessantly defied and denied.

Emma's feelings stem from denying the reality imposed on her senses, and lead her into the world of the absurd, where illusion and disappointment oscillate without end in the imprisoned mind of this woman.

Overall, Emma 2 is perpetually frustrated in her attempt to grasp her husband's real dimension, his affective or sensual side, always coming up against his wilful decision not to reveal anything real, while continually showing his wife the nullity of his existence. In this way, Emma is placed in the condition of being deprived of her capacity for autonomous vision, immobilised and controlled. The core of the perverse structure, which lies in a deep-seated defensive construction in which the other, the object, must be constantly controlled, is thus perfectly rendered. In preventing any representation of the other's image and her view of it, Emma 2, however, protects herself from the anxiety of castration, from fusional phantasies with her mother, and from every possible imitative game of identification.

This story finishes less well. I do not manage to successfully help Emma 2. She does not leave her husband, but accepts to go and live near her mother and sister, alone, far from her husband. It is a defeat, not a victory. It is a return to the original place of the trauma, from which she has not succeeded in detaching herself.

Here, too, it was not a choice, nor an act of reparation, but a profound and articulated repetition compulsion that has slowly closed the multiple ways out that this woman had initially managed to create for herself. I remained impotent, in this numb part of the patient's emotional reality; frozen in her immobility, she removes herself from every further possible line of enquiry or request for help.

Comment

However strange it might seem, and however much literature and film are full of stories of unfaithfulness and suffering, and however much we can say "After all, infidelity has existed since the dawn of time, ever since Eve ate the apple, ever since love exists!"—well then, despite all this and much more, there are no explicit studies in the psychoanalytic literature on a topic that is by no means secondary. This stems from the fact that, when all is said and done, men and women are monogamous, and love can end and a new love begin. And in the interval there may be superimpositions, betrayals, contrasting passions, but, in the end, for everyone, the fact remains that you cannot be in love with two or more people at the same time; in other words, you love only one person at a time.

In countries and religions where polygamy exists, more women get married (never more men), simply because a young woman, on whom the husband's attentions are then concentrated, is added to his circle of previous older wives. People who are with two women or two men at the same time do exist, of course, and we see them in analysis, but these are generally distressing and painful situations, or tied up with old bonds that have not been successfully broken, or new lives that cannot successfully be embarked on. And so it is no surprise that often the suffering caused by this impossibility to resolve the powerful archaic conflicts that generate these situations is the reason for asking for help and coming into analysis.

And yet, why—we can and should ask ourselves—is the human species monogamous? One says "for ever", and believes it, but it is a forever that is such only in the instant of the present moment, when one is gripped by the ecstasy of passion and wants it never to finish. Wagner places Tannhäuser in the gardens of the goddess Venus, where he can enjoy all the worldly pleasures, but after several years Tannhäuser is restless, hears the sound of the horns of his old comrades-in-arms, and the call to war boils in his veins. His "for ever" does not last forever.

And yet, to return to our initial question, even Tannhäuser, in the Venusberg, when he was with the goddess of love, loved only her. Odysseus, too, alongside Calypso, loves only the sweet nymph who offers her loved one nectar and ambrosia, sustenance of the gods. The fact that a love story ends, that the erotic, libidinal, passionate, and affectionate investment in the love object wanes, and that other passions take the upper hand—either for another love object or, as in the case of Tannhäuser, for the call to arms of his comrades' horns, and Odysseus, for Zeus's recalling him to the duty of taking up his journey once more—does not alter the fact that in that moment the investment is focused exclusively on that object.

Odysseus should have spent eternity with Calypso, on that marvellous timeless island, in a state of everlasting happiness, similar to Tannhäuser in the Venusberg, the Mount of Venus. It is interesting to note that both heroes spend seven years in these respective places. And yet after seven years, their eternal love ends, and the heroes' interests shift elsewhere.

Now the question about the exclusive nature of the investment is fundamental. Odysseus forgets Penelope, and Tannhäuser forgets Elisabeth, and for seven years both of them love another woman. In the daily life of ordinary people, and not just heroes, we also witness similar phenomena, of "sabbatical leave" taken away from the conjugal bond, to which one returns or which, instead, breaks, depending on the individuals and on the partners of the individuals concerned.

Freud, and other analysts after him, as we have seen in Chapter Two, have pondered "why we fall in love", or rather, why does the human being feel the irrepressible need to invest in an object outside the self?

However, what I am concerned with in this chapter is slightly different: in other words, why does the loving investment—apart from in serious pathologies, which we have also discussed in this book—focus on one object at a time? And yet, as far as other sorts of investment go, their plural nature at one and the same time is widespread: for example, parents can love several children; you can have numerous friends; you can play a number of different sports with equal passion; you can love the most varied works of art and types of art.

And so why does the love object, in the large majority of cases, have to be exclusive? Why has free love produced and produces huge amounts of suffering and distress, since at least one of the two partners is unable to accept the presence of the other? Why does the monogamous couple continue to be the accepted model of the love relationship, even if, as we have seen, it is not eternal? And it has been so down the centuries, and in different cultures and history, and in art.

What can psychoanalysis offer in terms of reflection about such persistence, about such an unvarying model? What can we say that is specifically psychoanalytic, and not sociological, or anthropological, or biological?

I believe that a plausible explanation can be traced back to the archaic, pre-oedipal event that, as we have seen, underlies every future adult love investment. We have seen how the need to love, and to be loved, can be considered the prototype of every human need, and of every relationship between human beings. The fusionality and dependence of the mother–child couple form a primitive matrix of the loving experience that is then lost as a conscious memory in early infancy and re-experienced in adolescence and in adulthood.

In this early matrix, which persists as a mnestic trace and an unchanging model, possession of the love object is fundamental. It is a cannibalistic merging, with a strong oral base, that is well expressed by the words that lovers often use: "I'm going to eat you with kisses/I want to eat you all up", and so on and so on.

The love object is desired with painful yearning, an overwhelming impulse for absolute possession, which excludes every other possession. To fuse with such an object, to incorporate it within oneself, to become one with it, are all emotional, passionate, and powerful issues that call into play the irrepressible nature of the exclusiveness of the investment. Desire for the other is so powerful, to the extent of engendering suffering for failing to possess, and, by definition, excludes any other desire for any other object. It is the return to the maternal breast as the infant's only possible means of satisfaction; it is the imitation that Eugenio Gaddini describes as the first form of knowing the other:

> From now on, the biological model "imitating in order to perceive" changes into the parallel psychic model, in which to perceive becomes "to be". "Imitating in order to be." Or rather, perceiving is still, as before, "being", but whereas this occurred previously on a prevailingly physical level, it now does so on one which tends towards the psychic.
>
> (Gaddini, 1969, p. 476)

* * *

> Concerning the psychic protomodel of imitation—"imitating in order to be"—it may be helpful to repeat that it installs itself not in the presence of the object but in its absence, and that precisely because of this, its aim seems to be that of re-establishing in a magical and omnipotent way the fusion of the self with the object.
>
> (Gaddini, 1969, p. 477)

* * *

> Imitation seems to be an essential element of the structure of identification, as is introjection, but it expresses a basic disposition towards the object, which should be distinguished from that of introjection. To imitate not only does not mean to introject, but may be a way of defending oneself from the anxiety provoked by introjective conflicts, even if this defence may in turn cause more serious pathological pictures. In the process of identification imitations and introjections are fused and integrated in the service of the aims of adaptation and of the reality principle.
>
> (Gaddini, 1969, p. 483)

Thus imitation has a homeostatic function because, if being the object means "simply being", this involves at the same time a strenuous defence against the threat of the object's otherness. It is the need to make one's own the otherness of the other that is experienced as a threat to desire.

How long this exclusiveness and absoluteness of the incorporated loved one persists is a question of imprinting, social adaptation, moral beliefs, sexual orientations, and environmental changes. It goes from Shakespeare's "But out! Alack! He was but one hour mine" to Penelope's twenty-year fidelity as sung by Homer in *The Odyssey*: "Your bed shall be ready the moment you wish, now that the gods have brought you back to your own country and your lovely home" (23, vv. 254–258).

Is fidelity a choice? Is infidelity a choice? It is difficult to say. As I have said before, I do not believe one is free to make choices in the affective realm. The world of the passions is set in motion or is extinguished thanks to numerous variants, as I have attempted to illustrate above. When we fall in love, we feel as though we are "in the throes of passion" and therefore subject to it, chained to it. If we do not fall in love, we feel repressed, stifled by a thousand internal and external bonds. It is difficult to talk of choice, and difficult to make choices. "I couldn't do anything else", we often hear our patients repeat. "It is not my fault", says Vicomte de Valmont in *Dangerous Liaisons* (by Pierre-Ambroise-François Choderlos de Laclos, 1782). The Vicomte is obliged to write a letter to his one true love, whom he is forced to abandon, and can only proclaim: "*That is the way of the world*. It is not my fault" (Letter 141, p. 346; author's italics). The novel claims to reflect the customs of the French nobility and upper middle classes on the eve of the French Revolution; in actual fact, it is a powerful analysis of savage passions within a very intense game, whose stakes, even if not all the characters realise this, are life itself.

CHAPTER TEN

Incapacity to love

Beauty (B93)

I
Like the sweet apple which reddens upon the topmost bough,
A-top on the topmost twig,—which the pluckers forgot,
somehow,—
Forgot it not, nay, but got it not, for none could get it till now.
—Sappho, "Fragment 105a" (seventh century BC, translated by
Dante Gabriel Rossetti)

As we have said in the Introduction, this chapter merits a book to itself. In fact, it is quite common for us to have patients who lament what Balint calls a "basic fault". These patients "can't love, but they expect to be loved". The demand that such a need is gratified is always decidedly problematic, and is often manifested violently and with a huge dissipation of energy, as though it were a question of life or death. They often come into analysis hoping that the relationship with the analyst may fill this gap and that the analyst, through analysis, can offer the love that they have failed to receive. However, the analysis is consequently lived as something that can guarantee an object that loves you, and

129

unconditionally so, like the primitive, fusional object that has been lost forever, rather than as the process by which you may be able to find the object that is waiting for you to love, worthy of receiving your love and withstanding the contempt that accompanies your weakness. These people in fact construct a theorem that is impossible to resolve: if he/she loves me, they think, there is something wrong with him/her. The object of the love investment is idealised as per childhood idealisations and so can never stand up to the disillusions of reality. As Kohut says:

> Man's capacity to acknowledge the finiteness of his existence, and to act in accordance with this painful discovery, may well be his greatest psychological achievement, despite the fact that it can often be demonstrated that a manifest acceptance of transience may go hand in hand with covert denials.
>
> (Kohut, 1966, p. 264)

And, further on:

> The acceptance of transience is accomplished by the ego, which performs the emotional work that precedes, accompanies, and follows separations. Without these efforts a valid conception of time, of limits, and of the impermanence of object cathexes could not be achieved. The ultimate act of cognition, i.e., the acknowledgment of the limits and of the finiteness of the self, is not the result of an isolated intellectual process but is the victorious outcome of the lifework of the total personality in acquiring broadly based knowledge and in transforming archaic modes of narcissism into ideals, humor, and a sense of supraindividual participation in the world.
>
> (Kohut, 1966, p. 268)

Although Kohut never explicitly discussed love, like Kernberg or Freud did, his works are nevertheless an excellent point of reference for observing the idealising events in love relationships. Kohut's work sheds light on the processes of the self's growth and evolution through the relationships of the self with the self-objects, throughout life. The self-objects are objects that are experienced as part of the self:

> The small child, for example, invests other people with narcissistic cathexes and thus experiences them narcissistically, i.e., as

self-objects. The expected control over such (self-object) others is then closer to the concept of the control which a grown up expects to have over his own body and mind than to the concept of the control which he expects to have over others.

(Kohut, 1971, pp. 26–27)

Kohut describes two types of self-object: an idealised parental imago and a grandiose mirror self. An idealised parental imago allows the child to experience a sense of fusion with the idealised parental object, calm and grandiose in its omnipotence. In the initial stages of romantic passion, this type of idealisation can be re-experienced, in the sense of the unique and unrepeatable fusional union that is described in such terms by the lover. At the same time, a grandiose mirror self can confirm the child's need to be strong and perfect. Reciprocal mirroring is not uncommon in the first stages of a love story, but in its turn places the relationship at the risk of suddenly breaking up if an intolerable discrepancy is perceived between the idealisation and the perception transformed by reality.

Now I do not want to excessively trivialise and maintain that each one of us is compelled to exist between two ways of functioning, or rather between childish idealising and adult reality, but, on a deeper level, would like to say that when in the presence of excessive differences between the idealisation and the perception of reality, then the intense frustration and resulting anger may risk completely destroying the love relationship with the other.

There is also another type of person who is incapable of loving. These are individuals who have suffered such extreme levels of deprivation in infancy that they cannot, as adults, let themselves trust in broaching a love investment that is inevitably destined, as their early experience taught them, to disappoint and to abandon them. For example, the difficulty that the so-called *hijos de rua*, or street children, experience in attachment is common knowledge, as, too, in some types of adopted children, who are capable of kindness, sympathy, and commitment towards the other but only on a superficial level, so that they never find themselves in the original situation of abandonment and desolation experienced in childhood.

Finally—and this is the situation most frequently observed in analysis—an incapacity to love can concern people (ordinary people) who have experienced an irremediably conflictual parental couple (two parents quite unsuited to each other), and who have therefore endured the incessant tension and conflicts that this parental relationship heaped onto the children.

These individuals dread a repetition of this conjugal unhappiness, the cold desperation that marked the life of their parents in their non-stop belligerent closeness, and in their request—at times explicit, at times implicit—for the children to take sides. These people fall in love, they feel libidinal impulses, but they cannot trust. Narcissistically, they fear that this love may hold more disadvantages than advantages; it may turn out to be more damaging than expected and plunge them back into the fear and suffering of their childhood. In this case, if finding an object is always a rediscovery of it, then we see that there is no desire to rediscover the traumatic object of their infancy.

There are, of course, also situations in which we assist relentlessly at a reconfirmation of the traumatic childhood experience. The repeated failures in love that these people bewail confirm the gravity of the original trauma and, at the same time, include an obvious feeling of relief for having managed to escape, yet once more, the snares of an unhappy union. What brings them to analysis is solitude, fear of the loneliness awaiting them, and the suffering due to missing out on being parents dictated by their obligatory choices.

Ordinary people: Antonella

At the start of analysis, Antonella does not narrate much about herself, nor let slip any clue for suspecting a particularly difficult or taxing story. Initially, Antonella presents herself as a simple young woman, slightly depressed, disheartened by an uninteresting job, with a limited number of friends.

Her father died two years ago, an authoritarian figure who was aggressive towards his wife and children. However, he is presented for a long time as strict but just, severe and harsh, but fundamentally good and loved by all the family. Her mother, instead, is presented immediately as weak, querulous, and complaining, often ill, incapable of reacting to her husband's frequent outbursts and verbal and physical aggression. Antonella is the rebel daughter who attracts most of her father's ire, especially in requests for greater freedom. As an extreme concession, she is allowed to go and study at university in a large city.

For the first six months, the analysis seems to unfold along paths apparently in keeping with our first encounters. Antonella seems interested in how the analysis works, and extremely grateful for the listening that her solitude and depressions are finally receiving.

However, I slowly become aware that I most oddly and unexplainably doze off during her sessions. The sessions are at different times, and so I find it difficult to explain why. I end up dreading these hours with Antonella, because I literally fall asleep, a sort of increasingly unexplainable blackout.

Meanwhile, through my dulled torpor, bizarre new elements of her story slip out. Antonella describes her maternal grandmother, an almost mythological figure, a living representation of persecutory ghosts, who tells her stories of local superstitions, of wreaths of flowers laid on the windowsill to placate the harpies, of legends and spells.

On several occasions, she says "she's ugly, she's ugly", this time alluding to her paternal grandmother, who seems to embody the image of a witch. I find it difficult to disentangle the old mountain legends from her current terrors, and I suspect a very well-hidden and well-organised delusional nucleus.

Little by little, Antonella manages to describe the phenomena of physical depersonalisation, of coenaesthetic misperceptions that assail her every time she lies down on the couch. She feels as though she is hovering in the air, or is glued to the couch, or turned to stone and unable to move; she, too, is frightened. I receive these communications with great difficulty because in the meanwhile my torpid state worsens. One day, I suddenly wake up, totally lucid. I think I dreamt that the lid was being taken off a coffin and that I was free to get out. In that very moment, I hear Antonella say: "I feel as though they have taken the lid off a coffin, I feel freer now." The nightmare had ended for both of us, and I would not experience those phenomena again, proper evil spells woven by witches.

Months later, the story was better clarified. During a session, Antonella dreams that she has a doll in her lap. To her great dismay, the doll begins to move; it drags itself about the room, and then begins to lose bits, and Antonella, with increasing horror, has to follow it around and pick up the pieces, realising that the doll is both alive but inanimate at the same time. Nothing comes to her mind, but something occurs to me. I ask her, very carefully, if by any chance she had ever had an abortion. Terrified, she confesses that as soon as she had got to the big city she had had a story with a boy, of no sentimental importance, but she had got pregnant. She had been obliged to have an abortion, without saying anything to her family, who were highly sex phobic. She had never dared confide in anyone, not even her girlfriends, and had thought of that incident of twenty years ago every day with shame and great sorrow: "Not a day passes that I don't think about it."

So I say to her then that it seems to me as though she had killed and buried a part of herself with that abortion, and that perhaps is why she has been feeling for such a long time now as though she was shut up inside a coffin. She agrees and adds that since that moment she has always felt "no longer vital" and that she has not had a relationship with a man since. She goes on to say that in these months she has had the impression, though, that she was no longer alone, and explains: "If I was in a coffin, you were also there with me." I confirm that I had also had the impression of a very suffocating period.

With regards to the unthought known, Bollas (1987) emphasises the importance of the mental process of recall, encouraging information to start emerging from the deepest parts of the self. Ogden also describes these countertransference sensations, referring them to what he calls "the autistic-contiguous mode of generating experience" (Ogden, 1989, p. 30).

> More specific to the autistic-contiguous mode of experience is countertransference experience in which bodily sensations dominate. Somatic experiences like twitching of one's hand and arm, stomach pain, feelings of bloatedness and so on are not uncommon. Very frequently the countertransference experience is associated with skin sensations such as feelings of warmth and coldness as well as tingling, numbness, and an exaggerated sensitivity to skin impressions.
>
> (Ogden, 1989, p. 44)

In the meeting between patient and analyst, this psycho-sensorial base, asserted in the countertransference when in the presence of unrepresentable traumatic areas, is activated.

At this point, I would like to make a brief comment on the memory/ trauma relationship. In Antonella's associations in the dream of the doll, all memories of early traumatic experiences were absent and only the experience of the abortion was represented. This event had taken shape inside the patient as a highly traumatic and persecutory experience, a repetition, in my opinion, of preceding early traumatic experiences that could no longer be evoked. She had not spoken about it with anyone for twenty years. A girlfriend she had lived with at that far-off time had soon become a permanent persecutory object in her nightmares. The abortion resulting from a casual, unplanned sexual affair had in fact confirmed her worst sex-phobic fears and her persecutory suspicions about relationships with others.

Antonella's dream does not in fact refer only to the abortion. She most effectively represents her perception of a growing and dramatic fragmentation of the self, accompanied by a transformation into an inanimate object. We are in the middle of what Gaddini defines as:

> non-integration, the first functional organization of the self, a fragmentary one, with which the infantile self finds itself at the moment of separation ... It may be useful ... to distinguish ... two contrasting and coexistent aspects of pathological anxiety of loss of the self, namely anxiety of non-integration and anxiety of integration. Obviously, it is the latter which represents the true pathological aspect; it is stronger than anxiety of non-integration, it prevents the natural developmental process, and contributes in an essential way to maintaining the non-integrative state as an extreme defence.
>
> (Gaddini, 1982, p. 381)

* * *

> The latter appear to be originally an expression of the fragmentary non-integrated early organization of the self, and to be related to the fear that this organization might go to pieces and get lost in space. This "anxiety of non-integration", as I call it, is one of two main aspects which anxiety of loss of the self gives places to, the other one being "anxiety of integration", which is instead related to the fear that whatever change in the non-integrated organization would lead to a final catastrophe. This anxiety may strongly oppose integration and the psychoanalytic process. Clinically, it may be important to distinguish non-integration from splitting.
>
> (Gaddini, 1982, p. 386)

* * *

> Patients often experience the anxiety of the loss of self in the form of
> a fear of physically going to pieces and getting lost in space. Frag-
> ments of the non-integrated self are related, most probably, to the
> experiences of bodily functioning by the primitive mind.
>
> (Gaddini, 1982, p. 381)

Analysis becomes the tool through which the never-born or aborted
parts of the self can be recovered, which would otherwise risk taking
on a life of their own as inanimate and perilously persecutory objects.

The experience that Antonella lives is absolutely terrifying. It can be
communicated only by means of contagion (projective identification)
that cannot possess any signifying or communicable ideational representations. In the analysis, the agony of the aborting experience reflects
her anxiety that the analytic experience might also suffer an abortive
failure. If the analyst continues to sleep, she can never modify the
patient's barrier of unreality and lack of signification.

The deep work of analysis with these patients must be carried out
with special attention to the microphenomena, to the microfractures in
the space and time of the setting during the session. As an example of
microprocesses, I would like to recount two fragments from sessions that
I believe are interesting since they clearly show the traumatic experience being recalled and its subsequent transformation.

Antonella begins the session particularly nervous and tense. It seems
as though she is falling into one of her introspective states, where she
is absent and withdrawn from her surroundings. She does not talk and
remains indifferent to my attempts to stimulate her. Slowly I, too, fall
silent without, though, losing my vigilance, and it strikes me that that
evening it is particularly noisy outside.

My counselling room is in a private street, where silence generally
reigns, but that evening, instead, people were arguing in the road,
babies were crying, and children were making quite a racket. Then
my entry phone started to buzz at regular intervals, but no one ever
replied. Antonella became more and more bothered and upset, almost
panic-stricken. At the end of the session, which she had spent in almost
total silence, having uttered only—"I don't really know what to say, I'm
not feeling very well"—she abruptly got up and left, clearly angry.

At the next session, Antonella seems much more relaxed and talks of
various episodes, but I know that I cannot let the atmosphere of the previous session go unnoticed. So I say to her that yesterday she seemed
very upset by outside noises.

Antonella seems surprised by my referring to it, but also relieved: "Yes, they really got on my nerves; it felt as though they were preventing me from concentrating on myself. Sometimes it happens that I am particularly disturbed by the outside." I ask her if it happened in the past too, and if she remembers anything in particular.

Antonella has no doubts: "Well, it's obvious, my father. He was always shouting, there was never a moment's peace when he was at home, and I was frightened of him, literally, because his outbursts were so violent and unexplainable. Anything could make him mad. I can't bear situations that are noisy. He showed absolutely no respect for me, for the fact that I was studying or doing something else. On Sundays, he decided to go to church, and it was all just one long shouting and screaming if we were even a tiny bit late. And if I wanted to go out alone, there was more shouting, because he didn't agree. I could never do anything."

Analyst: "It seems that the most traumatic element is the lack of respect, the constant humiliation. Perhaps here yesterday you also felt the noises from the street and the entry phone as an invasion of your space and time, exactly like the intrusions of your father."

Antonella: "It's something that happens to me always, not only here. I've always got the feeling that other people don't respect me, they don't consider me. Sometimes I think I'm exaggerating, that it's not possible that everyone's got it in for me, but then I have to accept the fact that it's really like that."

Analyst: "I think that yesterday you felt invaded in a particularly difficult moment when you needed a bit of introspection. And it seemed to you as though the same abuse and lack of respect that you felt at home was being repeated here in analysis."

At a level of transference repetition, Antonella relives her father's noisy invasiveness in the episode of the noisy counselling room and the insistence of the buzzing entry phone, and in that situation the analyst becomes the persecutory paternal figure. This experience would never, though, have been recalled, and certainly not remembered, if it had not been, all of a sudden, a disturbing external intrusion also for the analyst.

I would like to say that through the patient's projective identification, and the analyst's empathic sharing, a minute episode—a small microtrauma in the session—was able to be taken up in the analysis and connected to a precise sensorial mnestic trace. As I said at the beginning, the opportunity for differentiating the transferential and countertransferential elements of the present of the analytic situation from the experiences of the past can arise only after a different relational model has been produced, characterised by attention, understanding, and, above all, respect for the other.

This episode triggered a journey that included the activation of primitive somatic defensive barriers against relentless family invasion. Even the mother revealed a relational model of intrusion and lack of attention, based on different reasons from those of the father.

In the next session, Antonella says: "I had a dream yesterday. I was here in the session on the couch, but crossways, and I was asking myself: 'I wonder if the analyst realises there's something wrong in my position, that I'm all crooked.' Then the entry phone buzzed and you went to answer it and it seemed to me as though you were trying to prevent another person from coming in. I got up too, to help you, and I saw a shadow on the stairs, which seemed very threatening. You were trying to protect me and prevent it from entering." She then adds that she is feeling better, and also more trusting, and more courageous about the future, compared to recent days.

I comment that the dream seems to be a representation of what happened in the preceding session: "You felt the noises as a threatening intrusion of your time and space, and were afraid that they would insinuate themselves into the analyst's mind, distracting me and preventing me from thinking about you. Especially the entry phone, which you probably interpreted as another patient who was trying to occupy your time and your space." (The incessant buzzing of the entry phone was in fact the next patient—his first visit—who had arrived half an hour early, feeling very anxious, and could not manage to speak on the intercom.) The analyst was experienced as your father, who disturbed you with an utter lack of concern for privacy. In the next session, this experience was then recovered.

This had allowed Antonella to give a visual representation to the confused and nameless terrors that had so often crowded her phantasies and produced dramatic sensory experiences of fragmentation and depersonalisation. The man at the door (the next patient?) appeared as an explicit threat, seen and shared by the analyst even if perceived only as a shadow by the patient. The implicit sexual significance of the experience of terror was recognised by Antonella, also thanks to a long work carried out together previously about the difficulties of having sexual relations after the traumatic experience of a violent and abusive father.

Another image was interesting in the dream, the first. Antonella sees herself lying crookedly on the couch, across it, and wonders whether the analyst has realised how out of place she is. In this case, too, I think that the perception that something profoundly anomalous in her position was also activated; in other words, in the dream it becomes a represented and communicated reality, a sensation up until then expressed only as a somatic misperception. In fact, very often in the sessions, Antonella seemed to fall into almost hypnotic states of trance in which she complained she could no longer feel her arms or legs. She had had some episodes of hysterical paralysis in the past, for which she had gone to hospital, following particularly humiliating and depressing incidents.

Comment

Antonella came to analysis with an ordinary state of unhappiness, which she had not felt necessary up to that point to acknowledge as an element worthy of asking for help and change. She showed much faith in the transforming possibilities of an analysis and posed the main objective as that of finding a new work direction more suitable to her social and creative aspirations. However, these elements represented only one aspect of Antonella's personality, pathology, and suffering.

In the idyllic scenario of an upper-middle-class suburban family portrayed in the film *Ordinary People*, a dramatic reality soon emerges within the family, encapsulated aseptically in the treatment of a psychiatrist, who has to keep the persecutory demons of the past at bay.

Antonella's problem also soon appeared to be out of the ordinary, saturated with agony and suffering that was quite unimaginable to the analyst and also, on a conscious level, to the patient.

The idyllic representation of life in the small village of origin was disrupted by the progressive revelations of tragedy accumulated over the years and the generations.

The experience of solitude, of being abandoned, and constantly neglected emotionally and physically, the repeated paternal violence and verbal domineering, protracted exposition to her mother's periodic depression, the never-ending distortions of the primary objects' emotional and cognitive capacities, all this made up the weft and weave of Antonella's childhood and then expanded into mistrust, persecutory phantasies, and anxiety about the non-integration of her present life.

In this phase of Antonella's analysis, great patience was necessary not only to reconstruct the traumatic events but above all to transform in the transference the emotional quality of the welcome and listening given to both the early and later traumatic experiences that had occurred in her life. Only through acknowledging the unpleasant sensations, only through the possibility of empathetically sharing them—where possible—can you reach the deep level of the traumatic experience and highlight the different quality of the current experience. I would never have been able to truly understand the profound level of desolation and suffocation that Antonella felt in her intimate relationship with an absent object (the depressed and/or busy-elsewhere mother), if I had not in my turn experienced for such a long time that sense of torpor and sluggishness of the senses that had made me feel a victim of an evil spell. As a child, Antonella, too, had often felt herself to be the victim of witchcraft, the prisoner of overwhelming forces of evil. To be able to share them with the analyst in the present had given her access to a visual and communicable representation of absolutely terrifying disembodied demons.

The subsequent path of signifying and mentalising (understood as working through sensory and bodily experiences into precise mental representations) all the frequent episodes of depersonalisation and coenaesthetic sensations meant they could then disappear from the analysis and from the outside world. Their transformation into verbal communications, complete memories of personal and other family experiences, and meaningful dream representations (first only fixed constant persecutory figures were present in her dreams, with no history or meaning) meant, in short, access to a finally normal analytic path for herself and the analyst.

I cannot say that this analysis had a happy ending with Snow White holding her prince by the hand and walking off into the rising sun. But the successful conclusion of the analysis endowed the patient with greater internal equilibrium, a better management of her family and work relationships, and relationships in general. The persecutory aspects disappeared, and she was able to build relationships of trust and affection with many people, among whom also the analyst, who was no longer an object of anger for what had been missing in her childhood. But the sinister, frightening family atmosphere, traversed by flashes of incomprehensible aggression and suffering lived in total solitude, was too strong. The affective isolation and the difficulty of creating a relationship of trust and serenity with a partner have remained. Antonella is now a more solid and secure person, more capable of giving meaning to the everyday events and an aim to her life, but she is still a person alone, as she herself says.

Ordinary people: Andrea

For a long time, Andrea has been unhappy, irritable, and confused. He complains of a chronic migraine, which comes on especially at week-ends, and is disconsolately aware that he is becoming increasingly iso-lated as his affective and relational spheres shrink. Andrea defines his family as "a healthy, solid Catholic family". In actual fact, the family is dominated by the taciturn and dictatorial personality of the father, who has subjected his children to his domineering rule.

The only one who dared rebel was his sister, married to a man against her parents' will so that no one from the family went to her wedding. Vera paid a high price for her rebellion. She soon fell victim to a serious form of depression, with claustrophobia and panic attacks, that then led to a horrible death during Andrea's analysis.

Andrea is a very pleasant, affable man, capable of profound dis-cussion, an upholder of the values of solidarity and commitment, as well as a passionate lover of mountains. He made a curious request during our first meetings that perplexed me for a long time because I could not decipher it. He says that at this point in his life he needs an accomplice. This request shook me; it did not seem to be a request for change. I perceived its furtive and clandestine nature, and made a men-tal note of it as one of the characteristics of Andrea's personality that I thought would change. I still had no idea that at the end it would be I who would change, and accept real complicity with him, thus allow-ing Andrea to proceed towards his own autonomous path, even if it was initially clandestine.

The question I have often asked myself queried what this complicity actually involved. The answer I can give now is that it had to do with an attitude that I defined in the Introduction as the capacity to bear the "negative capability" for talking about the mysterious event of "when man is capable of being in uncertainties, Mysteries, doubts, without any irritable reaching after fact & reason" (Keats, 1817, p. 156). It is the capacity to tolerate "ignorance", mystery, doubt, and uncertainty, the "negative capability" that Bion has so rightly called our attention to, the capacity of the mind that depends on the ability of unconscious negative capability:

the capacity to bear negativity and withstand its persuasions to abandon a task, the ability to tolerate the pain and confusion of not knowing, rather than imposing ready-made or omnipotent certainties upon an ambiguous situation or emotional challenge.

(Bion, 1970, p. 125)

I was an accomplice in a dictatorial family context, fully aware of the impossibility of removing myself from this state but equally aware that a person could not be left alone in those conditions. An accomplice, a secret friend who knew and understood and was capable of being supportive and sympathetic to the difficulties and impossibility of realising one's own deepest desires.

The first years of Andrea's analysis were characterised by very long dreams, whose recounting often took up the whole session. In a certain sense, on a metaphorical level, one could say that the analysis had activated in him the possibility for having dreams and desires that could be shared, despite their contents being of profound defeat. At times, it was a repetition of the same dream, portraying a very complex and difficult arrival at a clearing, or in some empty space, near a river, or alongside a lake, and discovering that the caravan, or the camp, or the group that one was hoping to join had already left. These dreams were saturated with sadness and disappointment: "I arrived too late" was the dominant theme. They were the oneiric translation of a pitiful and invalidating life; a permanent oedipal defeat.

The father relentlessly persecuted his children, accusing them of lacking all initiative and discipline, and comparing his achievements with theirs. Andrea felt constantly attacked and never acknowledged by his father, or by any of the figures in authority he came across in his working environment. He is desperately alone: after an initial promise of happiness, everything he comes into contact with—work, affections—transforms into another prison, another duty to carry out.

Apparently, Andrea is the most successful sibling of the family: the only one to have got a degree, he quickly found an interesting and well-paid job. When young, he attended many basic Catholic communities, seeking an impossible ideal of life. Every time, he left these communities because he found it impossible to satisfy his ill-defined needs; in actual fact, he was unable to tolerate the celibacy imposed by such choices.

We often used one episode from his childhood to describe his affective relationships. When he was small, Andrea used to play with toy soldiers, but the game was all to do with putting them back into their box in the correct order, they never came out to be played with. His relationships with women seemed to follow a similar pattern: with great determination, he patiently paved the way for a meeting, but then promptly withdrew as soon as he was about to reach his goal (conquest of the chosen woman). Each time, there seemed to be valid reasons for not pursuing the matter.

Andrea suffers from an extreme form of "amorous anorexia", as we called it together in analysis. He can only assume the most minute doses of affection and investment from others, and can bear only infrequent and carefully gauged contacts. As soon as a woman interested in him appears on the horizon, Andrea pulls back, incapable of enduring such a libidinal indigestion. He cannot let himself love. Every pleasure is toxic because it makes him grow/fatten emotionally.

He often dreams he is with a woman but the telephone immediately starts to ring, or a doorbell, or the alarm clock, interrupting every possible encounter. The dreams at the start of analysis, of fantastic expeditions into the jungle, descending tropical rivers, sparked hope in his enthusiasm for undertaking an analytic journey towards unknown, wild shores. But his true request was quite another: for an accomplice. Together we would endure the solitude and impregnable isolation. The analyst had to be the mother-accomplice of the son in the irremediable conjugal and oedipal conflict. Once, in one of his dreams, he took a side road and arrived on the threshold of a church. There should have been a wedding, but he chose to run away. He got back into his car and turned back to the main road. The logical affective choice—marriage, which would have meant an untroubled state of affairs with the woman he was going out with instead of a state of sin—was not feasible. His father's imperious wish to reduce his children to a lay, and above all sterile, community won the day.

In the paternal family, only his father, among numerous brothers and sisters, had married and had children. Besides, his father had broken off relations with his siblings many years ago for ludicrous reasons, just as for many years no friend had been to their house. Many years earlier, his father had decided to live only in a small room next to the kitchen, basically separating from his wife. A short time afterwards, he fell victim to a deep depression and then suffered a stroke. Patiently, session after session, as Andrea had done as a child with his toy soldiers, we pulled out his memories of the past and the experiences of the present, not to play with them but to put them back into the box again in a well-ordered fashion. I often thought that at least now he had a playmate in this methodical and defensive ordering: the analyst. When I was beginning to resign myself to a progressive increase in the depressed part, and to a substantial defeat for me, after a year a new and unexpected phase of the analysis and his life began. His travel dreams were resumed and above all dreams of houses appeared: the first, an expression of his having got himself moving again, both in analysis and internally; the second, of his new possibility to access his own internal spaces, which had remained blocked for so long after the death of his sister and especially his father.

Andrea's problem is that he has a depressed nucleus, inherited from his father, from which he defends himself with increasingly wide-ranging retreats. Analysis helped him to survive, with my complicity, the persecutory threats of a primitive castrating father.

It was a very long, and also very frustrating, analysis, but it seems to have allowed the patient to overcome the progressively worsening depressive phase that had so worried me at the beginning.

Comment

An accomplice, a secret friend, or an eccentric uncle are often the elements in childhood that allow you to remove yourself from the impending compulsory family desperation, from the perception that you are missing a possible affective future due to a total absence of libidinal prospects, and of erotic, or affective, or simply relational desires finding any satisfaction. Andrea wanted to be called by name: "To hear my name said, simply that: 'Andrea'," he used to say. Somehow this miraculously happened in analysis. The complicity allowed recognition of a vital, generous, and strong identity that had long been repressed and suffocated. Castration had been successfully overcome at work, where he achieved the recognition he had never obtained at home. Even here, though, a satisfying and lasting loving relationship was not realised. Repetition of the family destiny not to procreate turned out to be absolutely invincible. However, Andrea's journey is by no means over, although his analysis ended some time ago. I believe that by adjusting his expectations to something more easily reachable, discovering an echo to his name and to his identity, thus having them confirmed in the light of day and not just in secret complicity, and finally being able to play without having to put the soldiers back in their box, is now within his grasp. It seems so simple, to love and be loved, in his words, so why is it so difficult to accomplish? What "basic fault" keeps Andrea from realising his dreams? Let us return to the origins, to the initial defective characteristics: the depressed mother, the hyper-controlling father. In this context, it now appears almost miraculous that Andrea succeeded in having an affective and relational life that was vital, not deathly. Granted, not the life he wanted; he, too, did not manage to walk towards the rising sun hand in hand with "someone to love". But he is still alive, thanks—I believe—also to the complicity of the analyst. Perhaps someone, in the end, will know how to pluck this fruit too, high at the end of the highest bough.

CHAPTER ELEVEN

The homosexual universe and physical perfection

> Brightness lit up the sky, the whole earth round about laughed
> at the glitter of bronze, and the land resounded to the thunder
> of marching feet./In the middle of all this, Achilles armed for
> battle. He ground his teeth, his eyes blazed like flames of fire and
> unendurable grief consumed him as he put on the divine gifts
> that Hephaestus had made for him, raging against the Trojans.
> —Homer, *The Iliad*, Book 19, 362–368 (eighth century BC)

I must confess to having had a certain number of misgivings before
deciding to include this section in the book. Some of the epigraphs
placed at the heads of the chapters have been written by professed
homosexual authors, and refer to homosexual love stories. It seemed
to me that the passions of love did not embrace any differences arising
from gender or object investment. And having had many homosexual
patients in analysis, I do not believe there is any specific otherness in the
object investment when compared to heterosexuals.

So, as Kenneth Lewes says: "In other words, there is no substantial
reason for thinking that *homosexuality* is a term that refers to a real, natural category of people" (1995, p. xviii).

Then I happened to read an interview of Jeffrey Tate, the great British conductor. Born with spina bifida and also suffering from a severe form of kyphosis that makes conducting a decidedly arduous occupation, Tate is gay, which he describes as being "an outsider on two scores" (in being both disabled and homosexual). In the same interview with Ben Holgate, Tate goes on to say: "The gay world is immensely hung up with physical perfection for some curious reason … Therefore, being disabled in that world is harder" (Holgate, 1998, p. 17).

This small parenthesis gave me much food for thought and led me to reflect on my gay patients—both men and women—whom I have had and still have in analysis. And certainly, the quest for aesthetic perfection and physical beauty is a much more common trait in the homosexual universe than in the heterosexual world.

In his autobiography entitled *My Father and Myself*, J. R. Ackerley (1896–1967) describes his difficult relationship with his father and the at times stifling atmosphere of a still profoundly Victorian England. A good-looking man and gifted with a lively intelligence, Ackerley was seeking that ideal friend, spurred on by a sort of adolescent impulse. For him, it was a long, extenuating, and fruitless quest that left him empty-handed and deeply embittered. In the Introduction to this beautiful book, W. H. Auden comments:

> In *My Father and Myself*, Mr. Ackerley strictly limits himself to two areas of his life, his relations with his family and his sex-life. His account of the latter, except for his happy endings, is very sad reading indeed. Few, if any, homosexuals can honestly boast that their sex-life has been happy, but Mr. Ackerley seems to have been exceptionally unfortunate. All sexual desire presupposes that the loved one is in some way "other" than the lover: the eternal and probably insoluble problem for the homosexual is finding a substitute for the natural differences, anatomical and psychic, between a man and a woman. The luckiest, perhaps, are those who, dissatisfied with their own bodies, look for someone with an Ideal physique; the ectomorph, for example, who goes for mesomorphs. Such a difference is a real physical fact and, at least, until middle age, permanent: those for whom it is enough are less likely to make emotional demands, which their partner cannot meet. Then, so long as they don't get into trouble with the police, those who like "chicken" have relatively few problems: among thirteen—and

fourteen-year-old boys there are a great many more Lolitas than the public suspects. It is when the desired difference is psychological or cultural that the real trouble begins. Mr. Ackerley, like many other homosexuals, wanted his partner to be "normal". That in itself is no problem, for very few males are so "normal" that they cannot achieve orgasm with another male. But this is exactly what a homosexual with such tastes is unwilling to admit ... Lastly, a homosexual who is, like Mr. Ackerley, an intellectual and reasonably well-off is very apt to become romantically enchanted by the working class, whose lives, experiences, and interests are so different from his own, and to whom, because they are poorer, the money and comforts he's able to provide can be a cause for affectionate gratitude.

(Ackerley, 1968, pp. x–xi)

Ackerley shares the fate of many gay men of his times in their unsuccessful quest for the love of a beautiful (and often poor) young boy and in being unable to live in a stable affective relationship happily, with shared passions and interests.

In my clinical practice, I have frequently come across another aspect of homosexual love, often described in the literature, for example by Ackerley. This is the desire to be *normal*, which at times is identified with the wish not to be homosexual (more often present in periods when homosexuality was illegal or in any case viewed from within a hostile and contemptuous social context), or—more commonly in our days—as a wish to be above reproach. Sometimes this is translated into an almost obsessive meticulousness at work, or into a particularly excessive attention to detail, or at other times into a search for a gay couple's way of life in imitation of the heterosexual model, therefore including also parenthood and in general an almost compulsive attention towards the home as a domestic place.

In another autobiography, *The Farewell Symphony* (1997), Edmund White comments at the beginning, almost as a sort of parenthesis:

I'd been to two psychiatrists for several years each, but I'd neither gone straight, as I'd hoped, nor accepted my homosexuality, as I'd feared. ... If marriage was my conscious but still deferred goal, I was less ready to admit I was always on the lookout for adventure.

(White, 1997, p. 10)

And so, after all, I have chosen to recount some stories of gay patients and to comment on their affective relationships. This time, the narrative path is guided by the appearance of two themes: the search for aesthetic perfection and the desire to be normal.

Francesco

Francesco is a successful young designer. He has a partner of long standing with whom he shares a home and an office. They have lived together for several years and have a good relationship, strengthened by sharing their creative profession, in which their roles are reciprocally and satisfyingly complementary.

Everything seemed to be going very well in Francesco's life. He is good-looking, urbane, and seductive. He came to analysis at the insistence of his partner, much disturbed by a recent episode. In recounting the event, Francesco also seemed frightened, much more than he had been during the episode itself. Briefly, this is the story he told me.

Quite unexpectedly, without knowing why, and without there being any problem with his partner, Francesco disappeared for almost a month, without saying where he had gone nor why. He left only a short message: "I've got to leave for a while, I'll explain when I get back".

On his return, he seemed confused and disoriented, to the extent of fearing a physical breakdown, which a period in hospital had however excluded. Soon back to normal, he was able to say where he had been and why he had disappeared. His story immediately seemed totally unexplainable and had driven his worried partner to persuade him to seek help.

In Italy, Francesco is a foreigner and during the many years he has lived in the country he has never been back to visit his family, nor have his numerous family ever come to Italy to visit him. He has always told his partner, friends, all acquaintances, and people at work that his mother is Sri Lankan, and very attached to her son, and that he has numerous siblings, a father very busy in his job (a small business), and that he left home in South-East Asia when he was about twenty to move to Europe.

In fact, his mother is the only one he very occasionally keeps in contact with. He says he resembles her a lot, especially in his fine, regular features, though they have nothing of the Oriental about them. And in actual fact, as he confesses to me, he does not know why he has been telling this story about himself, and for so many years; it is absolutely not true. His real story does not differ from it so much, except in some curious and specific details. In the first place, its location: Francesco is in fact American.

He comes from a small town in the so-called American Corn Belt, the area of cereal production in the United States, and from a very religious family. His father owns the only local supermarket and he has many brothers and sisters. He has always felt different from them:

> I understood only quite late that this feeling different meant being homosexual; before, I didn't know what it meant. I liked playing with my sisters and sewing dresses for their dolls. My mother used to ask me—even when I was quite young—for advice on what to wear, and I was very happy to play that role. I don't remember any particular difficulties with my father, nor any feeling of being scorned or attacked for my diversity, which, besides, was not evident then. I left home pretty young, but that was normal back then. I knew I wanted to work in fashion and my work experiences went hand in hand with my first sexual experiences. I've done a bit of everything in my life, all over the place, before coming to Italy.

What strikes me while listening to him is this "a bit of everything, all over the place". It's an all-embracing, sweeping statement but resounds within me as an intentionally generic part of the story, which I prefer to put to one side for the time being.

"And then"—he continues his story over several sessions—"I don't know why, at a certain point I arrived in Italy. Here I fell in love and remained, and decided that I needed a story to tell and roots to talk about, like everybody else, and I invented the whole story about Sri Lanka."

> And now my partner just cannot understand why I told him so many lies, to him and to everybody else. He says there was no need for them, that lying to him was absolutely absurd, but he can't understand that I wasn't lying, it was the story that I had built up for myself; it had been like this for years and there didn't seem to me to be any reason for changing it. Actually, I have to tell you that it was my story, which even I believed in; I had got used to it; I never thought of America; I didn't want to go there, but I never

said why, just that I'd lived for a long time in New York, which was true, and that I was bored with America. This was also true perhaps, I don't know; the fact is that for twenty years I have lived just as I'm describing it to you.

Here I pause, on this: "I have lived just as I'm describing it to you". It is absolutely extraordinary. It corresponds perfectly with "a bit of every-thing, all over the place".

In an article of 2005, Alessandra Lemma explores the psychic func-tions of lying and attempts to identify three self-object configurations. Each of these is associated with specific anxieties to which the lie offers an apparent solution. For the purposes of this case, I thought that the possible configuration of a lie might be particularly interesting. The second and third configurations are both forms of self-preservative lying, where the lie may be best conceived as a "symptom of hope" (Winnicott, 1984).

> In self-preservative lying, the lie represents a solution to interna-lised self-object configurations that are qualitatively different to those in the type of sadistic lying. ... In these cases the lies that are told are typically ones that allow the self to construct a lov-able or impressive version of the self and/or lies whose content aims to elicit the object's concern by placing the self in situations of invented danger. Here, the lie allows for the creation of a version of the self that is believed to provide a way through to the object who will certainly love, admire or be concerned about the self. It is as if the person acts as his own loving mother, comforting himself with this idealised version of the self now in relation with a loving, involved object.
>
> (Lemma, 2005, p. 744)

This is a form of self-preservation, where the lie may be used to create an attractive self that can arouse love, admiration, and attention from the object of investment. In this context, the lie would serve to eliminate any doubt the object might have regarding the self. In such a situation, the object is experienced as being not sufficiently willing or its move-ments are inscrutable.

It seems to me that when Francesco affirms "I have lived just as I'm describing it to you", he is referring to the old love objects of his infancy, especially his much loved mother, who do not seem able to come to terms with his homosexuality. Francesco can only lie to these figures, but the lie cannot simply consist in pretending to be heterosexual, but requires something far more elaborate. Francesco recreates another parallel universe to his own that he places on the opposing part of the globe (the East instead of the West, Hinduism instead of Evangelical Christians, and so on and so on). In this symmetrical universe, the original rules are respected because the number of siblings, the father, and mother correspond, even down to their characteristics and characters. However, the mechanism of disguise, camouflaging geographical and material aspects, appears to be very powerful. "A bit of everything, all over the place", he had said during our first encounters, alerting me immediately. What did this vagueness, these sweeping statements mean in a person who was otherwise so precise and almost obsessive in his narrating?

As will become clearer as the analysis progresses, in the first years after leaving his paternal home Francesco behaved very promiscuously, even turning to prostitution when economic needs dictated. This did not trouble him at all, but it was something that he absolutely could not reconcile with his family's mentality and religion. He could not lose his family, but nor could he risk exposing himself to their inexorable rejection, to being thrown out of their lives forever. In point of fact, he had left forever, and by strongly dissociating he had been able to lead a second homosexual life without any problems, successfully achieving what he had always wanted to be and have. And with such a well-constructed lie, he had protected his original love objects in his inner world so that, in his phantasy, they could continue to think of him as the calm, docile, obedient, and sensitive child he had in fact been.

Suddenly one day, the unexpected happened. He had met a person who also came from the same Corn Belt area, and he immediately found himself back in a world of memories that denial had kept at bay until that moment. Francesco had what we may call an acute dissociative episode, and although he left a message for his partner, he had got on the first plane and for the first time in more than twenty years he had returned home, to see his parents and family. He remembered practically nothing of the trip or of his stay there. At a certain point, he thought he should return home, and home was now in Milan, no longer in America. This time he did not leave unexpectedly, like twenty-five years ago. He said goodbye properly to everyone; he knowingly told plausible lies because he realised once and for all that it was not possible for his father, nor even for his mother, to conceive of having a gay son, and he left for Italy. Once back home, the worlds that he had kept apart with such nonchalance collapsed, and he found himself plunged into confusion.

Let us return to Lemma's function of the lie. What anxieties did Francesco's lie avoid? Regarding his partner and the social context he had lived in for years, the lie acted as a defence against the fear of being rejected and abandoned, when talking about his miserable and squalid origins—he called them "dusty", referring to the dust of the streets in his hometown. To have been born in the East—where he had never set foot—seemed much more attractive and mysterious. But the real original lie was the one concerning his family, as a defence against castration anxiety involving his taciturn, authoritarian father and the anxiety of being abandoned by a meek and submissive mother. As I mention in the Introduction, oedipal and pre-oedipal events, blended together, always come into play as our love life evolves. Much skill is needed to integrate the various aspects among themselves in order to be able to sustain the desired and hoped for libidinal investments in adult life.

Like many gay people, Francesco wanted to be *normal*. But his normality was not expressed in line with any official norm but had passed through a succession of elaborate protective lies with regard to the love objects that were experienced as emotionally not available or impenetrable. Lemma points out that:

> The linguistic roots of the words "truth" and "lie" shed further light on the possible functions of lying. The Greek etymology of the word "truth" is "open"; that for "lie" is "curved" (Forrester, 1997). These linguistic roots point to the way in which the lie involves a psychic detour—the lie allows the individual to "curve" round the truth. The use of lying indicates the difficulty, even danger, in being open and direct with one's objects. In psychic terms the lie then becomes necessary, we might say, when there is a need to bypass one's objects, to "work round them" in some way or even to swerve violently in order to avoid a head-on collision with them.
>
> (Lemma, 2005, p. 738)

During analysis, Francesco was able to experience an emotionally available analytic object and to allow himself to remember his past and put

together the various aspects of his life. His partner turned out to be loving and sympathetic, and—I suspect—also electrified and excited by the
complexity of his companion's life; quite the opposite of what Francesco
had feared. The analysis did not last long, about four years, but it was
very intense. At the end, I received a gift designed by Francesco, a piece
of clothing, with the word "Think" on the back, in English. I commented
that he had successfully achieved a dual outcome: he had clothed me, as
he used to do when young with his mother, and he had given me food
for thought, as he would have liked to have achieved with his mother
during his childhood years.

Giovanni

Giovanni asked for an analysis because he was confused. He had
already had other analytic experiences, but none had explored his
homosexuality. In the meantime, he had got married and had children,
but his family, although much loved, had not prevented his homosexual fantasies from persisting. He had not acted them out, though,
even if he had had various affairs, always with men, before his marriage and was well aware of his desires. But Giovanni too, like Edmund
White and many others, oscillated between the desire for a normalising
marriage and a promiscuous gay life with volatile object attachments.
As White says:

> The only two choices, it appeared, were marriage, cruel to the wife,
> stifling to the husband, and gay promiscuity, by definition transi-
> tory, sexy and sad for the young, frustrating and sad for the old.
>
> (White, 1997, p. 59)

Giovanni is a very intelligent, brilliant man. He has lived in a sort of
psychic bubble up until now, hiding his quiet desperation and his deso-
late affective solitude from himself, despite his family, friends, children,
and an enthralling job. Giovanni works the whole time, and apparently
tirelessly. He comes from a modest background, although not as poor as
he likes to recount. His parents never agreed about anything. Although
they never legally separated, they have often lived apart, due to his
father's quarrelsome and violent nature, his tendency to get involved
in nefarious business deals with disastrous economic results for the
family, and his frequent extra-marital affairs.

Giovanni grew up fearing and hating his quick-tempered and violent father with his brutally aggressive sexuality, and despising his submissive mother, finding happiness only at work. When young, Giovanni often hid in a wardrobe, a final retreat from the domestic shouting, and dreamt of flying to New York in first class, where he was offered an amazing meal. These flights into fancy, these daydreams, protected him from the domestic squalor; that, together with the company and affection of a kind, urbane, and homosexual uncle, the object of his father's scorn and derision.

Maturing, Giovanni was immediately aware of his homosexuality, but without any undue problems. What troubled him was the gay world that he frequented, its dark rooms, perverse aspects, the lack of any real bonds beyond the sexual relationship. He had not looked for different gay experiences that were more in tune with his need for affection and stability. And these encounters confirmed for him his father's sarcastic opinions about his uncle, who was actually revealed to be a weak man at the mercy of much younger boys who he maintained but who stole from him. Marriage seemed a decorous, and hoped for, solution.

The first years of marriage passed pretty well. There was a sort of *do ut des* pact between him and his wife, based on the fact that he went out to work and provided for the family, while his wife took care of its good name, thus he could preserve his childhood fantasies of escaping in first class. Unconsciously though, Giovanni became profoundly identified with his mother, and repeated the pattern of her marriage: he took refuge in work, as his only source of pleasure and satisfaction, and avoided any emotional relationship with his wife and children. How much this was also due to intensely repressing his homosexual urges did not worry him in the slightest.

In recent years, however, Giovanni had begun to feel a nagging irritation, especially about himself. He had periodic headaches, and his work started to be less gratifying. For a long time, he devoted a great deal of energy to furnishing his house and enriching his family. Inside himself, he noted a yearning for aesthetic perfection that was expressed in heightened care for clothes and furnishings. And yet something was missing. Finally he had a fatal meeting. He fell head over heels in love with a younger, very beautiful man.

At this point, he asked to come to analysis. Confused, he once more found himself confronted with the gay world he had fled from twenty years ago. He feared its squalor; he was afraid he would lose everything—social standing, decorum, the carefully constructed domestic peace. And yet he could not resist the reappearance of passion: "Why can't I be happy, at least once in my life? Why aren't I allowed to be happy while others are?", he used to ask me disconsolately.

Giovanni's analysis was long and complex. He left his wife and made a life with his new partner. But this did not resolve aspects of his old desperation, dating back to his fear of poverty and squalor, to the fighting and emotional abandonment of his infancy.

Giovanni cannot give up idealising, the meal in first class: "Everything I touch turns into shit, I'm like King Midas" is one of his stock phrases. And his new partner is invested with the scorn and emotional harshness that has characterised his life. Giovanni accepts his homosexuality but cannot accept the everyday aspect of existence, which, every time, inexorably, takes him back to the experience of his original family. In his idealising, being gay means belonging to a blighted world. You do not have a family, a boat, a dog, the normal life of heterosexuals. At every moment you are exposed to solitude, to old age, and to sickness. Squalor is not acceptable in his idealising of the ego; however, everything risks becoming squalid because it is subject to decay and decadence, or to brutality and betrayal—just like what had happened with his parents. The search for physical perfection, beauty, is the only safeguard against these elements. Beautiful objects, beautiful lovers are a safe haven, a defensive bulwark against the decay of time, against the immorality of your own choices. Giovanni occasionally betrays his partner with other lovers, in his impossible quest for perfection. He never finds it.

He gets angry with me, the analyst, because I do not understand, because he thinks I am translating his experiences into a heterosexual language. He has trouble accepting being normal. In a certain sense, this word cannot exist for him because it contrasts starkly with his primitive aspirations. And yet the time does not pass in vain during analysis. Gradually, he discovers he is genuinely fond of his partner, despite the many defects he seems to have. He loves him, as he discovers with a sort of painful surprise. This man does not correspond to any ideal; on the contrary, Francesco manages to argue with him all the time. And yet, for some strange reason, he is attached to him and despite everything feels good with him; together they have set up house. But Francesco fears this bond; he does not want a gay marriage. He is afraid it might represent the sadness of his previous marriage, the squalor of that of his parents. He shuns promiscuous experiences, even though they tempt him. His past eroticism is disturbing. The dark room of some of those gay meeting places mirrors a dark room in his mind, in his inner psychic reality. He dreads these phantasies materialising, that his life may be transformed, and letting go of his idealising. The dark room does not contain anything aesthetically perfect or physically beautiful. Instead, it is dark and encounters, however exciting, are clandestine, furtive, and dangerous; they are encounters in the dark, in the dark of his mind and thought. Analysis no longer allows him to have them. A new superego has replaced the primitive one. Now homosexuality is allowed, and, perhaps, he will not transform everything he touches into shit any more. Certainly, he feels lighter and calmer, even though we cannot place any bets, in his case as in the case of many patients described here, that he will walk forwards forever hand in hand with his partner, as in the fairy tales.

Comment

Homosexual love lends itself well to a consideration made in the Introduction: every impassioned love story needs a mimetic model. Gay love stories are profoundly subject to changes in law, morals, and social conventions. Obviously, it is a very different thing to be able to openly love the object of your choice compared to clandestinely living such a passion. Despite this, however bizarre it might seem, the two elements I have singled out above—yearning for physical perfection and an urge for normality—are aspects that I have found again and again over the years, in differing ideological tones and social openness regarding homosexuality.

What I—in my turn ideologically conditioned—thought at the beginning, that there is no difference between homosexual love and heterosexual love, however correct that is from a general and objective point of view, must, despite this, come to terms with some specific elements that are certainly in part due to the persistence of archaic homophobic conditioning, both in the individuals directly involved and in the environment in which they live, and partly reflect vestiges of ancient cultures.

I deliberately chose to include Homer's description of Achilles at the start of this chapter, the undisputed hero of the *Iliad*: beautiful as only heroes can be, and deeply in love with Patroclus, to the extent of taking up arms once again to avenge his death. At the death of Patroclus, Achilles' fatal ire and just wrath against Agamemnon wane; his heroic, warlike narcissism lessens. They are replaced by intense grief for the beloved's death, anger towards Hector, and a desire for revenge. The ego's narcissistic protection accompanies the defence of the object of the love investment. Armed Achilles who climbs the hill before battle is a poetic and psychological masterpiece: everything resounds within him, the arrows in their quiver, the lance, his bleeding heart. Amorous passion prevails over political and strategic considerations. Achilles goes forward to meet his destiny, as everyone hurries to remind him, but destiny is also what made him fall in love with Patroclus. Homosexual love has ancient roots, in collective knowledge and culture. It accompanies the smell of blood and the sound of arms, of battles to fight and those already fought.

Despite this, in times of peace, gay love is difficult to integrate into everyday life. It is still like this today, however much you want this and attempt to normalise it. It escapes such a path, for ancient, extremely ancient reasons.

Today, as analysts, we can only proceed in our professional role of respectful listening, fully aware of the many battles that these loves must fight and the infinite defeats they suffer every day.

Since the times of Freud, the analytic approach has been based on the contemporaneously empathic and neutral act of listening. Since listening to the patient provides us with the necessary information for understanding the special experiences of his life, the analyst must put to one side all expectations and moral prejudices in his respectful listening to the patient in order to be able to truly enter fully into sharing that patient's inner world.

The objectives of an analysis are understanding and treating, not judging or modifying. The transformation that we always observe during analysis must happen along an evolving path that respects the patient's nature. Having said this, I have found it interesting to single out along this path some of the special traits of homosexual love, which disregard ideological inferences and current morals and have more to do with the primitive archaic roots of the first loving investments, well rooted in the patient's inner world, no different to all the other situations observed so far.

CHAPTER TWELVE

Love on the silver screen*

> She was in the cinema where doors
> keep opening and closing.
> At that noise she thought
> He was coming back;
> But he was not.
>
> —Sandro Penna (1976, p. 13; author's translation)

It gives me great pleasure to begin this chapter with Sandro Penna's poem, and thus directly at the cinema, inside its darkened interior, "where doors keep opening and closing". How many love stories have we seen on those screens and inside those halls? How many dates have started out with a "What about going to see a film?" How many love stories have been conducted in the darkened halls of the cinema, one eye on the screen, the other on the beloved, closely entwined in the protective darkness of the auditorium? But that eye never left the

---

*The fourth section of this chapter was previously published in 2009 in a longer article entitled "The skin house: a psychoanalytic reading of 3-Iron", *International Journal of Psycho-Analysis, 90*: 647–660, translated by Andrea Sabbadini.

screen, and long languid kisses alternated with enraptured immersions in memorable stories, in unforgettable scenes. Life at the cinema, cinema in life, love for the cinema, love at the cinema, love on the screen, furtive loves, clandestine loves, some barely begun, others drawing to an end. To hear on screen what you do not dare say yourself, being at the cinema with the right person, realising that you are at the cinema with the wrong person, weeping copiously at love stories on the screen that are more real than life and crying at the cinema about love stories that have ended and that no film will ever manage to narrate... All this resounds in the analytic consulting room in a constant play of mirrors and references, of doors that open or close forever; what nostalgia, what regret for when the cinema was a whole world in itself and we "bright and pensive, ... arrived/at the threshold of youth", as evoked by the words of Giacomo Leopardi (1828).

Let us return now, directly from the cinema to the consulting room.

Today, the dialogue between film and psychoanalysis appears to be particularly lively and intellectually stimulating, and the relationship between the two disciplines is developing in an increasingly rich and complex exchange. The stories recounted at the cinema make it possible to identify single individuals with broader collective destinies, contained within the cinematographic narrative. The individual and unique story of the protagonist allows the spectator to project onto the screen different aspects of his self. The screen then becomes a special mirror, where past tragedies are re-read in the light of present and current perspectives. In fact, thanks to its special temporal nature, film possesses the specific and unique capacity for both being a witness of the past and bearing a message for the present and future. The cinema has always provided an extraordinary opportunity for working through traumatic losses when encountered on the screen, at "a safe distance", thus allowing us to give new meanings to old memories and experiences.

In this chapter, I have chosen to discuss four films, two classics—which I have already mentioned above—and two more recent, in which the passions of love are declined in both a traditional and original way at the same time. The style of each film is original, the story is traditional; bits of the preceding chapters can be glimpsed in them.

In discussing the films, I will alternate considerations on the cinematographic language with others that are more specific to psychoanalytic technique and clinical practice.

Les Amants

The Lovers is a film by Louis Malle of 1958 starring Jeanne Moreau and Jean-Marc Bory. Its plot is very simple: a middle-class woman from the provinces—bored and snobbish, stuck in a marriage full of ritual and social engagements, with a Paris dandy for a lover—is suddenly struck by *l'amour fou* for the first time in her life thanks to a young man met quite by chance when her car broke down, and she leaves her marital home for him.

At the cinema, we have seen how love is the *subject of subjects*, particularly where the carnal aspect is inseparable from feelings. Louis Malle made the film that everyone harbours in their hearts and dreams of living: a detailed story of love at first sight, the burning "contact of two bodies" that only later will appear as the "exchanging of two phantasies".

Rightly or wrongly, François Truffaut maintained that with this film Malle had dared to do something never attempted before, to portray on film a whole night of love. To express the full range of feelings experienced during the long scene, as the two lovers live out their idyll in the gorgeous countryside illuminated by the moon, the director chose Brahms's *Andante ma moderato* of the *Sestetto in si bemolle*, Op. 18, as the soundtrack. Malle had perceived that the music contains a concentration of erotic and sentimental feelings that are inexpressible in words. When the film came out, in 1958, it was claimed to be scandalous in France and attempts were made to prevent it from being shown and from taking part in the Venice Film Festival (where it won the Special Jury Prize). It was highly controversial in the United States, resulting in a long series of court cases that culminated in the US Supreme Court drawing up definitions in 1964 for "obscenity" and "hard-core pornography".

In the film, Louis Malle dissects the middle-class microcosm of the French provinces—as Balzac had done in his time in literature—showing a husband completely involved with his job, and a lover suspected of exploiting the situation and not really in love with Jeanne Moreau. But the romantic and sensual aspect, which sparked the wrath of the morality camp, comes in the second part of the film: long shots in the mist, bodies tenderly leaning against each other, and even the hint of a nude scene (Jeanne Moreau in profile without a bra!).

More than fifty years after it came out, the film no longer seems scandalous, and in fact one tries hard to glimpse the elements that triggered such furore. It is still a very beautiful film, a bit dated, but all the same an art film, with a marvellous Jeanne Moreau who laughs wholeheartedly, extraordinarily erotic, even beyond the love scene that shifted the canons of the public's sense of modesty.

For the public opinion of the 1950s, it was in fact unthinkable to accept that a woman of a certain social standing, cultured and reasonable, would decide to abandon her role of wife and mother in exchange for a future that was all too uncertain in the name of a night of passion. While the narrating voice in the last scene says "She was afraid, but had no regrets", we see the car with the two lovers moving off into the future.

I am presenting it here for two reasons. The first concerns the moral concept, which changes with the times, and which we as analysts have always to keep an eye on: right there, within us, where a moralistic seething can be felt while listening to the patient. The second because it offers a different narrative solution to passion, to the *amour fou*: no longer the inevitable death of Madame Bovary & Co. but a journey towards an uncertain future, one in any case preferable to a present lacking passion and feeling.

Leaving aside the contents of the film, I would like to pause on its almost excessive repetition of the nocturnal stroll that had struck Truffaut so greatly. Several times above, I have said that repetition represents a stylistic code for romance and passion; compulsively it recalls the obsession that engulfs you when invaded by the presence of your beloved. It is something that absolutely cannot be expressed in words, but which we analysts need to keep clearly in mind because in our consulting rooms we often assist, fortunately, at the flowering of loving passions that are often perceived with difficulty in their pure and simple state by the analyst, used in general to words, to feelings expressed through reasonable measured words and not to lightening strikes of passion or to misty nights. Once again, I think it is better to remain suspended, waiting, in a participated listening that does not quench the passion but at the same time does not reduce the analysis to ashes.

The libidinal re-awakening that Malle's film attempts to describe occurs frequently. It happens especially where transformations are occurring in the analysis, softening repressions and defences that have frozen over time. Like Jeanne Moreau, patients can and should be able to say in analysis: "She was afraid, but had no regrets", and feel themselves supported by the analyst in proceeding towards an uncertain future, but with an internal solidity they have never experienced before. At times, the analyst may be jealous, or even envious of the patient's happiness and rediscovered freedom. He may experience it as being abandoned, or as an attack on the analysis. Instead, it is a product of the analysis, which has liberated old repressions and permitted emotions and feelings that are no longer devastating to the patient's ego to unfurl and take wing.

L'année dernière à Marienbad

Last Year at Marienbad, Golden Lion at the Venice Film Festival of 1961, was directed by Alain Resnais. The screenplay and dialogues are by Alain Robbe-Grillet, a detail that should not be forgotten. At the time the film was shot, the two Alains were both exponents of the Nouvelle Vague. Set inside and outside a huge, luxury, international hotel, with sumptuously grand but frigid decorations, the film describes an unknown man incessantly courting a woman with repeated references to last year, in the same hotel, where they had met and had had a love affair. The woman does not seem to recall the episode and the spectator can never know the truth, nor if one of the characters is lying. The man tells her they had an intense love story and that he has returned to take her away to live with him. The woman replies that she does not know him, and even that she had not been at Marienbad last year. "But you can't not remember! You're afraid to remember!", the man vehemently replies, showing her a photograph of last year. Who is right and who is wrong? What really happened last year at Marienbad? Every object, every stucco that the hotel is full of, every detail is fundamental in a film in which the dialogue is so dry and reduced to the bare essentials, quite the opposite of its excessive baroque sets. The film is a symbolic journey within a space, the space of the hotel and its extremely long, never-ending enfilade of corridors, in a constant alternation between past, present, and future, sustained by the presence of an equally infinite number of mirrors, in which the characters are continually reflected in an inexorable game. We move from the falsely realistic representation of the cinematographic mirroring to the confusion of a space in which the protagonists seem to be imprisoned. The mirror that should in fact reveal what lies behind their intentions, offering the spectator a parallel point of view, not unlike the games of mirrors, illusions, and deceptions of baroque painting, does not perform its task of representation and restoration but, in constantly referring back to other mirrors, other rooms, or other corridors, instead describes a mental time that is always and only present, where the past and the future flatten out into a single dimension, the internal one of the unconscious world, which by definition is a-temporal.

The imagined is represented in cinematographic reality by doing away with the two levels of representation: the real one and the one reflected by the mirror. In the film, inner reality is reflected by the mirror, simultaneously present in the external reality placed in front of the mirror, which is constantly asymmetrical in its specular reflection.

In a recent interview, Giorgio Albertazzi, extraordinary star of the film, describes how he felt alienated during the shooting of the film, incapable of understanding the plot and the sense of what was being filmed. His partner, the sophisticated and enigmatic Delphine Seyrig, said to him: "It's simple; we're objects".

This process of objectivisation performed by the director has a disturbing effect on the spectator too. Along with mirrors, it is aided by the hotel gardens lacking any flowers or plants, by the geometric sharpness heightened by the black and white of the film, and by the foreign accent of both leading actors (perceptible in the French, original-language version). And yet this film, which seems dated to today's eyes and so terribly slow, both telling its story and in its filming style that was so modern at the time it was shot, beautifully represents the sense of alienation one feels when living an intense love story.

That state of agitation, seeing reality through pink-tinted spectacles, thinking it is bizarre that everything goes on as usual when our inner world is in such tumult, that sense of feeling stunned or bemused, so often evoked in novels and poetry, all this is gathered and translated into images in this powerful film.

Throughout, the spectator is constantly frustrated in his attempt to grasp the characters' real dimension, their affectivity or sensuality, colliding with the director's obstinacy in never showing anything for real, while allowing the perpetual existence of the characters to be continually seen in the mirrors. The spectator is given the task of choosing the reality he wants. Did the characters really meet last year? Was there really a passionate love story between them? Did the husband kill his wife or was it only a phantasy? Is the narration of the facts a nostalgic invention of the leading lady or the meticulous recollection by the lover of a real passion that she would prefer to forget?

Conversations and events are repeated in various, always different places in the chateau and, through a long series of tracking shots down the corridors, the spectator takes part in the mental continuity of nostalgia that stylistically can only exploit repetition.

As in the film, also in the human psyche we observe the relentless repetition of words and gestures that should ensure the unchanging continuity of our passion. Passion is there to last forever, for the whole night, from one year to the next, down all the corridors of all the castles. We are merely the objects of our passion; in overwhelming us, it makes objects of us and causes us to lose our dimension of subjects capable of choosing and deciding our fate.

Just as we are not masters of our passions, so—the film would seem to suggest—we are not masters of our memories and recollections. Symbolising this, a game with matches was played by the man and the husband, and then obsessively repeated, with different moves but always ending in the same way (the game would quickly become popular among the general public, and spread everywhere).

The main character in the film describes their relationship of the previous year in the same hotel to the woman he loves; he proposes memories and emotions that may or may not really have existed.

But in the emotional reality of each one of us, we know very well how memories of past loves are never the same within a couple. The person who continues to love and to keep the other's cherished memory in his heart will have much stronger and more intense mnestic traces compared to the other who loves no longer. While the dialogues between ex-lovers are heart-rending: "Do you remember? Really, you don't remember? That's not possible! You were there, and you said, and I replied, and then... And do you remember that time in the train? And Rome? What! You don't even remember Rome?" In French, they say *par cœur* and in English *by heart* to mean "from memory", placing the seat of our memories in our heart. In actual fact, one remembers what has left a trace in our hearts. The trailer of the film is very explicit on this point: "You yourselves will be at the heart of this love story, such a story as you have never imagined. You will see things never before seen, images never before projected on screen; but which you will perhaps have lived in your life."

Passion is described boldly, striking right to the heart, as in the repeated scene in the film of a group of men who turn round and shoot at the outline of a cardboard heart.

The film quickly made a name for itself, and very soon became a cult movie, despite scarce initial public acclaim. Whoever has seen it cannot forget the long corridors, the enfilade of mirrors, or the geometries in the gardens. One is continually lost in the enormous space of the film. It is the place and time of love—eternal and interchangeable.

Two Lovers

Two Lovers, a film of 2008 by the director James Gray, is located in Brighton Beach, Brooklyn, the last appendage before Coney Island, one of the most famous beaches of New York, a district largely populated by Jewish immigrants of first, second, and now third generation, mainly of Russian descent. In fact, the director, who comes from this milieu, likes to shoot films in his Little Odessa featuring representatives of these European Jews, with their rites and traditions. Not all of this is made clear in the film; in fact, a good part of the film's attraction lies in the unsaid. For example, the passing mention to the rare, inherited, genetic disorder of Tay-Sachs disease, a pathology about one hundred times more common in Ashkenazi Jews than in other world populations, and that prevented him marrying his first girlfriend—something that spurs the main character to attempt suicide in the film's opening shots. Or the hint to the long period in hospital following this attempted suicide. Together we will see these omissions, these unsaid aspects, which contribute so much to the film's appeal.

We could call this film "The Choice", or "The Need to Love", or "Between Fusionality and Separateness", because these are all central components in the plot.

To be more precise, three significant and revealing elements stand out in the film—very clear examples of its weft and weave and its comment. First, the urban environment where the story unfolds, the film's framework—a New York divided in two between a popular, sepia-coloured Brighton Beach, squalid like automatic laundries or the fire stairs of American films, and a sparkling, exciting Manhattan seen only at night, with the subway running between the two, with its stations, tunnels, and elevated tracks. To note, for example, in order to understand the colossal difference between these two worlds, the scene in which Leonard, the lead character, comes out of the metro with Michelle and then sees her getting into a luxurious black limousine, with the door held open by the driver. A second example is the beautiful photographs taken by Leonard, in which all the surrounding urban squalor is represented, contrasting with the equally beautiful photos of the bar mitzvah, which, though, do not have any backgrounds; they are merely portraits of happy people.

There is a constant contrast in the film between claustrophiliac and agoraphiliac aspects, the first represented by Leonard's parents' apartment, rich in memories, photographs, and objects brought over from Eastern Europe, deeply imbued with that Yiddish-mum preoccupation so beautifully expressed by Isabella Rossellini (aged here perhaps more than in reality) who anxiously spies on her son from beneath his closed door. For example, the marvellous scene in which he notices his mother's shadow between two slats of the door and is terrified that she will barge into his room uninvited. On the contrary, the agoraphiliac aspects can be found in the crowd scenes, external shots full of sunlight, in which we see Leonard walking about among a throng of people, all different from each other, all anonymous characters in an immense choral metropolis, where dissimilarities between individuals are nullified. These scenes are always long shots in which it is difficult to locate the face of the main character; we can only hear his voice, talking on his mobile phone. This is an example of what I said at the beginning: individual tragedies that get lost in the meeting with other infinite collective stories.

Lastly, there is the protagonist's need to love, the cause, in the first place, of his attempted suicide and consequent hospitalisation and then, in actual fact, of the whole unfurling of the film. In the film, love is represented as the choice between two opposites: blonde and brunette; Arian and Jew; tragic and disturbing Gwyneth Paltrow, tranquil and domestic Vanessa Shaw; the possible illusionary symbiosis with Michelle, the passionate, reflective, and separate experience with Sandra. Sandra represents the pull towards family and domesticity, towards growth and development of the self, away from past experiences of flight and immigration towards common experiences of present integration and differentiation. Michelle represents a flight from all this, even, if possible, aided by drugs, shared madness, and the theatricality of the opera, which, besides, is the *Cavalleria Rusticana*, in the film, with its tragic conclusion of the love triangle. Michelle was born in America, she is American but does not share the American dream of the immigrant; instead, she appears like Manhattan, sparkling and external, very beautiful, unreachable, but desperately unhappy and condemned always to take the wrong path. In the end, the character does not choose between the two because, even if he has chosen Michelle, he loses her straight away, in the metaphor so well expressed by the waves of the ocean that uninterruptedly break on the shore. But among the waves he finds the gloves that will restore his courage and his desire to return home, to his own people, to Sandra, and to normal life.

Concerning the first two elements, the urban and the claustrophilia/ agoraphilia, I would like to quote two excerpts from an interview of some years ago by the director James Gray:

> I can only say like the one thing you're really striving for I think—at least I am—in what [you're] trying to do is to bring a certain emotional authenticity to the work. And a certain authentic emotion to the work. And I guess the best avenue I have is to make it as personal and as autobiographical as I can. I grew up in a semi-attached row house in Queens in New York. And my family and my grandparents and my father's from Brooklyn and so you're essentially an outer boroughs kid, you're growing up. You're trying to view the world really through rose-colored glasses. It's difficult because Manhattan is so fantastic and it's 9 miles away and all these cool rich people live there and have great lives and you live in a semi-attached row house in Queens. So I suppose that you try to steal from your past and try and make it as personal as you can. So that's part of who I am and I suppose that's why it's made its way into movies. And New York is very different from anywhere else in the country ... The idea of a certain Jewishness to my movies is extremely important. I'm thinking consciously about things that didn't originally come to me that way. I suppose I'm always trying to break down the wall between my characters and myself. I'm trying to make the film as expressive and personal as I can, even if I can't explain, for example, how important it is for me to be Jewish. It's important for me to try to remove the wall and reveal myself in the hopes that it's interesting. Being Jewish is part of who I am.
>
> (Weintraub, 2009)

Gray's Little Odessa is populated with refugees from Eastern Europe, who are partly arranged as in a theatre of the absurd, a Pirandellian *Characters in Search of an Author*, who knock on the director's memory in search of a representation/witness of their past existence (see the photographs hanging on the wall).

Watching the film, we become involuntary witnesses of a process of remembering and consecrating, in our turn photographers and observers of the protagonist's unconscious phantasies.

We know very well that the desire for fusion, for being one whole with the beloved can be understood as intense longing and regret for the primitive symbiosis with the mother, even if this has not left any conscious memory. This yearning can never be satisfied in a state of love. As we have seen, Kernberg (1995) would sustain that a certain capacity for being alone is necessary in order to be able to love and to be two. There is a subtle difference between a genuine search for non-duality and a desire sustained by symbiotic or fusional phantasies. The wish to merge with the loved person may be a pathological defence against difference and solitude. Certain pathological modes of insecure attachment lead to such an adhesive sort of identification with the other that every type of separateness and difference with the other is negated.

In my opinion, this is the film's main character's pathological state. Because it is certainly a pathology, we are told that right at the beginning. When Michelle asks him for help, he is thrown off balance: "I was in hospital for a long time and really believed I would never fall in love again. But I love you. I understand you; I'm just like you." But this is not true because Leonard never has the nerve to tell himself the truth. Except at the end, when he musters up the courage to turn back from the beach, after having lost Michelle, and to begin again with Sandra. We could say that a potential that remains unexpressed, or a separation that remains incomplete, is being relinquished. Instead, I believe we are witnessing a maturing and an adult capacity to change, thanks to which we assist at unreachable infantile ideals being given up that are, after all, dangerous for the lead character's ego.

Bin-jip

Kim Ki-Duk is a sophisticated South Korean director of subtly lyrical films, often dealing with philosophical and moral subjects in a rarefied, extremely formalised style, who has achieved considerable critical and public acclaim in the West.

With 3-Iron, a work of full artistic maturity, Kim Ki-Duk seems to be trying to push to its extreme consequences the use of symbols and metaphors as expressive and narrative devices.

The female protagonist had been locked into a marriage dominated by violence, and she seems to be waiting for the moment to at last leave her husband and a home which, emotionally, she no longer inhabits, even if her portraits cover most of the wall surfaces. However, she is unable to free herself on her own, as is often the case with victims of domestic violence trapped inside humiliating claustrophobic relationships.

The house reflects such experiences: it is almost waiting for someone to move in, maybe through small loving gestures towards its objects and their owners, just like our female character who is waiting for someone to fill her emotional void.

It is this empty house that the young man moves into. He is a splendid specimen of a silent rebel, a cuckoo who invades someone else's nest, who enters empty houses to live emotionally inside them and to obtain from them a warmth and a structure which he seems unable otherwise to create for himself. Every aspect of him aims at what is essential, with a kind of extreme minimalism. The film is the narrative of a new Oriental Diogenes who, with a golf club on his shoulder (the 3-iron of the title—the club least commonly used by golfers) roams the world in search of Man—a Man being searched for in his houses, in his living spaces.

Throughout the film, we are witnesses of surreal, dreamlike situations, in stark contrast with such ritualistic everyday gestures as doing the laundry, or repairing broken objects—gestures almost identically repeated in every household.

This beautiful film could be used as a key to give us access to a psychoanalytic home—a home inhabited by complex concepts—to help us understand the real meaning of *representing* the human soul with images, and why we can talk about a genuine Skin House. For Didier Anzieu:

> The Skin Ego is a reality of the order of phantasy; it figures in phantasies, dreams, everyday speech, posture and disturbances of thought; and it provides the imaginary space on which phantasies, dreams, thinking and every form of psychopathological organisation are constituted. ... The Skin Ego is an intermediate structure of the psychic apparatus.
>
> (Anzieu, 1985, p. 4)

At times, psychic reality risks being confused in psychoanalytic parlance with internal reality. I believe that this film admirably demonstrates the difference and does it, in my opinion, with rare sophistication. What is extraordinary is that the director manages to express these elements from an artistic and a completely non-psychoanalytic point of view, which only goes to confirm that psychoanalysis has not invented anything new but has merely given names to basic aspects of the workings of the human mind.

Psychic reality is the area where we reflect on what takes place in our inner reality, on the sensations we perceive, on the feelings we feel. In other words, our potential for the mentalisation of our inner world's sensory and emotional experiences is located in psychic reality. But in order to achieve this—that is, to possess a psychic reality—we need some kind of representation of such experiences. A good part of an analyst's work lies in helping patients to create and widen their psychic reality—that is, the space where their inner subjective experiences can be represented. Such a representational activity is what we call the capability for symbolisation.

It is quite extraordinary that the film's characters remain altogether silent (a reference, perhaps, to the silent movies of the past). Sounds, on the other hand, belong to the external world. As soon as our male protagonist enters a new home, his first move is to listen to its answering machine in order to find out where its dwellers are, but also in order to provide the house with some sound. Then he puts on his CD, always the same one, which is the music of his own home, the soundtrack of his own film.

It is impossible to reach the internal world of that house directly, but we can try to find out about its psychic reality, that is, the way in which it represents itself, in order possibly to change it. Thus each house has its own character, and we can perceive how it is represented from its furniture, its paintings, its plants, the clothes in the wardrobes, the food in the refrigerator, the dirty linen. And if houses, as I was trying to explain before, are representations of the self in a symbolic form, if they are Skin Houses, then the inner world of their dwellers finds its expression in the psychic reality of their houses.

Thus, for instance, Kim Ki-Duk conveys the image of houses whose internal world is impregnated with violence, and the first image we come across is the portrait of its owner, a boxer wearing boxing gloves. As a confirmation of that first impression of violence, we later hear on the soundtrack the noise of the couple arguing, despite having just come back from celebrating their wedding anniversary in Hawaii. Or we have the beautiful scene in another house where the main character fixes a toy-gun in order to shoot some balloons but then, when the family who owns the house comes back, that same gun is used by the child to "pretend" to shoot his parents who are having an argument, although this is no longer quite a game.

Watching *3-Iron* we continuously come into contact with symbols which refer back to feelings and emotions, which in turn contain unconscious meanings. In symbolic representation, the symbol represents the object, but is not entirely identified with it, whereas in symbolic equation, the symbol is identified with the object to such an extent that symbol and represented object become identical (see Segal, 1957, 1991).

In *3-Iron*, the female protagonist understands immediately the symbolic meaning of certain activities that the young man performs in the houses he occupies, such as taking pictures of himself surrounded by objects, or doing the laundry, and she repeats them herself, thus generating a shared language, a style, a culture. In the film, she becomes the person for whom the symbol acquires a meaning.

In order to have a symbolic relationship, the ego and the object must be sufficiently differentiated; otherwise the symbol, which is created by the ego, gets confused with what is symbolised, that is, with the object. For example, if I say: "I want to have you", I do not mean that I want to possess you literally, but only symbolically.

In *3-Iron*, we come across certain characters, such as the woman's husband, to whom we apply the concept of symbolic equation, that is, they are incapable of freeing themselves from concrete thinking in which the objects and the symbols representing them are equivalent. Occasionally, material reality forcibly overlaps with symbolic phantasy, the symbol then collapses, and this leads almost inevitably to disaster like in the manslaughter episode, in which the golf ball that the young man uses to practise his shots is released from its tie and ends up hitting and killing an innocent car-driver.

The young man does not want to own anything, but only to use the objects he comes across as symbols that can give linguistic meaning to his existence. The woman, who according to her husband has everything, is unable in her psychic reality to use any of those objects and be engaged in a relationship with them because she feels alienated from them, turning them into non-objects. It is only when our male character enters a house and uses the objects that they acquire a symbolic life of their own and therefore can also have a meaning for her. Take, for example, the scene with the scales, which are modified so that they no longer indicate the weight of an external reality, but the more important weight of the inner reality in which the two of them are immaterial and weightless.

Even the husband's violence against the female protagonist has not so much to do with his beatings, of which she carries the marks, but rather with a lack of symbolic representation: for him, she is an object to be possessed, a true symbolic equation between the symbol and the thing itself. For her husband, it is not as if she belonged to him; she does belong to him. When he realises that this is not true, that he does not possess her, he loses his mind. In this sense, it would be interesting to contrast this couple with the one in the house with a fish pond, where both husband and wife focus on activities intended to create harmony and beauty around them. The objects they use, such as teacups and bonsai plants, are invested with love and care: symbolic representations, I believe, of the love and care they mutually feel towards each other and towards the external world. This is a house where one can find peace and also respect.

Symbol formation also dominates the characters' ability to communicate, in so far as all communication occurs through symbols. The ability to communicate using symbols is at the basis of verbal thinking—that is, communicating through words—but it is also behind artistic creativity, because the symbol is not a copy of the object it represents but something created completely anew. The world created by the artist is a new one. It is related to the objects that it describes, but such a narrative takes place through their symbolic representation which, as such, can always be different and original, while objects remain constant and consistent. We could say that symbols are entirely a product of our creation, but at the same time they are also something that already existed and which we merely discover, and creativity would then relate to what we do with them.

To get back to the film, the symbols used by Kim Ki-Duk can to a large extent be shared by his spectators (even if I suspect that the meaning of some of them might escape Western viewers) and, if this were not so, *3-Iron* would be incomprehensible and lose its function as a vehicle of communication.

In the film too, as in life, the thought-houses of the two protagonists evolve as they themselves grow. To think means to hold together, to stand up on a solid foundation; the emergence of thought requires support and a certain stability, conditions also needed to build a house. The reflective capability of our psychic reality is enriched by the passing of time: we build new and more complex relationships; we devise compromises; we tolerate ambiguity; we cultivate the skill to bear hatred and love. Our potential for symbolic thought grows as we grow and allows us to cultivate illusions that coexist side by side with our increasingly complex realities.

Our film's two characters stop ceaselessly moving from house to house and settle for a compromise that, while being surreal, also contains a core of absolute truth precisely for being a compromise. This is what Anzieu (1994) calls the move from the Skin Ego to the Thinking Ego, and which we can conceptualise as a move from an Ego-House-Skin (the effect of primitive primary narcissism) to a more mature I-Thou that reaches the potential for symbolisation of the object precisely because it has succeeded in separating and differentiating the subject from the object.

In 3-Iron, we can also find another aspect, interesting in relation not only to psychoanalytic practice, but also because of its sociological and anthropological implications. I am referring here to phantasies about invisibility, which often play a leading role in the love stories of timid or repressed individuals (for a detailed discussion on phantasies of invisibility, see Kilborne, 2002).

The film's main character tends towards invisibility; he tends to become a ghost, to exist only in the minds of those he wants to be seen by. Often, the house-dwellers guess his presence from certain signs, such as a cushion placed somewhere else or a poster removed. In fact, most of the time they sense a presence, an invisible one that the human eye cannot see. This becomes very obvious in the prison-cell scenes, where our young man tries to disappear in a space of around three square metres. Eventually, he draws an eye on his hand, in the attempt to be seen only by a symbolic eye, not by a real one.

The phantasies of invisibility express the wish, but also the fear, of not being seen or known. In a way, they defend us from the terrifying experience of being exposed and put to the test (it is not a coincidence that the young man never builds his own house, but contents himself with occupying other people's homes). Those who try to make themselves invisible are afraid that there is no room in the world for them and imagine disappearing or at least controlling how others will see them. However, while being protected from any castration threats derived from being seen, by becoming invisible, they end up isolating themselves from others (see Lansky, 1997).

Phantasies of invisibility are closely related to castration anxiety (Rangell, 1991). For Freud, castration anxiety originated in a fear of retaliation on the part of the father for the son's attempt to compete with him (both sexually and otherwise) for the mother (Freud, 1905d, 1923b, 1924d, 1925j, 1926d). From this perspective, we could suggest a strictly Freudian reading of *3-Iron*, by showing that its main character is struggling with an oedipal scenario that creates huge problems for him. He fails to engage in a direct confrontation with his father (represented here by the girl's violent husband), even if at the beginning he challenges him to a contest in which he believes himself to be stronger and more original: a game of golf, to be played with the 3-iron, a club rarely used by golfers. However, he inevitably ends up defeated when openly confronted with the socially accepted parameters of wealth and power. Our young man, who never speaks or expresses any wish to possess things, in fact does not possess anything, only his golf ball, and can do nothing against his rival who, on the contrary, is visibly wealthy and arrogantly shows off his power.

The initial oedipal defeat in the film allows our young man gradually to move away from his original anarchic and nihilistic tendencies towards a proud choice of diversity, towards a rejection of consumerism and of possessions, towards a recovering of traditions from the past (for instance, in the episode in which he buries an old man found dead in one of the squatted houses), in a crescendo of symbolic re-significations in which the condition of being excluded from others could be turned into an autonomous, creative, and alternative choice.

Those who have phantasies of invisibility also express the refusal to be like others (parents, teachers, society in general) would wish them to be. The fear of what others might see in you, however, can reinforce your difficulties in relating to the world. In *3-Iron*, the character who never speaks does not defend himself, not even when accused of murder, though he also remains silent when he should instead accuse himself of manslaughter, having hit the woman in the car with a golf ball. Avoiding violence by trying to become invisible, he ends up creating another kind of violence, resulting from not allowing himself to be exposed.

Anxieties about making ourselves visible stem from a fear of being exposed and recognised, while on the other hand, the compulsion to be seen at any cost, so common in our society, might be related to a need to control what others see in us. The fear of being seen might conceal a fear of being understood, approached, and loved in a way that is beyond our control. A serious trauma may evoke intolerable experiences of shame and impotence.

We do not know why the film's character wants to make himself invisible, nor what may have happened earlier in his life. What we do know is that he has suffered violence, because he practises it and becomes a victim of it. From our analytic work, we have learned that those who tend to make themselves invisible are people running away from feelings of pain and shame. By hiding away, they avoid the risk of coming across more suffering, but they also end up avoiding love and being loved, as we have seen throughout this book.

The ending of 3-Iron is remarkable indeed. The young man triumphantly succeeds in becoming invisible, choosing to exist and be visible only to his girlfriend, and managing always to avoid her husband's presence. The way he moves around to achieve this result reminds one of dancing, the gestures of mimes, or ancient Japanese theatre. As he gets back inside the world of others, this time our character chooses to live no longer in isolation, but nevertheless to be visible only to those he wants to be seen by. We may think that his creative skills allow him to invent a different reality, located in a phantasy world that he shares with another person, who is presumably as unhappy and traumatised as he is himself. I believe that such a creative quality allows him to find an original solution to the Oedipus complex—a compromise that would protect him from castration anxiety. In his world, he does not compete with his father because, not unlike the oedipal child, he would be doomed to defeat. Instead, he invents a different world (see Winnicott, 1971) where he can triumph over the father and come to possess the mother, thus imposing his spiritual and moral superiority over him.

To return to Freud, the film's two protagonists start loving once again in order not to get sick and, loving each other, they come back to the world where they had made themselves invisible. One could object that we are still dealing with a phantasy world in which that house and that space still do not belong to the young man, who seems to fail to build a place that could be entirely his own.

I believe that this ending, which I described as remarkable, is of special interest to us psychoanalysts, in as much as we often ask ourselves how patients will be able to resolve their conflicts, and how their repetition compulsion may give way to defences better suited to their instinctual needs and superego demands.

While playing with reality, the film's protagonist creates a house-environment that represents him in the best possible way, and he proves he can live better than its legitimate owner in the space he occupies.

The creative solution he arrives at transforms that opulent and vulgar space, depressing for those who have to live in it, into a delicate and lyrical environment that puts a smile back on its dwellers' faces and clears away the violence that had once characterised it.

At the end, even the house's legitimate owner finds a smile and some happiness in this restored space. It is an incomplete, partial, and only provisional solution, which is probably what the director intended; we could also describe it as open and unsaturated and, as such, being a provisional compromise among different psychic forces, it could make future developments available to the spectators' minds.

I would like to remind you of Betty Joseph's beautiful article of 1986, in which she proposed to consider psychic change not only as a durable and long-term change, that is, a sort of final state of permanent well-being, but rather as moment-to-moment changes, "seeing them as our patient's own individual method of dealing with his anxieties and relationships in his own unique way" (Joseph, 1986, p. 192).

Symbolism and unconscious phantasy can indeed be used to avoid contact with external reality (Parsons, 2000; Steiner, 1993), but they are also essential for establishing a dynamic, creative relationship with it and for discovering original solutions for extricating oneself from the problems of love.

CONCLUSIONS

Kiss me on my mouth, my last summer.
Tell me you will not go very far away.
Come back and carry love on your shoulders,
and your weight will no longer be in vain.
                    —Sandro Penna (1976, p. 10; author's translation)

A Midrash tells the story of a rabbi many centuries ago in a far-off place in Eastern Europe who used to go to a certain place, in a certain forest, every time he wanted a miracle to take place. There, after having burned a certain sort of wood, he recited some well-known words in the form of a prayer, after which the miracle took place. The next generation of rabbis, increasingly pious and religious, used to go to the same forest, burn the same sort of wood, and recite the same prayer, but they no longer remembered the secret place where this used to take place. Despite this, the miracle still happened. The subsequent generation of rabbis had forgotten not only the place but also the type of wood to be burned in sacrifice. However, they remembered the words of the old prayer, the forest, and the miracles wrought by their fathers. And the miracles they asked for also came true, within reasonable limits. But by the time of the next generation, apart from no longer knowing the location of the secret place or the sort of wood to use, they had also lost, in their oral transmission of traditions, the name of the forest and the region in which it was located. And yet, the words of the prayer, always faithfully repeated, sufficed, and the necessary miracles were wrought. Finally, they arrived at the generation that had lost everything forever in the upheavals of persecutions, great changes, and transmigrations, even the holy words of the necessary prayers for making miracles happen. However, all alone, within the confines of his home, the rabbi remembered: actually he remembered nothing, but the memory clearly remained within him, handed down through the generations, about the possibilities for making that miracle happen. And that was enough. The memory transmitted from generation to generation sufficed for something sacred and miraculous to happen and be transmitted under any conditions.

As an analyst, this is what I believe happens with our patients. We have lost the place of our original love, the words that were said, the fire that fuelled them, and the forest that welcomed them. But we have not lost our memory of them, our recollection that one day it had been like this. And if it had once been like that, then it could possibly be re-ignited and blaze anew in our hearts and in the hearts of those we love.

As I have often stated, some patients are particularly needy of love. These individuals generally function quite well, especially after years of analysis, and yet they are frozen, their hearts spent. Although their analysis is an important and fundamental emotional and cognitive experience in their lives, it does not manage to spark any significant transformations in their long-established, familiar behavioural patterns. Unexpectedly analyst and patient find themselves locked in impasses that are difficult to shift, in never-ending repetitions of unpleasant yet well-known situations, in humiliating and belittling emotional experiences that both analyst and patient are all too familiar with. To quote Morris Eagle:

> The analytical process has not simply to do with the strengthening of the Ego but its primary function should be, generally speaking, "a replacement of maladaptive representations and cognitive-affective schemas with more adaptive representations and schemas."
>
> (Eagle, 2011, p. 272)

And we analysts know only too well how we labour to trigger this process. But let us also turn to Ferro's words, in his book *Seeds of Illness, Seeds of Recovery*:

> Psychoanalysis is the method that allows emotions to be "broken down" into narrations, whereby they can be endowed with "bodily form" and "visibility". For the analyst what matters is not the individual narration as such, but grasping the emotions that lie upstream of it, the narration being their "narrative derivative". If we are able to "grasp" the emotions we create a new situation for the patient, where the emphasis is not really on the traumatic event it relates, intolerable, unbearable and without any apparent way out, but rather on a mood, in its turn intolerable and unbearable, which can however open up towards new processes.
>
> (Ferro, 2002, p. 100)

With these patients, we must succeed in going beyond the narrative that they recite like a mantra about their life—an unchanging and unchangeable story—and ingeniously work through its basic, underlying elements. Finding the right words—those that are specific, logical, clear, and suitable—for recounting what has been really lived and experienced and going beyond the myths and narrative legends (habitual schemas used from generation to generation) that are easier to follow are essential for combatting the long-entrenched habit of expected defeat and disaster that some narratives contain by default. It is difficult to perform these tasks, since it is much easier to pursue the ideological and cultural *main stream* of every narrative. The skills of being an analyst lie in our ability to penetrate the obvious, and to listen out each time for the detail that differs, the strident note, the silence within that apparent melody.

At a certain point in his book *A Star Shines over Mt. Morris Park*, Henry Roth describes in rare detail the moment in which he realises that there is a specific, particular, and unique word for describing the distinct atmosphere and emotion he is feeling at that very moment:

> And he passes below the hill on Mt. Morris Park in autumn twilight, with the evening star in the west in limpid sky above the wooden bell tower. And so beautiful it was: a rapture to behold. It set him

a problem he never dreamed anyone set himself. How do you say it? Before the pale blue twilight left your eyes you had to say it, use words that said it: blue, indigo, blue, indigo. Words that matched, matched that swimming star above the hill and the tower; what words matched it? Lonely and swimming star above the hill. Not twinkling, nah, twinkle, twinkle, little star—those words belonged to someone else. You had to match it yourself: swimming in the blue tide, you could say ... maybe. Like that bluing Mom rinses white shirt in. Nah, you couldn't say that... How clear it is. One star shines over Mt. Morris Park hill. And it's getting dark, and it's getting cold—Gee, if instead of cold, I said chill. A star shines over Mt. Morris Park hill. And it's getting dark, and it's getting chill...

(Roth, 1994, p. 81)

Sometimes it happens just like this in analysis too. We seek for a phrase, a word that specifically relates to that particular situation, chosen deliberately to suit the material the patient is listening to and describing. This word sparkles and reveals our attentive, participated listening. But most of all it discloses the subjective, profound, and personal working through accomplished by the analyst, pertinent to describing that distinct emotion and particular atmosphere.

In the majority of the stories recounted in this book, the patients appear to need something specific and particular from the analyst, something that is subjectively unique; I have called this an act of specific sharing that springs from the analyst's individual experience. In order to be truly listened to and understood, these patients seem to require a mutual "give and take" with the analyst. By this, I intend a subtle, indistinct experience that develops the function of the countertransference to a much greater degree than might have been imagined in the past.

Several of the patients I have chosen to discuss here appear to have in common an elementary, archaic need to love and be loved. They seemed to nurture unconscious phantasies about love and to believe that love alone is enough to help and cure them. At times, they seemed to think that if only their parents had loved them enough, they would not have suffered constantly from the low self-esteem that seemed to have persecuted their lives and their unsuccessful attempts to combat it. Or they appeared convinced that it would have been enough if their parents had been less emotionally ambivalent towards them to escape the sufferings and repeated failures in their affective lives that they were unable to avoid. Their phantasies about repairing damaged internal objects went hand in hand with a powerful desire for compensation.

The original unconscious phantasy of many of the patients described in this book could well have been summed up like this: "I was worthy of being unconditionally loved. I was worthy of being at the centre of my parent's life in my childhood." Unexpressed and clearly unconscious, this deeply buried phantasy was also addressed to the analyst: "I should be at the centre of my analyst's thoughts, affections, and life as compensation for not having been the central focus of my primary love objects."

In my experience, if the analyst maintains a constant, unchanging stance of almost sacrificial attention and attitude towards these patients, because of their fundamental need to be loved and disregarding their everyday disposition and behaviour in the sessions, we run the risk of creating disastrous consequences. We must be very attentive in the analysis of these unusually needy and dependent patients, and capable of distinguishing between reality and phantasy in the transference and countertransference dynamics. From another point of view, as analysts we cannot take on and treat these patients so genuinely needy of attention and affection in the same way as patients who are less needy because then we would risk missing some of the fundamental elements and not reaching the core of their deepest suffering.

When we are struggling in analysis with experiences of desperation and despondency, due to an unexplainable immobility or a never-ending repetition of behaviours and attitudes that have no way out; when we exhaustedly ask ourselves: "What is it that I'm not seeing? What is it that I'm not managing to grasp?", this is the moment when it is a good idea to look more carefully at our own countertransference. To be more precise, we should pay more attention to the experiences pertaining to our own internal world that are triggered by the patient's internal world. The analyst's subjective quality that I am illustrating here differs slightly from our customary subjective stance that we normally employ and talk about, which offers indispensable links to the patient's internal world for our analytic listening and understanding. In my opinion, it also differs from the question of empathy or being in tune, which are also essential elements that I have spoken about at length in the preceding chapters. Obviously, not all the analyst's internal experiences during the session significantly link up to the clinical material proffered by the patient. At times, though, there is something, a level of empathy sparked by some unconscious transmission that originates with the patient, which activates memories, feelings, and phantasies that belong only to the analyst's private life. I do not believe that such phantasies or memories necessarily have to be shared with the patient, but I do believe that they should be registered and referenced to the analyst's personal and private life, so that the patient's corresponding memories or emotions can be more readily perceived. This requires a necessary level of harmony and empathy. Both these qualities are essential with these patients, who, as I have already said, seem to have a need to love and be loved and an above-average level of attention that is more intense than what normally occurs in the analytic process. Indeed, I believe that these patients' heightened neediness and deprivation literally trigger those flashes of temporary, fragile union between their needs and the long-buried memories and experiences in the analyst's unconscious. I would like to express my gratitude here not only to the patients who with patience and tenacity managed to let me reach and perceive these aspects, which by definition are so fleeting and transient, but also to my mentors who, with equal patience and tenacity, showed me the path to listening: Luciana Nissim and Giuseppe Di Chiara (Di Chiara, 2003). From different perspectives, both taught me how to listen to the patient and to comprehend the potential of theories to represent facts, together with something else that has no price: passion for the creativity inherent in our work.

We know only too well in fact that analytic listening always entails some form of creativity on the part of the analyst: the memories, phantasies, and intuitions triggered in the analyst's unconscious call for—as I have attempted to illustrate in the preceding chapters—a patient act of weaving and attention to the form and colours of the material that is being woven on the loom. This particular state of mind focused on listening to both the patient's and the analyst's internal worlds is an essential analytic tool, especially with those patients who seemingly cannot make any effective use of the analytic process.

Armed with our proven skills and our awareness that every story can have a different ending and a different character can always be interpreted, then the sufferings of love that resound so frequently in our consulting rooms, the repeated illusions and delusions that we come across, the betrayals of innermost intimate convictions, feelings, and trusts, and the oscillation of hope and despair can all be tackled with greater vigour and conviction. Too often, we let ourselves get caught up in the external plot of the story, weighed down in our listening by ideologies and prejudices. Love and its consequences are a constantly evolving and changing topic in our consulting rooms and in the lives of both patients and analysts. Without the libidinal capacity to invest and to risk loving, one slowly and quietly suffocates. On the contrary, excessive love, *amour-passion*, as we have seen, risks leading to the deadly repetition of the alternative between Eros and Thanatos, so that passion finds relief only in death, in death for love, the German *Liebestod*. The difficulty in repairing lost love objects and pardoning unpardonable betrayals leads to a solitary desert of diffidence and despair, where the body inexorably sickens, since the psyche finds no release for its pain.

In this book, I have illustrated various moments from a number of analyses in which I have managed to intimately grasp my patients' unexpressed and overflowing pain, through being able to resound within my own internal world the same feelings of despair and disappointment, of futile waiting, of the need for reparation. The rabbit, the little girl hanging over an abyss, the doll that fell to pieces, the wrong clothes for the party, and many other moments omitted for lack of space were all, indeed, instant flashes of shared illumination. Not being thoroughly understood, not being able to communicate the intimate truth of one's despair, not managing to write together another story with a more joyful ending or at least one that is less predictable in its vain suffering are all elements that risk ruining our daily work with these patients and undermining the opportunities for reparation that they are seeking.

The passions of love require the listener to have the same potential for lightness as expressed by Sandro Penna:

> The limpid air is coming back
> and with me stays
> this no longer limpid
> melancholy
>
> (1976, p. 49; author's translation)

Idealisation is central to love, one of its most important components. We have seen how the beloved is idealised, and how, through projective identification, the person who loves also feels idealised. We have seen how one can love love, the mere act of loving rather than the object of one's love. We have seen how every love object is a re-found object, a sort of surrogate for the original lost love, or, and also, a therapeutic aid for old wounds of love, for unsatisfied needs finally fulfilled. If the original relationship with the primitive love object was painful and frustrating, the re-found love object will be an object that repeats the old sufferings of childhood. Furthermore, we have seen how one can never really re-find the symbiotic fusionality of early infancy, and how this, if experienced, can only inexorably lead to suffering for its loss and one's disappointment. Love always remains balanced between the desire to re-find the original lost object and the need to find a profoundly different object from the first one. Life passes in the expectation and promise of a happy love, like a river that flows towards the sea. We can maintain the idealisation, which is indispensable for love, but we have to transform it to suit the multiple changes of the reality we live in, to the time that flows, to the events that happen to us. We can also idealise reality to make it suit our needs for idealisation. After all, it is all about finding new and different narrative modes that might be more in tune with new experiences, different poems, new seasons, or old summers that may not go too far, but will do so lightly, so that we will be able to carry the weight of love on our shoulders, sharing sufferings and memories, but also joyful moments and recollections.

REFERENCES

Abraham, G. (1976). The sense and concept of time in psychoanalysis. *The International Review of Psycho-Analysis, 3*: 461–472.

Ackerley, J. R. (1968). *My Father and Myself*. London: Bodley Head.

Ambrosiano, L., & Gaburri, E. (2008). *La spinta a esistere*. Rome: Borla.

Anzieu, D. (1985). *Le moi peau*. Paris: Dunod. [*The Skin Ego*. New Haven: Yale University Press, 1989.]

Anzieu, D. (1994). *Le Penser*. Paris: Dunod.

Auden, W. H. (1938). "O tell me the truth about love"/"Funeral Blues". In: "Four Cabaret Songs for Miss Hedli Anderson", *Another Time*. New York: Random House, 1940.

Aulagnier, P. (1967). *Le désir et la perversion*. Paris: Seuil.

Austen, J. (1811). *Sense and Sensibility*. Cambridge: Cambridge University Press, 2013.

Balint, M. (1952a). *Primary Love and Psychoanalytic Technique*. London: Karnac.

Balint, M. (1952b). On love and hate. *The International Journal of Psycho-Analysis, 33*: 355–362.

Balint, M. (1960). Primary narcissism and primary love. *The Psychoanalytic Quarterly, 29*: 6–43.

Barthes, R. (1977). *Fragments d'un discours amoureux*. Paris: Seuil. [*A Lover's Discourse: Fragments*. Translated by R. Howard. London: Vintage, 2002.]

Bayly, T. H. (1844). "Something to Love". In: *Songs, Ballads, and Other Poems*. London: R. Bentley.

Beck, U., & Beck-Gernsheim, E. (1990). *Das Ganz normale Chaos del Liebe*. Frankfurt: Surhkamp Verlag. [*Normal Chaos of Love*. Hoboken, NJ: Wiley, 1995.]

Beckett, S. (1936). "Cascando". In: S. Lawlor & J. Pilling (Eds.), *The Collected Poems of Samuel Beckett*. New York: Grove Atlantic, 2014.

Bédier, J. (1902–1905). *Le Roman de Tristan par Thomas: poème du XIIe siècle*. 2 vols. Paris: Firmin Didot. [*The Romance of Tristan and Iseult*. Translated by H. Belloc. London: George Allen & Company, 1913.]

Bell, D. (2006). Existence in time: development or catastrophe? *The Psychoanalytic Quarterly, 75*: 783–805.

Benjamin, J. (1998). *Shadow of the Other*. New York: Routledge.

Bergmann, M. S. (1987). *The Anatomy of Loving*. New York: Columbia University Press.

Bion, W. R. (1957). On arrogance. In: *Second Thoughts*. London: Karnac, 1993.

Bion, W. R. (1962a). *Learning from Experience*. London: Heinemann.

Bion, W. R. (1962b). The psycho-analytic study of thinking. *The International Journal of Psycho-Analysis, 43*: 306–310.

Bion, W. R. (1965). *Transformations*. London: Karnac.

Bion, W. R. (1966). Catastrophic change. *Bulletin of the British Psychoanalytical Society*, no. 5.

Bion, W. R. (1967). Notes on memory and desire. *Psycho-analytic Forum, II, 3*: 271–280.

Bion, W. R. (1970). *Attention and Interpretation*. London: Tavistock.

Bion, W. R. (1992). *Cogitations*. London: Karnac.

Blum, R. P. (1973). The concept of erotized transference. *Journal of the American Psychoanalytic Association, 21*: 61–76.

Bollas, C. (1987). *The Shadow of the Object*. New York: Columbia University Press.

Bolognini, S. (1994). Transference: erotised, erotic, loving, affectionate. *The International Journal of Psycho-Analysis, 75*: 73–86.

Bonaparte, M. (1940). Time and the unconscious. *The International Journal of Psycho-Analysis, 21*: 427–468.

Borgogno, F. (1999). *Psicoanalisi come percorso*. Turin: Boringhieri. [*Psychoanalysis as a Journey*. London: Open Gate Press, 2007.]

Boris, H. (1984). Working with an anorexic patient. *The International Journal of Psycho-Analysis, 65*: 435–442.

Brecht, B. (1927). "Remembrances of Marie A". In: *Die Hauspostille*. Berlin: Suhrkamp Verlag. [*Manual of Piety/Die Hauspostille*. New York: Grove Press, 1966.]

Britton, R. (1998). *Belief and Imagination*. London: Brunner-Routledge.

Butler, J. (1990). *Gender Trouble: Feminism and the Subversion of Identity*. London: Routledge.

Caproni, G. (1995). "Battendo a macchina". In: "Versi Livornesi", *Poesie 1932–1986*. Milan: Garzanti.

Carroll, L. (1865). *Alice's Adventures in Wonderland*. London: Ward, Lock & Co. (n.d., 4th edn.).

Catullus. (*c.* 57–56 BC). "Poem 109". In: *The Poems of Catullus*. Translated by D. Dunn. London: William Collins, 2016.

Céline, L.-F. (1932). *Voyage au bout de la nuit*. Paris: Denoël & Steele. [*Journey to the End of the Night*. Translated by R. Manheim. Richmond, UK: Alma Classics, 2012.]

Choderlos de Laclos, P. A. F. (1782). *Les Liaisons dangereuses*. Paris: Editions Norph–Nop, 2011. [*Dangerous Liaisons*. Translated by H. Constantine. London: Penguin, 2007.]

Da Ponte, L. (1785). *Le nozze di Figaro* (Wolfgang Amadeus Mozart). [*The Marriage of Figaro*. Translated by E. Beatty & M. Bona, The Royal Opera House, Covent Garden, London.]

Dante Alighieri. (1304–1321). *La Divina Commedia, Inferno*. Venice: Dolce-Giolito, 1555. [*The Divine Comedy, Hell*. Translated by D. L. Sayers. London: Penguin, 1949.]

Dante Alighieri. (1304–1321). *La Divina Commedia, Paradiso*. Venice: Dolce-Giolito, 1555. [*The Divine Comedy, Paradise*. Translated by M. Musa. London: Penguin, 1984.]

De Masi, F. (1988). Idealization and erotization in the analytic relationship. *Rivista di Psicoanalisi, 34*: 76–120.

De Rougemont, D. (1939). *L'Amour et l'Occident*. Paris: Plon. [*Love in the Western World*. Translated by M. Belgion. Princeton, NJ: Princeton University Press, 1983.]

De Troyes, C. (12th–13th century). "The Poetical Romances of Tristan". Edited by F. Michel. London: William Pickering, 1835.

Di Benedetto, A. (2001). Ascoltare chi non sa parlare. L'inconscio e l'infante. *Richard e Piggle, 19*(3).

Di Chiara, G. (2003). *Curare con la psicoanalisi*. Milan: Raffaello Cortina.

Dickinson, E. (1863). Poems F586/J1739 and F588/J536. In: R. W. Franklin (Ed.), *The Poems of Emily Dickinson*. Cambridge, MA: The Belknap Press of Harvard University Press, 1999.

Diena, S. (2004). Difficoltà tecniche nel trattamento psicoanalitico dell'anoressia e della bulimia. In: M. Curi Novelli (Ed.), *Dal vuoto al pensiero. L'anoressia dal vertice psicoanalitico* (pp. 80–81). Milan: Franco Angeli.

Diena, S. (2008). Trauma, memoria e transfert: gente comune. In: A. Ferruta (Ed.), *I transfert. Cambiamenti nella pratica clinica* (p. 115). Milan: Borla.

Eagle, M. (2011). *From Classical to Contemporary Psychoanalysis: A Critique and Integration*. New York: Routledge.

Eissler, K. (1963). *Goethe: A Psychoanalytic Study, 1775–1786*. Detroit: Wayne State University Press.

Eliot, T. S. (1935). "Burnt Norton". In: *Four Quartets*. New York: Harcourt, 1943.

Ellis, H. (1937). *On Life and Sex: Essays of Love and Virtue*. Garden City, NY: Schuyler Press, 2000.

Fachinelli, E. (1989). *La mente estatica*. Milan: Adelphi.

Faimberg, H. (1981). *The Telescoping of Generations*. London: Routledge, 2005.

Faimberg, H. (2007). Plea for a broader concept of Nachträligeit. *The Psychoanalytic Quarterly, 76*: 1221–1240.

Ferenczi, S. (1949). Confusion of tongues between adults and the child: the language of tenderness and the language of passion. *The International Journal of Psycho-Analysis, 30*: 225–230.

Ferro, A. (2002). *Fattori di malattia, fattori di guarigione*. Milan: Raffaello Cortina. [*Seeds of Illness, Seeds of Recovery*. Hove: Brunner-Routledge, 2005.]

Ferruta, A. (2012). A reconsideration of Freud's essays on sexuality and their clinical implications. *The Psychoanalytic Quarterly, 81*: 259–278.

Flaubert, G. (1857). *Madame Bovary*. Paris: Michel Lévy Frères. [*Madame Bovary*. Translated by G. Wall. London: Penguin, 2003.]

Flaubert, G. (1869). *L'Éducation sentimentale*. Paris: Michel Lévy Frères. [*Sentimental Education*. Translated by R. Baldick & G. Wall. London: Penguin, 2004.]

Fonagy, P. (1999). Memory and therapeutic action. *The International Journal of Psycho-Analysis, 80*: 215–223.

Fontane, T. (1894). *Effie Briest*. Berlin: Deutsche Rundschau. [*Effie Briest*. London: Penguin, 1976.]

Forrester, J. (1997). *Truth Games: Lies, Money, and Psychoanalysis*. Cambridge, MA: Harvard University Press.

Freud, S. (1900a). *The Interpretation of Dreams. S.E., 4 & 5*. London: Hogarth.

Freud, S. (1905d). *Three Essays on the Theory of Sexuality. S.E., 7*. London: Hogarth.

Freud, S. (1910h). A special type of choice of object made by men (Contributions to the psychology of love, I). *S.E., 11*. London: Hogarth.

Freud, S. (1912d). On the universal tendency to debasement in the sphere of love (Contributions to the psychology of love, II) *S.E., 11*. London: Hogarth.

Freud, S. (1914c). On narcissism: an introduction. *S.E., 14*. London: Hogarth.

Freud, S. (1915a). Observations on transference-love. *S.E., 12.* London: Hogarth.

Freud, S. (1917a). A difficulty in the path of psycho-analysis. *S.E., 17.* London: Hogarth.

Freud, S. (1920g). *Beyond the Pleasure Principle. S.E., 18.* London: Hogarth.

Freud, S. (1921c). *Group Psychology and the Analysis of the Ego. S.E., 18.* London: Hogarth.

Freud, S. (1923b). *The Ego and the Id. S.E., 19.* London: Hogarth.

Freud, S. (1924d). The dissolution of the Oedipus complex. *S.E., 19.* London: Hogarth.

Freud, S. (1925j). Some psychical consequences of the anatomical distinction between the sexes. *S.E., 19.* London: Hogarth.

Freud, S. (1926d). *Inhibitions, Symptoms and Anxiety. S.E., 20.* London: Hogarth.

Freud, S. (1937d). Constructions in analysis. *S.E., 23.* London: Hogarth.

Gabbard, G. (1996). *Love and Hate in the Analytic Setting.* Northvale, NJ: Jason Aronson.

Gabbard, G., & Lester, E. (1995). *Boundaries and Boundary Violations in Psychoanalysis.* New York: Basic Books.

Gaddini, E. (1969). On imitation. *The International Journal of Psycho-Analysis, 50*: 475–484.

Gaddini, E. (1982). Early defensive fantasies and the psychoanalytical process. *The International Journal of Psycho-Analysis, 63*: 379–388.

Gammaro Moroni, P. (2003). Precisazioni teorico cliniche sul trattamento psicoanalitico dell'anoressia. In: M. Curi Novelli, *Dal vuoto al pensiero* (pp. 87ff). Milan: Franco Angeli, 2004.

Girard, R. (1961). *Mensonge romantique et verité romanesque.* Paris: Hachette. [*Deceit, Desire and the Novel: Self and Other in Literary Structure.* Baltimore: Johns Hopkins University Press, 1966.]

Goethe, J. W. (1819). "Selige Sehnsucht"/"Blessed Longing". In: *West-östlicher Divan.* Stuttgart: Cottaische Buchhandlung. [*West–East Divan.* Translated by M. Bidney. Albany, NY: State University of New York Press, 2010.]

Graves, R. (1954). *Greek Myths.* Cambridge: Cambridge University Press.

Green, A. (2002). *Time in Psychoanalysis: Some Contradictory Aspects.* London: Free Association Books.

Green, A. (2005). *Love and Its Vicissitudes.* London: Routledge.

Grotstein, J. (2000). *Who Is the Dreamer Who Dreams the Dream?* Hillsdale, NJ: Analytic Press.

Hill, D. (1994). The special place of the erotic transference in psychoanalysis. *Psychoanalytic Inquiry, 14*: 483–498.

Holgate, B. (1998). Tate à Tate. *The Weekend Australian Review, 17*: 26–27.

Homer. (8th century BC). *The Iliad*. Translated by E. V. Rieu, P. Jones, & D. C. H. Rieu. London: Penguin, 2003.

Homer (8th century BC). *The Odyssey*. Translated by E. V. Rieu & D. C. H. Rieu. London: Penguin, 2003.

Joseph, B. (1985). Transference: the total situation. In: M. Feldman & E. Bott Spillius (Eds.), *Psychic Equilibrium and Psychic Change* (pp. 156–167). London: Brunner-Routledge, 1989.

Joseph, B. (1986). Psychic change and the psychoanalytic process. In: M. Feldman & E. Bott Spillius (Eds.), *Psychic Equilibrium and Psychic Change* (pp. 192–202). London: Brunner-Routledge, 1989.

Keats, J. (1817). Letter to George Keats. Sunday, 21 December 1817. In: G. F. Scott (Ed.), *Selected Letters of John Keats* (p. 156). Cambridge, MA: Harvard University Press, 2002.

Kernberg, O. F. (1974a). Barriers to falling and remaining in love. *Journal of the American Psychoanalytic Association, 22*: 486–511.

Kernberg, O. F. (1974b). Mature love: prerequisites and characteristics. *Journal of the American Psychoanalytic Association, 22*: 743–768.

Kernberg, O. F. (1994). Love in the analytic setting. *Journal of the American Psychoanalytic Association, 42*: 1137–1157 (reprinted as chapter seven in Kernberg, 1995).

Kernberg, O. F. (1995). *Love Relations: Normality and Pathology*. New Haven: Yale University Press.

Kilborne, B. (2002). *Disappearing Persons: Shame and Appearance*. Albany: State University of New York Press.

Kohut, H. (1966). Forms and transformations of narcissism. *Journal of the American Psychoanalytic Association, 14*: 243–272.

Kohut, H. (1971). *The Analysis of the Self*. London: Hogarth.

Kristeva, J. (1983). *Tales of Love*. New York: Columbia University Press.

Lacan, J. (1949). Le stade du miroir comme formateur de la function du Je. In: *Écrits*. Paris: Seuil, 1966. [The mirror stage as formative of the function of the I as revealed in psychoanalytic experience. In: *Écrits: A Selection*. London: Tavistock, 1977.]

Lacan, J. (1953). Some reflections on the ego. *The International Journal of Psycho-Analysis, 34*: 11–17.

Lansky, M. (1997). *The Widening Scope of Shame*. Hillsdale, NJ: Analytic Press.

Laplanche, J., & Pontalis, J. (1983). *The Language of Psychoanalysis*. London: Hogarth.

Lemma, A. (2005). The many faces of lying. *The International Journal of Psycho-Analysis, 86*: 737–753.

Leopardi, G. (1828). "A Silvia". In: *Canti*. Florence: Piatti. ["To Silvia", Canto XXI. In: *Canti*. Translated by J. Galassi. London: Penguin, 2010.]

Lewes, K. (1995). *Psychoanalysis and Male Homosexuality*. London: Aronson.

Lucretius (mid 1st century BC). *The Nature of Things*. Translated by A. E. Stallings. London: Penguin, 2007.

Maggini, C. (Ed.) (2001). *Malinconia d'amore. Frammenti di una psicopatologia della vita amorosa*. Pisa: ETS.

Merleau-Ponty, M. (1945). *Phénoménologie de la Perception*. Paris: Gallimard. [*Phenomenology of Perception*. London: Routledge & Kegan Paul, 1962.]

Milite, T. (2005). *L'intermittenza del giallo*. Savona: Sabatelli.

Nietzsche, F. (1886). *Jenseits von Gut und Böse. Zur Genealogie der Moral*. Munich: Deutscher Taschenbuch Verlag, 2002. [*Beyond Good and Evil*. Translated by R. J. Hollingdale. London: Penguin, 2003.]

Ogden, T. (1989). *The Primitive Edge of Experience*. London: Jason Aronson.

Ogden, T. (2004). On holding and containing, being and dreaming. *The International Journal of Psycho-Analysis, 85*: 1349–1364.

Ovid, P. N. (AD 8). *Metamorphoses*. Translated by M. M. Innes. London: Penguin, 1955.

Oz, A. (2003). *A Tale of Love and Darkness*. Translated by N. de Lange. London: Vintage, 2005.

Parsons, M. (2000). *The Dove that Returns, the Dove that Vanishes*. London: Brunner-Routledge.

Paz, O. (1974). *Teatro de signos/transparencias*. Madrid: Editorial Fundamentos.

Penna, S. (1976). *Stranezze 1957–1976*. Milan: Mondadori Libri. [*This Strange Joy*. Columbus, OH: Ohio State University Press, 1982.]

Perelberg, R. (2008). *Time, Space and Phantasy*. London: New Library of Psychoanalysis, Routledge.

Person, E. S. (1988). *Dreams of Love and Fateful Encounters: Romance in Our Time*. New York: Norton.

Person, E. S. (1991). Romantic love: at the intersection of the psyche and the cultural unconscious. *Journal of the American Psychoanalytic Association, 39S*: 383–411.

Plato. (*c*. 384 BC). *The Symposium*. Translated by C. Gill. London: Penguin, 1999.

Plato. (*c*. 350 BC). *Philebus*. Translated by B. Jowett. http://classics.mit.edu/Plato/philebus.html, last accessed, 25 August 2017.

Pontalis, J. B. (1977). *Entre le rêve et la douleur*. Paris: Gallimard. [*Between the Dream and Psychic Pain*. London: Hogarth and the Institute of Psycho-Analysis, 1981.]

Propertius. (*c*. 28 BC). *The Poems*. Translated by G. Lee. Oxford: Oxford University Press, 2009.

Proust, M. (1919). *À la recherche du temps perdu: À l'ombre des jeunes filles en fleurs*. Paris: Gallimard, 1954. [*Remembrance of Things Past (Vols. 3–4): Within a Budding Grove*. Translated by C. K. Scott Moncrieff. London: Chatto & Windus, 1966.]

Quinodoz, D. (2009). Growing old. *The International Journal of Psycho-Analysis,* 90: 773–793.

Rangell, L. (1991). Castration. *Journal of the American Psychoanalytic Association, 39:* 3–23.

Rilke, R. M. (1923). *Duineser Elegien.* Leipzig: Insel–Verlag. [*Duino Elegies and the Sonnets to Orpheus.* Translated and edited by S. Mitchell. New York: Vintage, 2009.]

Rose, J. (1997). Distortion of time in the transference: some clinical and theoretical implications. *The International Journal of Psycho-Analysis, 78:* 453–468.

Roth, H. (1994). *Mercy of a Rude Stream (Vol. 1): A Star Shines Over Mt. Morris Park.* London: Phoenix.

Sabbadini, A. (1989). Boundaries of timelessness: some thoughts about the temporal dimension of the psychoanalytic space. *The International Journal of Psycho-Analysis, 70:* 305–313.

Sandler, J. (1976a). Dreams, unconscious fantasies and "identity of perception". *The International Review of Psycho-Analysis, 3:* 33–42.

Sandler, J. (1976b). Countertransference and role-responsiveness. *The International Review of Psycho-Analysis, 3:* 43–47.

Sandler, J., & Sandler, A. (1978). On the development of object relationships and affects. *The International Journal of Psycho-Analysis, 59:* 285–296.

Sappho. (7th century BC). "Fragment 105a". Translated by Dante Gabriel Rossetti. In: J. McGann (Ed.), *Dante Gabriel Rossetti: Collected Poetry and Prose.* New Haven: Yale University Press, 2003.

Schafer, R. (1977). The interpretation of transference and the conditions for loving. *Journal of the American Psychoanalytic Association, 25:* 335–362.

Segal, H. (1957). Notes on symbol formation. *The International Journal of Psycho-Analysis, 38:* 391–397.

Segal, H. (1991). *Dream, Phantasy and Art.* London: Brunner-Routledge.

Shakespeare, W. (1595–1600). "Sonnet 33". In: *The Complete Works of Shakespeare.* London: John Dicks, 1867.

Singer, I. J. (1932). *The Sinner/Yoshe Kalb.* Translated by M. Samuel. New York: Schocken Books, 1988.

Spinoza, B. de. (1677). *Ethics.* Edited and translated by E. Curley. London: Penguin, 1996.

Steiner, J. (1993). *Psychic Retreats.* London: Brunner-Routledge.

Stendhal (M.-H. Beyle). (1822). *De l'amour.* Paris: Pierre Mongie. [*Love.* Translated by G. & S. Sale. London: Penguin, 2004.]

Stern, D. (1985). *The Interpersonal World of the Infant.* New York: Basic Books.

Tolstoy, L. (1877). *Anna Karenina.* Moscow: Rousky Vestnik. [*Anna Karenina.* Translated by R. Pevear & L. Volokhonsky. London: Penguin, 2003.]

Tustin, F. (1981). *Autistic States in Children*. London: Routledge.

Tustin, F. (1986). *Autistic Barriers in Neurotic Patients*. London: Karnac.

Weintraub, S. "Frosty". (2009). "Director James Gray Interview—Two Lovers". 11 February 2009. http://collider.com/director-james-gray-interview-two-lovers.

White, E. (1997). *The Farewell Symphony*. London: Chatto.

Winnicott, D. W. (1953). Transitional objects and transitional phenomena: a study of the first not-me possession. *The International Journal of Psycho-Analysis, 34*: 89–97.

Winnicott, D. W. (1956). Primary maternal preoccupation. In: *Collected Papers: Through Paediatrics to Psycho-Analysis* (pp. 300–305). London: Tavistock, 1958.

Winnicot, D. W. (1960). The theory of the parent–infant relationship. *The International Journal of Psycho-Analysis, 41*: 585–595.

Winnicott, D. W. (1965). *The Maturational Process and the Facilitating Environment*. London: Karnac, 1990.

Winnicott, D. W. (1967). Mirror-role of mother and family. In: *Playing and Reality*. London: Tavistock, 1971.

Winnicott, D. W. (1971). *Playing and Reality*. London: Tavistock.

Winnicott, D. W. (1974). Fear of breakdown. *The International Review of Psycho-Analysis, 1*: 103–107.

Winnicott, D. W. (1984). The antisocial tendency. In: *Deprivation and Delinquency*. London: Routledge, 1984.

Winnicott, D. W. (1987). *The Spontaneous Gesture: Selected Letters of D. W. Winnicott*. Edited by R. Rodman. Cambridge, MA: Harvard University Press.

Wright, K. (2009). *Mirroring and Attunement*. New York: Routledge.

INDEX

For Product Safety Concerns and Information please contact our EU
representative GPSR@taylorandfrancis.com
Taylor & Francis Verlag GmbH, Kaufingerstraße 24, 80331 München, Germany